W0114769

SAGE was founded In 1965 by Sara Miller McCune to support the dissemination of usable knowledge by publishing innovative and high-quality research and teaching content. Today, we publish over 900 journals, including those of more than 400 learned societies, more than 800 new books per year, and a growing range of library products including archives, data, case studies, reports, and video. SAGE remains majority-owned by our founder, and after Sara's lifetime will become owned by a charitable trust that secures our continued independence.

Los Angeles | London | New Delhi | Singapore | Washington DC | Melbourne

Modi's foreign POLICY

Thank you for choosing a SAGE product!
If you have any comment, observation or feedback,
I would like to personally hear from you.
Please write to me at **contactceo@sagepub.in**

Vivek Mehra, Managing Director and CEO, SAGE India.

Bulk Sales

SAGE India offers special discounts
for purchase of books in bulk.
We also make available special imprints
and excerpts from our books on demand.

For orders and enquiries, write to us at

Marketing Department
SAGE Publications India Pvt Ltd
B1/I-1, Mohan Cooperative Industrial Area
Mathura Road, Post Bag 7
New Delhi 110044, India

E-mail us at **marketing@sagepub.in**

Get to know more about SAGE

Be invited to SAGE events, get on our mailing list.
Write today to **marketing@sagepub.in**

This book is also available as an e-book.

Modi's foreign POLICY

Reeta Chowdhari Tremblay

Ashok Kapur

Los Angeles | London | New Delhi
Singapore | Washington DC | Melbourne

Copyright © Reeta Chowdhari Tremblay and Ashok Kapur, 2017

All rights reserved. No part of this book may be reproduced or utilised in any form or by any means, electronic or mechanical, including photocopying, recording or by any information storage or retrieval system, without permission in writing from the publisher.

First published in 2017 by

SAGE Publications India Pvt Ltd
B1/I-1 Mohan Cooperative Industrial Area
Mathura Road, New Delhi 110 044, India
www.sagepub.in

SAGE Publications Inc
2455 Teller Road
Thousand Oaks, California 91320, USA

SAGE Publications Ltd
1 Oliver's Yard, 55 City Road
London EC1Y 1SP, United Kingdom

SAGE Publications Asia-Pacific Pte Ltd
3 Church Street
#10-04 Samsung Hub
Singapore 049483

Published by Vivek Mehra for SAGE Publications India Pvt Ltd, typeset in 11/13 pt Optima by Diligent Typesetter India Pvt Ltd, Delhi and printed at Chaman Enterprises, New Delhi.

Library of Congress Cataloging-in-Publication Data

Names: Tremblay, Reeta Chowdhari, author. | Kapur, Ashok, author.
Title: Modi's foreign policy/Reeta Chowdhari Tremblay and Ashok Kapur.
Description: New Delhi, India; Thousand Oaks, California: SAGE Publications,
    2017. | Includes bibliographical references and index.
Identifiers: LCCN 2017016983| ISBN 9789386446589 (print (hb)) |
    ISBN 9789386446596 (e-pub) | ISBN 9789386446602 (e-book)
Subjects: LCSH: India—Foreign relations—21st century. | India—Politics
    and government—21st century. | Modi, Narendra, 1950–
Classification: LCC DS449.T74 2017 | DDC 327.54/0090512—dc23 LC
    record available at https://lccn.loc.gov/2017016983

ISBN: 978-93-864-4658-9 (HB)

SAGE Team: Supriya Das, Alekha Chandra Jena and Ritu Chopra

Contents

Preface

Like any other observers of Indian politics in May 2014, we were curious to see whether and, if so, how Prime Minister Narendra Modi was to translate his decisive electoral victory into achieving a transformative agenda, both at home and abroad. And like most others, we were quite taken by surprise when, given his palpable hesitancy to speak about foreign affairs during the electoral campaign, he was not to waste a single moment to put foreign policy on the front burner—sending a signal to both regional and extra-regional powers that India, as a self-confident country, intended to play a strategically leading role in the world affairs. Prime Minister Modi's invitation during his swearing-in ceremony to the neighbouring countries' leaders, notably Pakistan's Nawaz Sharif, followed by an exceptionally busy foreign policy agenda during the very first year (a series of visits to strategically selected foreign countries, inviting President Obama to the Republic Day festivities, engaging the India diaspora, etc.) signalled a new direction in India's foreign policy. It would also underline Modi's favourable reception by the leaders of the great powers in which all was forgotten about his troubled days and his visa denial by several countries, including the United States. Our interest was further piqued by the fact that, although the Modi government was facing obstacles to pursuing some major objectives of its domestic agenda given the opposition in the Rajya Sabha, it was in the domain of foreign policy that Modi and his team seemed to be enjoying a relatively free hand. As we followed the Prime Minister's speeches and the activities both within and outside the neighbourhood, we began to see a new pattern in India's foreign policy. And while the discussion in the Indian media and among foreign policy experts generally limited itself to analyses of policy changes or policy continuities with the past, we were seeing something else—a foreign policy emerging from a new cognitive script with its own specific discursive contours. Without much fanfare, the Modi government had effectively replaced the normative discourse of non-alignment and strategic autonomy with what in this book we have called a fluid, dynamic multilevel alignment cognitive script and strategy. Abandoning an inherited policy framework, the Modi government was bringing in a full-fledged paradigmatic shift in India's foreign policy.

This book is partly in response as well to the unfortunately myopic perspective of much of the extensive Indian literature on Indian foreign policy, diplomatic and strategic affairs: largely as a result of a long span of rule of India by Nehru and the Congress party, Indian scholarship was/is largely cast in the Nehruvian mold with little assessment of Nehru's/Congress party's assumptions about the character of the world system, the key elements that constitute power and influence in the modern world. In our opinion, there were two main reasons for the lack of development of serious debates about Indian external affairs. First, what could be called the 'logic of appropriateness', consisting of the cognitive rules, more or less prescribed, according to what the scholarly community perceived, as appropriate, that is, in line with the institutionalized practices and understanding of the right and reasonable. Then, it logically follows—why bother with the formation of a non-Nehruvian discussion when the Nehruvian narrative was widely accepted in Delhi intellectual circles, the Congress party, and by the institutional pillar of Indian diplomacy, the Ministry of External Affairs. Second, there has been traditionally and historically a hesitation to venture a critique of the Nehruvian framework, with the fear of being labelled right wing, anti-socialist and pro-West. Our book is in no way a critique of liberalism or secularism—rather it openly endorses these important values. The book makes a significant point that there must be diversity in scholarship research and competing intellectual traditions in world history. We hope our work will lay the groundwork for an active theoretical and empirical debate on India's foreign policy without any ideological bias.

Narendra Modi's impressive election victory, the marginalization of the Congress party in national affairs and Modi's desire to modernize India's economic, military and diplomatic arrangements, and to unwind further the Nehruvian legacy in foreign affairs, further motivated us to write this book. It should be viewed as an attempt to interpret Modi's diplomacy and approach to strategic affairs. It is meant to contribute to a debate about an alternative paradigm in the study of Indian diplomacy and strategy. It no doubt rests on two contextual elements: India's strong economic performance and future because of the recognition that there is an organic connection between economic modernization and national power as evidenced, for example, by the growth of the United States, Japan and China that emerged on that basis. An aspect of this connection is the link between developing policies that engage the outside world and subordinating rhetoric to the deeper purpose of actually changing the thinking and policies of friends and foes.

The book recognizes Modi's success thus far to expand India's economic and strategic presence in a wide geostrategic sphere which includes Muslim Middle Eastern countries to India's west and extends to the Indo-Asian-Pacific region up to East Asia, including the South China seas. Modi's willingness not to shy away from adopting mildly controversial positions on Tibet, the South China seas or Taiwan and his decision to project the role of measured military actions against Pakistan and China along with the attempt at a diplomatic discourse in his geostrategic world—taken together with the widespread global acceptance, even endorsement, of the legitimacy and value of this approach—clearly warrant an attentive study of Modi's approach to external affairs. We feel that it is appropriate to speak of 'Modi's policy' because he is the main architect of the new orientation. Of course, its execution lies in the hands of officials in various ministries, especially External

Affairs, Home, Defence, Economic and Intelligence Affairs as well as the Prime Minister's Office itself. It is true that Modi is benefitting from important policy changes engineered by two recent predecessors: Prime Minister Narasimha Rao who took several initiatives such as opening up to China, starting economic reforms, opening up to Israel and the 'Look East' policy; and Prime Minister Vajpayee who took India into the nuclear weapons age to ensure that neither China nor Pakistan would have a cost-free option to escalate conflict with India. And we characterize these changes in the book as 'punctuated incrementalism'—bold developments in Indian foreign policy but changes nevertheless that kept intact the historic normative framework of non-alignment and strategic autonomy. Modi, however, is an architect in a fundamentally more radical sense than either Rao or Vajpayee in that, for the first time in India's history, he has eschewed that hallowed framework. But we also recognize that the new cognitive institutional structure of multilevel alignment foreign policy cannot become firmly established nor even sustained in the medium term if the Modi government fails to deal with two major domestic challenges: the ever increasing rhetoric of Indian/patriotism/Hindu nationalism and the growing political and religious alienation of the Kashmiri Muslim population. However, Modi's latest resounding electoral victories at the state level, particularly in the state of Uttar Pradesh, which have significantly enhanced his domestic political capital, hopefully will allow him to apply it successfully towards the resolution of these two challenges.

For research for this volume, we acknowledge the support of Social Science Humanities Research Council of Canada which has generously provided funds to support our research during the last 30 years on India, security issues, South Asian regional politics and secessionist movements. Most of the research for this book was carried out at the libraries at the University of Victoria, the University of Waterloo in Canada and the British Library in London. Ashok would like to thank a number of Indian practitioners who provided valuable insights about Indian strategic affairs over a number of years during his numerous research visits to India—Ambassador Kanwal Sibal, former Foreign Secretary; Ambassador Sudhir Devare, formerly Ambassador to Indonesia; the late S.K. Singh, former Foreign Secretary and Governor of Arunachal Pradesh and later of Rajasthan; the late Professor M.L. Sondhi and Mrs Madhuri Sondhi; H.K. Dua and Hiranmay Karlekar, two distinguished journalists; Vice Admiral (retired) A.R. Tandon; D.C. Nath, former Director in IB; and Major General (retired) Afsir Karim. They kindly shared their expertise with Ashok, but none of them bears any responsibility for the contents of this book. In addition, a huge thank you goes to Mike Tremblay for his meticulous editing of each chapter. We would also like to acknowledge Supriya Das of SAGE who has patiently guided us through the different processes of publishing this book. Finally, we would like to dedicate the book to our respective spouses, Mike and Deepika, in gratitude for their understanding, patience and moral support in this as in all our endeavours.

Reeta Chowdhari Tremblay
Ashok Kapur

Introduction

In the 2014 Indian Parliamentary elections, Narendra Modi and the Bhartiya Janata Party (BJP) received an overwhelming electoral mandate. And after a 30-year period of governance by different political coalitions, Prime Minister Modi formed the first majority government. During the election campaign, Modi had confined himself to purely domestic issues such as inclusive development, policy-oriented governance, growth and employment, eradication of corruption and removal of dynastic ruling elites.[1] But it is foreign policy which, during and after the formation of the new government, has come to occupy centre stage in Modi's governance agenda—dramatically so with the Prime Minister himself driving foreign policy and putting his distinctive stamp on it in terms of both substance and style. Since taking office, Modi's hectic, proactive foreign policy agenda has covered a great deal of ground, whether actively engaging with India's immediate and extended neighbourhoods or deepening India's relationship with all major global players. This has meant multiple foreign visits, engagement with global and regional multi- and mini-lateral institutions and forums, cultivation of strategic partnerships leading to diplomatic and military-to-military agreements with, most notably, the United States, France, Australia, Canada and Japan. But mostly, Modi has been able to bring about a shift in the global thinking from a perception of Indian foreign policy that lacks direction to one that is coherent, well articulated and proactive.

True, the media, both national and international, have been granting massive coverage to Modi's foreign policy (given the at times rather frantic foreign policy statements that have emanated from the Prime Minister and his government and given as well the panache with which Modi has conducted his highly publicised foreign visits), but a scholarly discourse has yet to emerge about the goals that guide India's present foreign policy, the instruments employed to achieve these goals and the precise settings of these policy instruments. Notable exceptions are two excellent and thought-provoking books which have captured Modi's foreign policy activities. C. Raja Mohan's *Modi's World: Expanding India's Sphere of Influence*, structured around his columns in the newspaper *The Indian Express*, gives us some clues about Modi's foreign policy; however, the time frame is confined to the first year of the National Democratic Alliance (NDA) government. But it does give us a hint that foreign policy under Modi administration might be transformative in both style and content and that it most probably constitutes what Raja Mohan describes as 'a consequential moment in India's international evolution'.[2] There is also Harsh V. Pant's 2016 book *Indian Foreign Policy: An Overview* which describes India's foreign policy, including the 'Modi Doctrine', in relation to four evolving relationship dynamics between India and the major powers, India and its neighbourhood, India and its extra-regional outreach, and India and the global order. While the book, in the present context, does not pretend to go beyond a detailed historical analysis of India's foreign policy, Pant perceptively notes that 'Modi seems to be redefining the terms on which India is likely to engage with the world in the coming years.... Most significantly, Modi is gradually, but surely, marginalizing the idea of non-alignment as the bedrock of Indian foreign policy'.[3]

While continuing with some themes developed by Raja Mohan as well as Pant's valid contention that Modi, in pushing aside the ideological rhetoric, 'is dismantling India's default foreign policy legacy of non-alignment', in this book, we advance the argument that, under Modi, there is a new interpretative framework of foreign policy ideas, which is best described as a 'paradigm shift'. In a departure from various scholarly characterizations of India's foreign policy in terms of idealism, hyper-realism, neoliberalism, etc., we focus instead on the underlying cognitive and discursive structure of non-alignment which over time, despite pragmatic and incremental adjustments, had resulted in continuity in Indian foreign policy until Modi's arrival on the Indian national scene. We suggest that the institutionalization of that cognitive non-alignment structure has, in fact, been successfully replaced by Modi's multilevel alignments.

As is to be expected, such a move from non-alignment to multilevel alignments entails quite substantial changes in the accompanying policy discourse, goals and instruments. The new discourse is about inter-linkages—alignments aimed at avoiding zero-sum outcomes by pursuing a course of integrative bargaining among diverse powers with diverse interests. This shift, on the one hand, responds reactively to previous policy anomalies and failures, and, on the other hand, proactively seeks to adjust existing lines of policy to the newly articulated goals. Moreover, it leads to a blending of foreign policy strategies, without necessarily generating any contradictions. Kanti Bajpai refers to this approach as a 'hybrid neoliberal-cum-hyper-realist grand strategy'[4]—deepening economic relationships with China yet getting tougher on border issues and more assertive in the Indian Ocean. Other examples of this approach are simultaneous military and defense alignments with the United States, France, Australia, Japan and Russia, and tripartite agreements regarding energy security with Afghanistan and Iran.

Indeed, given the three challenges which Bajpai has identified as 'China, asymmetric and unconventional conflict, and border management', Modi's foreign policy team does not see any contradiction in intermingling strategies underscored in the Nehruvian (with its emphasis on diplomacy and soft power), neoliberal (putting economies at the core of India's relationship with external powers) or hyper-realism (maintaining balance of power) approaches.[5] It is a radical departure from the historical legacy within which India has been trapped despite changes in the domestic political–economic–military as well as external geo-political environments. It is a departure from what A.P. Rana has described as Nehru's intellectual construct of non-alignment which was 'an attempt to avoid commitment, as much as possible, to a defense-oriented security policy, for fear that the sort of power politics that would then be generated would do the world grave harm'.[6] The multilevel alignment discourse, while freeing Indian foreign policy from the rhetoric of non-alignment and strategic autonomy, allows the Modi government to push forward on his agenda of redefining India's global identity as one of the world's leading powers while still subscribing to India's traditional and ongoing emphasis (some might call this Nehruvian) on India's primacy in the South Asian region and, to a limited extent, on the security concerns in the Indian Ocean.[7] This is to be accomplished by creating transactional relationships—balancing India's measured demands (e.g., the need for modern defence equipment) and seeking support for the other side which appeals to their interests and values (commercial and strategic interests, e.g., of Japan) in order to present a positive-sum game (mutual benefit of both sides). Our objective in this book is to explore the new paradigm, the ushering in of an era of new cognitive/normative structures and its implications for India's foreign policy.

It is also important to note that we use the term *multilevel alignment* rather than *multi alignment*, a distinction with a very real difference. First, for us, a multilevel alignment strategy not only entails a broader focus and scope but, most significantly, it includes an engagement with diverse set of actors with a diversity of interests: it means aligning India's interests and ambitions with those of global parties which might perceive each other's interests with contradiction, thereby allowing India the prospect of moving beyond limited coordination in pursuing its strategic interests. It is true that Indian foreign policy goes beyond what Ian Hall describes as: 'three interlinked foreign policy practices: bids for membership of a range of established and new multilateral institutions and forums; the pursuit and management of informal and formal partnerships with multiple states in multiple issue areas; and what is termed, in what follows, normative hedging'.[8] But what Hall's description fails to capture is that at the centre of all these three aspects of multi-alignment strategies lies the traditional core cognitive structure of non-alignment or of its later incarnation, strategic autonomy. In contrast to the multi-alignment case, a multilevel alignment strategy and its accompanying discourse point to the discontinuities, not only with a traditional past but also with the recent past where changes in foreign policy have come about due to an altered global geo-political and economic environment. Our analysis, therefore, takes issue with Hall's suggestion that the shift towards multi-alignment began a decade ago, and the foreign policy under the Modi government is basically just the consolidation of 'an approach that has evolved for at least a decade, which is judged by India's foreign policy-making elite as the best means to achieve what they perceive as its core interests and ideals in an increasingly uncertain global context'.[9] Second, for us, a multilevel alignment process may actually serve to inhibit rather than encourage the pursuit of rigid national policy positions, thus both creating flexibility and opening windows of opportunity for India to innovate, while adhering faithfully to its domestic and strategic priorities. And although past policy decisions remain points of reference, the multilevel alignment process frees the discussions about foreign policy from those past decisions, particularly if they were embedded in a negative relationship.

Our assertions in explaining this shift are meant in no way to de-emphasize or underestimate the import of the changes which have occurred, particularly after the 1962 Indo-China war, the end of the cold war and the opening of India's economy. Indeed, India's foreign policy has evolved in response to India's internal conditions and its external environment. Foreign policy scholars have been consistent in pointing out major changes—largely occurring during the 1990s, that is, 'a shift from a high minded, pious but ultimately impotent idealism to a sober and more effective pragmatism'; getting rid of 'the always somewhat hypocritical stance that militarism is not a proper ingredient of foreign policy' to coercive diplomacy; India's integration into the world economy and the rise of economic thrust in India's foreign policy; and India's strategic partnership with the United States.[10] Irrespective of party politics at the national level, significant changes have been brought about by different governments. Rajiv Gandhi's visit to China in December 1988 after a standoff in the Sumdoronghu (Chinese: Wangdong) Valley paved the way for the 1993 Boundary Agreement with China. The Agreement on the Maintenance of Peace and Tranquility was signed during Narasimha Rao's visit to China.[11] This has resulted in an expansion of commercial dealings with China without resolving the border disputes. During the early 1990s, in order to re-engage the Association of Southeast Asian Nations (ASEAN) countries, Narasimha Rao launched the *Look East* policy. India's post-1990 economic reforms and liberalization required a dynamic engagement with East Asia. In 1998, the Vajpayee government pushed India beyond the nuclear Rubicon by conducting the Pokhran II nuclear test and making its nuclear doctrine explicit with 'a no-first-use' policy. Other noteworthy changes include Japan's increasing involvement in infrastructural development as well as its emergence as the largest donor of official development assistance to India and one of the largest sources of foreign direct investment (FDI), and, most significantly, a transformation of its relationship with the United States. And the 123 Agreement (the US–India Civil Nuclear Agreement) signed during Prime Minister Manmohan Singh's visit to Washington in July 2008 led to a transformative relationship between India and the United States. However, these post-1991 changes in Indian foreign policy, entailing as they have policy-by-policy adjustments, can best be categorized by what has come to be known in policy scholarship as, to use

David Prindle's term, 'punctuated incrementalism'—marked equally by punctuation and stasis. The term picks up on Bryan Jones and Fran Baumgartner who describe change and stasis as 'encompassing incremental adjustments within policy subsystems and nonincremental, punctuated change when the subsystems assigned the policy could no longer contain the demands for change'.[12]

Changes in Indian foreign policy have without a doubt been substantive. But, as Pratap Bhanu Mehta points out, as India was changing, so was the world during this period. And India's integration or a move towards a more pragmatic policy can be viewed as 'more an artefact of the structure of power in the international system'.[13] Whenever there were non-incremental changes, these have typically been reactions to the external environment (e.g., the collapse of the Soviet Union in which India lost its largest trading partner, a new unipolar reality to which India responded by liberalizing its economy), what we have therefore identified in the Indian foreign policy regime as 'punctuated incrementalism'. Some evidence of punctuated incrementalism can be found in Shivshankar Menon's recent book, *Choices: Inside the Making of India's Foreign Policy*, which covers policy decisions in which Menon participated either directly or indirectly during the prime ministerships of Narasimha Rao, Atal Bihari Vajpayee and Manmohan Singh. It points to both changes and continuity in policy. Menon aptly observes that (a) 'there was a remarkable continuity in policy among these three prime ministers, with each building on his predecessor's work' and (b) all policy changes, moreover, brought about by the choices made by each one of them (India's relations with the United States, integration of the neighbourhood, an attempt to resolve issues with Pakistan and stabilization of the relationship with China) have been internalized into the Indian policy culture. With regard to the latter point, he notes, 'the fact that the policies represented by these choices have been continued by the successor government suggests that the shifts they represent have now been internalized, and absorbed into the practice of Indian foreign policy and the common understanding of what India's interests are'.[14]

Responding to the external environment, the expressed worldview of the political leadership ranged from Nehru's articulation of India's national interests 'in high-flown phrases of world peace and cooperation' to Indira Gandhi's stress on 'security, territory, and prestige'.[15] However, the foreign policy continued to be asserted within the traditional framework of autonomy and non-alignment—'preserving India's decision-making autonomy in the realm of international affairs'.[16] Despite its increasing irrelevance in a unipolar world, it was reframed as strategic autonomy, reflecting 'Nehru's emphasis on avoiding all unnecessary entanglements with major powers that might risk a degree of subordination of India's national interests those of others'.[17] If one were to agree with Rajen Harshe's assertion that 'non-alignment, for India, was a policy and a strategy to survive and negotiate with a world that was getting dragged into the politics of cold war', why then one might ask, did the post–Cold War Indian leadership continued to adhere to this traditional framework?[18] Harshe's answer to this question is that two foundational principles have sustained the policy of non-alignment: the defence and promotion of peace, and the principle of flexibility allowing India to pursue its national interest:

> Especially when the security interests of India were threatened, the apparatus of non-alignment provided room for seeking military assistance from either of the super-powers to repel an aggression No wonder, the foreign policy analysts, while presenting the changes in Indian foreign policy particularly after 1991, point to the political leaderships' framing of the changes with the framework of non-alignment.[19]

We suggest that the continuity path was largely due to the institutionalization of non-alignment as a normative and cognitive structure, which once created, proceeded to take Indian foreign policy on a particular course of continuity. Keeping the national interests at centre in policy design, we assert that Indian foreign policy practices, until Modi's appearance on the national scene, were the products of this cognitive structure of non-alignment or strategic autonomy, pushing Indian foreign policy onto a path-dependent course where decisions not only depended on past knowledge but also future decision-making would find itself constrained as policymakers were unable to break free of the mold and take bolder steps towards changes that would betray the obligatory set of venerable expectations. No wonder then that India's foreign policy epistemic community, brought together by the Centre for Policy Research and the National Defence College, was occupied between November 2010 and February 2012 with producing a forward-looking foreign policy strategic document, *Non-Alignment 2.0*. The authors of this document were Sunil Khilani, Rajiv Kumar, Pratap Bhanu Mehta, Retired Lt. Gen. Prakash Menon, Nandan Nilekani, Srinath Raghavan, Shyam Saran and Siddharth Varadarajan, and had benefited from discussions and input from important members of the policy community, such as the then National Security Advisor, Shivshankar Menon, and the Deputy National Security Advisors, Alok Prasad and Latha Reddy. Given the changing nature of the global geopolitical and economic structure and the accompanying uncertainty and the 'extraordinary' transformational trajectory of Indian economy, this informal epistemic community's document was intended to present a strategic approach whereby India would enhance both its strategic space and its capacity to act as an independent agent—'two core objectives of non-alignment in a changing world'. The aim of this thinking piece was clear— the preservation and sustenance of the prevailing cognitive structure of non-alignment and strategic autonomy:

> The core objective of a strategic approach should be to give India maximum options in its relations with the outside world—that is, to enhance India's strategic space and capacity for independent agency—which in turn will give it maximum options for its own internal development. Such an approach will preserve and sustain two core objectives of non-alignment in a changing world. This policy can therefore be described as 'NONALIGNMENT 2.0'—a re-working

for present times of the fundamental principle that has defined India's international engagements since Independence. The core objectives of Non Alignment were to ensure that India did not define its national interest or approach to world politics in terms of ideologies and goals that had been set elsewhere; that India retained maximum strategic autonomy to pursue its own developmental goals; and that India worked to build national power as the foundation for creating a more just and equitable global order.[20]

Much has been written about non-alignment both as a cognitive structure and a policy instrument, and a variety of explanations have been provided by foreign policy scholars for its adoption by Nehru and for its survival thereafter. It is seen variously, according to some of the more notable explanations, as a strategic policy pursuing national security objective of India putting itself in an advantageous position by creating an independent maneuvering space between dominant global powers;[21] an ideational foreign policy;[22] a protest against power politics;[23] a balancing strategy in trying to fashion a third bloc;[24] a survival strategy in the Cold War as well a response to the north–south divide; a strategy for opposing imperialism and racism in global politics and maintaining a moral distance from the European imperialism;[25] a pre-emptive policy for newly independent nations to ensure their independence in conducting foreign relations;[26] an independent policy to pursue India's own developmental and economic needs and counter-hegemonic critique to the post-colonial world; or a 'the contingent outcome of a sophisticated analysis of the world order' given the difficult political choices confronting the post-Independence leadership.[27] While noting changes in Indian foreign policy during the Janata rule in 1978 meeting the needs of national security, Bimal Prasad referred to non-alignment as 'the bedrock of the foreign policy enunciated by Nehru'.[28] Similarly, Peter Lyons also noted that Janata government's 'foreign policy pronouncements are not significantly different from those of Mrs. Gandhi and that much of the Nehru legacy lives on, at least in the declaratory dimensions of India's foreign policy'.[29] In their 2007 essay, Subrata Mitra and Jivanta

Schöttli, while suggesting that the old Panchsheel doctrine was getting a new makeover by Manmohan Singh's UPA government (from 'idealistic evocations' to 'an instrumental approach to abstract goals'), aptly and perceptively trace India's ambiguities in major Indian foreign policy issues which 'find resonance in the repeated references to non-alignment in the foreign policy pronouncements of India's leaders'.[30] In July 2009, Indian Prime Minister Manmohan Singh attended the 15th meeting of the Non-Aligned Movement in Egypt, giving further credence to the outdated foreign policy legacy. Similarly, in 2008, Harsh Pant, reviewing Indian foreign policy within the contexts of the global balance of power, India's nuclear status, its bilateral relations in the Middle East and competition and cooperation with China along with India's emerging energy needs for developmental purposes, concludes that despite an intense debate 'in the Indian polity and the strategic community' during the regime of different coalitional governments, irrespective of their ideologies, foreign policy has shown a remarkable continuity.[31]

There is a paucity of explanations for the continuity of this framework; however, among the more convincing ones offered by can be found in Itty Abraham' 2007 Economic and Political Weekly essay, 'The Future of Indian Foreign Policy'. Abraham notes that during its post-Independence history, India's foreign policy has 'held firm to a plank of strategic independence' (meaning non-alignment). During the loud debate on India's proposed nuclear relationship with the United States, probably the safest bet was to stick, at least rhetorically, to the cognitive non-alignment frame, thus allowing the centrist government to move beyond the debate over the future of Indian foreign policy whether to align with the US or not'. In this debate, the left was

[C]learly concerned about the anti-China tilt that comes with closer ties with the US; the right worries loudly about the possibility that India's future nuclear weapons development will be held hostage by restrictions imposed by the US. The broad centre that is in favour of the agreement is defined by a pragmatic approach that sees the India-US agreement as returning tangible benefits in the short- and medium-term. The centre argues that this agreement does not imply a permanent loss of sovereignty and comes with real returns that will lead, eventually, to India achieving desire of joining the inner circle of world power and influence.[32]

Baljit Singh had a slightly different take in his 1965 study, where he surveyed a number of government and political leaders, including cabinet ministers and members of legislatures, and came to the conclusion that foreign policy was the creation of India's first Prime Minister, Nehru, and his 'policy of nonalignment in world affairs received the overwhelming support of India's intellectuals',[33] resulting in its subsequent institutionalization. It is no exaggeration to say that the Indian intellectual community has been the driving force behind the furtherance of the strategic autonomy cognitive script. Furthermore, Indian interest and professional groups uncritically 'accepted Nehru's policy as correct, and they proceeded to justify it'.[34] What has been missing in these explanations is that, once created, the non-alignment normative and cognitive structure took on a life of its own, becoming formally institutionalized as a set of internal and external relationships, and led Indian foreign policy on a path-dependent trajectory that had the effect of continually reproducing this normative institution over time.

Under Modi, there has indeed been a paradigm shift. We may ask what it is that has enabled such a fundamental change, ushering in this new cognitive/normative structure that we have termed a multilevel alignment discourse. We have identified three major factors that have made the paradigm shift in foreign policy possible: the 2014 electoral outcome; a top-down foreign policy-making institutional structure; and Prime Minister Modi as a policy entrepreneur.

As a result of the Indian parliamentary system and the first-past-post electoral rules, the outcome in the 2014 general elections has vested a tremendous amount of power in Modi's majoritarian government which has been able, as a result, to exercise greater institutional control. Modi himself, as a Prime Minister who was able to deliver a majority government after thirty years of coalitional electoral outcomes has power commensurate with that accomplishment. It is an important but unintended consequence of the Indian parliamentary and electoral institutions that they allow a political leader with such tremendous electoral power to pursue, virtually untrammelled, his/her policy agenda. Modi is not the first leader to do so—Nehru and Indira Gandhi did indeed exercise virtually absolute power. And in the foreign policy arena, this power is further enhanced by the foreign-policy-making structure. Historically, foreign policy-making is based in the PMO with the Prime Minister playing the leading role and Parliament and the Cabinet relegated to minor parts. In their leadership capacity, as Shivshankar Menon points out, the personalities of Prime Ministers matter in making strategic foreign policy choices:

> Each of India's Prime Ministers made—chose to make—significant strategic decisions that had long-term impacts on the future of India: Jawaharlal Nehru and non-alignment, Indira Gandhi and the birth of Bangladesh in 1971, P.V. Narasimha Rao on Border Peace and Tranquility Agreement and economic reform, Atal Bihari Vajpayee to test Nuclear weapons in 1998 and in diplomacy with Pakistan, and Manmohan Singh with the Civil Nuclear Initiative and settling issues with Pakistan.[35]

Majority government Prime Ministers, along with a chosen team, have historically remained in full control of the institutional and cognitive dimensions of the foreign policy process. When to these unintended consequences of the Indian institutional arrangements vesting total control in a majority-supported, elected leader, are added Modi's exceptional entrepreneurial talents, his charismatic and persuasive manner of discourse and the positive response of the general population (both at home and abroad), the result is a degree of power, unparalleled in recent history, to bring about an institutional change in the foreign policy regime. As well, communicative discourses gain further significance where the policy agenda is controlled by a restricted elite, since a reform agenda, to be successful, must gain legitimacy amongst the population. Modi's freedom to implement a shift in policy has as much to do with his ability to convey policy ideas through a persuasive discourse as much from the power he derives by virtue of his position and electoral credentials. No one can deny that Modi, with his superb oratorical skills in Hindi, has effectively coined and used new slogans and created new narratives by reinterpreting traditional idioms and myths and given these new meaning, thereby successfully mobilizing the citizenry to his new agenda.[36] Starting from his self-described position as an outsider with no conception or experience of how Delhi functions, Modi sought legitimacy for his ideas on the grounds that his national agenda was not 'a political platform, rather it is a platform of a national policy and, therefore, my views should not be evaluated from a political perspective'. In short, his message was clear: his ideas were essentially non-political and were entirely directed towards public service.

Policy entrepreneurs are, as per J.W. Kingdon's label, policy/political leaders with 'the knowledge, power, tenacity and luck to use an instrumental approach to policy-making by using windows of opportunities, reframing issues, undertaking calculated risks and pursuing heightened levels of attention to policy problems to promote their 'pet solutions' to policy makers'.[37] The decisive victory of the BJP was based entirely on the domestic agenda where the public clearly weighted the economy as the most important factor. However, the massive popular mandate has enabled Modi to set on the course of a proactive foreign policy agenda in accordance with his personal policy preferences and only to a limited extent those of the winning party. The moment he was sworn in, Modi enunciated a symbiotic relationship between domestic and foreign policy—domestic goals of development. It was to be growth and employment through the pursuance of a different kind of foreign policy. But in his very first speech as a Prime Minister, he chose to send as a first message to the world:

> [I]t is not important that millions of people have made some party victorious or made someone a prime minister. But it is important that millions have given a good mandate and have held India's position high in the world that is the message of these elections.[38]

In his first independence message, he laid out his foreign policy goals—to connect with the Indian diaspora and global powers to invest in India's manufacturing sector, to adopt a multi-dimensional foreign policy that included working with India's South Asian neighbours to move forward the region's economic and strategic significance in the world. With characteristic oratorical brilliance, he noted that in a new globalized world,

> India cannot decide its future by remaining isolated and sitting alone in a corner. The economics of the world have changed and, therefore, we will have to act accordingly.... I say to the world 'Come, Make in India' ... from electrical to electronics ... from automobiles to agro value addition ... paper or plastic ... satellite or submarine.... Brothers and sisters, our foreign policy is a much talked about issue. I clearly believe that India's foreign policy can be multi-dimensional.... I seek cooperation from neighbouring countries for fighting against poverty in concert and cooperate with them, so that together with SAARC countries we can create our importance and emerge as a power in the world.[39]

The Modi discourse was now in full swing and he had set the stage for a proactive shift in foreign policy agenda.

By connecting complementary policy processes—the problem stream to identification of issues, the policy stream to the solution or response to problems, and the political stream to the policymaker's opportunity to turn the response into a policy—Modi, as policy entrepreneur, has been able easily to move the foreign policy agenda to the 'decision agenda'.

He is effectively guiding the new (multilevel alignment and transactional framework) normative positive-sum game.[40] Despite the fact that during the 2014 elections Modi campaigned exclusively on a domestic platform, he assiduously supplemented his own beliefs with what he was able to glean from continuous exposure to the national mood. The BJP's electoral victory created both opportunities and conditions for Modi's success. One of the most important characteristics of a policy entrepreneur, is sheer persistence in promoting 'their ideas in all ways and in several fora, and are willing to invest large resources in order to promote their solutions'.[41] One instance of Vajpayee's persuasive abilities is mentioned by Menon when he 'single-handedly used his powers of persuasion to make the idea of the United States as an ally actable to India' but Modi's persistence and persuasiveness are evident across the total policy process—encompassing the three streams as noted above and moving beyond the domestic constituency.[42] He has carried his policy messages (among others, combating terrorism, India's three 'D' advantages, concerns about South China Sea) with him during his more than 50 foreign trips on six continents, visiting 45 countries, attending several international forums and addressing the large diasporic gatherings in major western and Asian cities. In this last instance, Modi's expectations have been that the policy messages being sent to the diasporic community will drill down to the audience at home.

In order to succeed, a policy entrepreneur needs to attract the support of key players, particularly where the entrepreneurial activity carries a calculated risk. The paradigmatic shift in foreign policy, which has been successfully spearheaded by the Prime Minister himself, has been possible, as mentioned above, because of the foreign policy-making structure institutionalized in India since Independence. Modi has been able to play his entrepreneurial role by controlling the foreign policy-making agenda in the PMO and by marshalling the support of the vocal informal epistemic policy network. With Parliament and the

Cabinet playing a minimal role, Modi is able to introduce and promote his ideas in many different fora, without worrying about domestic political contestation. Although, due to the constraints of coalition politics of the last three pre-Modi decades, foreign policy-making became subject to a somewhat weakened centralized control that resulted in the enfeebling of India's foreign policy, the majority BJP government has effectively and categorically reverted the locus of authority to the new Prime Minister and his team, effectively precluding a wider contestation between competing paradigms.

In this book, our goals are modest. We do not intend to provide an exhaustive or detailed examination of India's foreign policy but rather to concentrate on the paradigmatic shift and the new Modi doctrine which is emerging as a game changer and moving Indian foreign policy away from its traditional cognitive script of non-alignment. The first chapter engages with the theme of continuity and change in Indian foreign policy; within the broader theme of a paradigm shift, we outline the Modi government's priorities, policy goals and policy instruments. The second chapter sets up the context— the legacy of non-alignment and strategic autonomy, in relation to which the paradigm shift has taken place under Modi's leadership. It focuses particularly on the Nehruvian legacy and the foundational discourse, past policy failures and anomalies. The subsequent three chapters deal with three significant aspects of Indian foreign policy and trace the Modi government's policies within the framework of a break from the past and the ushering in of a new paradigm. Chapter 3 intertwines the discussion of neighbourhood with the multilevel alignment strategy, suggesting that Modi's policy of neighbourhood must be viewed within the larger context of policy priorities in relation to the great powers. Chapters 4 and 5 look at the two most pressing and significant Indian foreign policy issues: India and China, and, India and Pakistan. In Chapter 5, we also introduce India's domestic dilemma of Kashmir: the domestic governance agenda of the coalition partners, the Peoples Democratic Party (PDP) and the BJP, and the ongoing unrest in the Kashmir Valley and its relevance for Modi's Pakistan policy. In the concluding, essentially forward-looking, Chapter 6, we briefly explore external and internal challenges to Modi's transformative policy agenda as well as the opportunities it may bring about.

Notes

1. It is not unusual that foreign policy is not mentioned by leading candidates in Indian general elections. Partha S. Ghosh, writing after the 10th Lok Sabha elections in 1991, points out that

    > Foreign policy, it is clear, plays an extremely limited role in India's electoral politics; in all ten parliamentary elections held so far, its role has never been more than marginal. Several factors contribute to this apathy, the most important of which are societal backwardness, an inward-looking economy, lack of a strategic culture, and limited interaction between the foreign policy establishment and academia. (See Partha S. Ghosh, 'Foreign Policy and Electoral Politics in India: Inconsequential Connection', September 1994, p. 814)

2. Raja Mohan, 'Modi's World: Expanding India's Sphere of Influence'.
3. Pant, 'Indian Foreign Policy: An Overview'.
4. Bajpai, 'Modi's Foreign Policy—How's It Going?'
5. Ibid.
6. Rana, 'The Intellectual Dimensions of India's Nonalignment', 312 (fn. 32).
7. Raja Mohan, 'India's Foreign Policy: Nehru's Enduring Legacy'.
8. Hall, 'Multialignment and Indian Foreign Policy under Narendra Modi', 272.
9. Ibid.
10. See Mehta, 'Review: A New Foreign Policy?', 3173.
11. See Menon, 'Choices: Inside the Making of India's Foreign Policy', Chapter 1, 7–33.
12. Jones and Baumgartner, 'From There to Here: Punctuated Equilibrium to the General Punctuation Thesis to a Theory of Government Information Processing', 3; see also Prindle, 'Importing Concepts from Biology into Political Science: The Case of Punctuated Equilibrium', 21–44.
13. Ibid., 3175.

14. See note 11, p. 4.
15. Mansingh, 'India's Search for Power: Indira Gandhi's Foreign Policy, 1966–1982', 26.
16. Pant, 'Indian Foreign Policy: An Overview', 5.
17. Dalmia and Malone, 'Historical Influences on India's Foreign Policy', 1046.
18. Harshe, 'India's Non-Alignment: An Attempt at Conceptual Reconstruction', 399.
19. Ibid.
20. Khilnani et al. 'Nonalignment 2.0: A Foreign and Strategic Policy for India in the Twenty First Century', 6.
21. See Rana, 'The Imperatives of Non-Alignment: A Conceptual Study of India's Foreign Policy Strategy in the Nehru Period'.
22. See Brecher, 'India and World Politics: Krishna Menon's View of the World'; Ganguly, 'India's Foreign Policy: Retrospect and Prospect'; Harsh, 'Introduction'.
23. Misra, 'Studies in Indian Foreign Policy'.
24. Subrahmanyam. 'Nehru and the India-China Conflict of 1962'.
25. Sen, 'Goodbye to Non-Alignment and All That', 4456.
26. Rana, 'Nehruvian Tradition in World Affairs: Its Evolution and Relevance to Post–Cold War World Order'.
27. Abraham, 'From Bandung to NAM: Non-Alignment and Indian Foreign Policy, 1947–65', 195–219.
28. See Prasad, 'India's Foreign Policy: Studies in Continuity and Change', 461.
29. Lyon, Review of B.R. Nanda's 'Indian Foreign Policy: The Nehru Year', 718.
30. Mitra and Schöttli, 'The New Dynamics of Indian Foreign Policy and Its Ambiguities', 31.
31. Pant, 'Contemporary Debates in Indian Foreign and Security Policy: India Negotiates Its Rise in the International System', 3–10.
32. Abraham, 'The Future of Indian Foreign Policy', 4209.
33. Singh, 'Pundits and Panchsheela: Indian Intellectuals and Their Foreign Policy', 127.
34. Ibid., 126.
35. See note 11, p. 126.
36. For a discussion on the role of discursive institutions, see Schmidt. 'Taking Ideas and Discourse Seriously: Explaining Change through Discursive Institutionalism as the fourth "New Institutionalism"', 1–25.
37. Cairney, 'Understanding Public Policy: Theories and Issues', 271.
38. For the full text, see http://timesofindia.indiatimes.com/news/Full-text-of-Narendra-Modis-speech-in-Central-Hall-of-Parliament/articleshow/35420762.cms (accessed on 17 May 2017).

39. 'Narendra Modi's First Independence Day speech: Full Text'. http://indiatoday.intoday.in/story/narendra-modi-independence-day-speech-full-text-red-fort/1/377299.html (accessed on 17 May 2017).

40. For Policy Streams, see Kingdon, 'Agendas, Alternatives, and Public Policy'.

41. Guldbrandsson and Fossum, 'An Exploration of the Theoretical Concepts of Policy Windows and Policy Entrepreneurs at the Swedish Health Area', 435.

42. See note 11, p. 3.

1

A New Interpretative Framework of Foreign Policy: A Paradigm Shift

During the 2014 Indian General Election campaign, Narendra Modi confined himself to domestic issues such as inclusive development, policy-oriented governance, growth and employment, and the removal of corruption and the dynastic ruling elites. His only comment on foreign policy, by Modi's own admission, was in response to persistent questioning by journalists that the only thing he could confidently say about his approach to Indian foreign policy was that India was to engage with the world on equal terms, '*na hum aankh jhukakar ke baat karenge aur na hum aankh dikhakar ke baat karenge. Hum duniya se aankh milakar baat karenge*' (India is neither to meet the world by casting down its eyes, nor will it glare at the world, but India will meet the world 'eye to eye').[1] However, the BJP 2014 election manifesto, *Ek Bharat Shreshtha Bharat*, does provide a short glimpse of the foreign policy which the Modi government was to undertake. Under the heading, 'Foreign Relations–Nation First, Universal Brotherhood', the manifesto reads

> The vision is to fundamentally reboot and reorient the foreign policy goals, content and process, in a manner that locates India's global strategic engagement in a new paradigm and on a wider canvass, that is not just limited to political diplomacy, but also includes our economic, scientific, cultural, political and security interests, both regional and global, on the principles of equality and mutuality, so that it leads to an economically stronger India, and its voice is heard in the international fora.[2]

Some of the specific goals mentioned in the manifesto are as follows: building a strong, self-reliant India and participating in the global community guided by the tradition of *Vasudhaiva Kutumbakam* (the world is one family); pursuing friendly relations with the neighbours, including strengthening regional forums like South Asian Association for Regional Cooperation (SAARC) and the Association of Southeast Asian Nations (ASEAN); developing Brand India by harnessing the valuable resources of Indians living abroad; and 'Instead of being led by big power interests, we will engage proactively on our own with countries in the neighbourhood and beyond'.[3]

During and subsequent to the formation of the new government, it is indeed foreign policy which has come to occupy centre stage in Modi's governance agenda, with the Prime Minister himself driving foreign policy and putting on it his distinctive stamp in terms of both substance and style. Immediately upon coming into power, the new government declared its commitment to building 'a strong, self-reliant and self-confident India; regaining its rightful place in the community of nations'. Modi's very first act was to invite to his swearing-in ceremony all eight members of SAARC along with the leaders of Tibet-in-Exile and Mauritius, with the open message that India would henceforth be paying serious attention to its immediate neighbourhood. It reflected India's desire for a stable and secure regional environment in order to pursue its own economic growth and handle the issue of poverty in India. In this one symbolic action, the new Prime Minister signalled the intertwining of domestic priorities with the external agenda. Foreign visits by the Prime Minister and the Minister for External Affairs, Sushma Swaraj, to both Asian and non-Asian countries, have emerged as an important instrument of foreign diplomacy. In addition, Modi has participated in several multilateral meetings, including BRICS, G-20, EAS (ASEAN), the Shanghai Cooperation Organisation (SCO) and SAARC. Indeed, he would appear to be the first Indian leader since Nehru to have gained prominent notice outside India. To both the domestic and international audience, Modi's message has been simple and clear, namely that the pursuance of the domestic agenda is closely related to and even contingent upon the success of a proactive and strategically oriented foreign policy. In placing foreign policy at the centre of the governance agenda, Modi has generated a huge set of expectations from a government that is the first in three decades to rule with a single-party majority.

All this raises the question: Should we interpret these developments as indicating a full-fledged paradigmatic shift in India's foreign policy under Modi or do they reflect mostly a continuity with the past? C. Raja Mohan in his recent book *Modi's World: Expanding India's Sphere of Influence* suggests that Narendra Modi's approach to foreign policy marks a break from the past and is so seminal as to mark the beginning of the 'Third Republic' in India. Taking issue with the claims of foreign policy continuity asserted by analysts suggesting that Modi is little more than energetically pursuing Indian diplomacy within an inherited policy framework, Raja Mohan cautions that these claims of continuity miss 'elements of change'. For him, five elements of change can be identified: a renewed focus on economic diplomacy to pursue national interests; a shift in the Indian discourse on globalization (from the 'enduring fear' of globalization to 'confident globalization'); a political approach to the neighbourhood policy; the infusion of new cultural norms of civilizational identity in the foreign policy discourse, and the positioning of India as a 'leading power'. He also suggests that the new domestic political context generated by Modi's massive electoral mandate received in the 2014 parliamentary elections 'could turn out to be an important discontinuity in the evolution of Indian politics that has begun to have a significant impact on how Delhi engages the world'.[4] Similarly, Harsh V. Pant, in his 2016 book, *Indian Foreign Policy*, laying out an overview of Indian foreign policy, points to Modi's dismantling of the traditional non-alignment strategic and intellectual framework. He introduces us to some of the major Modi's initiatives in the security arena with a 'purposeful response towards China'—

balancing economic relationships with military deterrence, a 'refreshing focus on immediate neighbourhood', enhancement of closer ties with the United States and military collaboration with 'Australia, Japan and Vietnam while working to regain strategic space in the Indian Ocean'. Pant, who does not hesitate to allude to Modi's confidence in India's ability to emerge as a global power, concludes that 'Modi seems to be redefining the terms on which India is likely to engage with the world in the coming years'.[5]

But with the exception of C. Raja Mohan and Harsh V. Pant, foreign policy scholars have generally been hesitant to accept the notion that Modi's foreign policy might represent such a change from the past, let alone that it could signal the ushering in of a new era.[6] Indeed, such is the conventional view, and we believe that it is mistaken. We do not hesitate to assert that we are witnessing, and for the first time, a foreign policy discontinuity with what we describe in the following chapter as the Nehruvian legacy. We suggest in our analysis that not only has Modi succeeded in breaking with the past but that certain essentially irreversible policy actions, particularly in the security arena, have the potential to constitute a new legacy—Modi's legacy.

A New Interpretative Framework: Electoral Outcomes and Policy-making Architecture

Under Modi there is a new interpretative framework for foreign policy ideas which can be described as a 'paradigm shift': it entails substantial changes in the policy discourse, goals and instruments. This shift, on the one hand, responds to previous policy anomalies and failures, and, on the other hand, adjusts existing lines of policy to the newly articulated goals. To use Peter Hall's categorization, this is a 'third-order change', entailing simultaneous changes and *adjustments* of three policy components: 'the instrument settings', 'the instruments themselves' and 'the hierarchy of goals behind policy'.[7] In the absence of any society-wide contestation over foreign policy goals, the policy shift has emerged from above. Modi has consistently articulated his worldview, both at home and abroad, that pursuing of successful economic diplomacy and security policy is the answer to India's inclusive economic growth which will, in turn, ensure India's role as the leading power of the world. Moreover, Modi has taken personal charge of conveying this shift, and it is through assertive leadership that a new policy paradigm specifying major shifts has been made visible. Despite his unapologetic usage of religious symbolism and the appropriation of secular leaders to tailor his policy message, his personal leadership, with its distinctive confident style and impressive oratory, has proven to be an excellent tool for inaugurating paradigm change. No doubt, conditions were congenial and well suited to bringing about such a change. A strong electoral mandate, India's growing economic significance, the political appeal/ acceptance of the new economic global agenda at home, as well as the inherited foreign-policy-making architecture, have made possible the transition from a Nehruvian legacy to a Modi-generated new world.

Harsh Pant argues that the absence of effective foreign-policy-making institutions in India has in the past produced largely ad hoc foreign policy responses and a lack of both intellectual and strategic coherence, resulting in a counter-productive strategic culture deficit.[8] One of our assertions in this chapter is that it is precisely this institutional shortcoming that has helped Modi to shift the foreign policy agenda in such a short period of time. Paradoxically, the deinstitutionalized highly personal foreign-policy-making structure, established in India since Independence, has shown itself to be an important adjuvant for the new prime minister so proactively to initiate a new policy agenda. Not only has it allowed him to dismantle the traditional non-alignment framework but also it has made it possible for him to perform his role as a successful policy entrepreneur. In that role he has also set new bureaucratic rules for the foreign-policy-making team as well as the Ministry of External Affairs and introduced a new culture of performance monitoring. It is interesting to note that a senior Congress leader and the former External Affairs Minister Salman Khurshid, now sitting on the other side of decision-making, expressed dismay over the fact that Modi was not allowing the Ministry of External Affairs 'the freedom to work independently as the prime minister is trying to directly or indirectly run it as per his whims and fancies'.[9]

Historically, foreign policy-making is based in the Prime Minister Office (PMO) with the prime minister playing the leadership role.[10] Walter Anderson suggests that the reason why Indian prime ministers have maintained a free hand in the conduct of foreign policy is 'due to the lack of effective parliamentary restraints on the prime minister; to the inability of associational groups to mobilize popular support on foreign policy questions; to the lack of a bipartisan tradition between the ruling party and the opposition; to the pervasive view that criticism of official policy is somehow illegitimate'.[11] While Nehru was the major architect of post-Independent India, Indira Gandhi and Rajiv Gandhi exercised total control over both the content of foreign policy and its implementation; and only a handful of advisors, both political and bureaucratic, were admitted to the inner circles of these prime ministers.[12] Parliament and the Cabinet play a minimal role.[13] However, the control of the prime minister was undermined whenever coalition governments were formed and varied depending upon the strength or the fragility of the coalitions. For example, during the very brief tenure of Janata rule (mid-1977–79), the Parliamentary Consultative Committee on Foreign Affairs and the Cabinet Committee on Political Affairs exercised significant influence on the formulation of policy, but this was largely due to the influential membership of these committees (such as the former Foreign Ministers Y.B. Chavan and Dinesh Singh). Mrs Gandhi, after returning to power in 1980 with a majority government, together with a small inner coterie (prominent among them, the principal secretary, P.C. Alexander; former senior official at the MEA and special advisor in the prime minister's secretariat, G. Parthasarathy; chairperson of the Economic Administrative Reforms commission, L.K. Jha and former head of the RAW, K.N. Kao) undertook the control of foreign policy decision-making. In this centralized and leadership-driven foreign-policy-making process, the mediation between decision-makers, policy experts and the public at large takes place through 'an informal network that is led by a small but shifting group of activists within and outside the government'.[14] Some of the entities of this informal epistemic policy network are state-created, such as the prominent Indian Council of World Affairs (the Vice President of India is the ex-officio President while the Minister of External Affairs is the Vice President) or the 1965 initiative by the then Defence Minister Yashwantrao Chavan's which led to the establishment of the prestigious Institute of Defence Studies to undertake the assessment of national and international security issues.

However, due to the constraints of coalition politics during the past three decades, India's foreign policy inevitably lacked an insightful, coherent strategic formulation and this resulted in political and bureaucratic inertia.[15] The present majority BJP government has categorically and effectively reversed the process and once again pushed the locus of authority towards the new prime minister and his team, thereby avoiding any wider contestation between competing paradigms. Modi and his self-selected 'Muscle Team', comprising Ajit Duval, Advisor, the National Security Council; Sushma Swaraj, Minister of External Affairs; Nripendra Misra, Modi's Principal Secretary; Finance Minister Arun Jaitley who had initially held the portfolio of Defence as well; and Subrahmanyam Jaishankar, Foreign Secretary, are the architects of the new interpretative framework of foreign policy ideas.[16] Modi's team, along with the informal epistemic community network, are in full control of the institutional and cognitive dimensions of the foreign policy process. Television anchors such as the NDTV's Burkha Dutt, Times Now's Karan Thapar and Arnab Goswami have come to create a public arena for the foreign policy discourse with familiar faces from Indian think tanks, some with close party affiliations and others supported by the Indian bourgeoisie, openly supportive of Modi's economic agenda. Doval and Misra, two influential members of the muscle team, were closely associated with the Vivekananda International Foundation.[17] Ram Madhav, the National General Secretary of the BJP and Modi's ambassador at large, who has played a prominent role in Modi's foreign visits, serves as the Director of the India Foundation research centre along with Suresh Prabhakar Prabhu, Minister of Railways; Nirmala Sitharaman, Minister of State; and Jayant Sinha, Minister of State for Civil Aviation. Another influential director of the India Foundation is Swapan Dasgupta, a well-known political columnist who has worked in almost all the leading publications in India in senior editorial positions. He can be seen and heard on major TV channels discussing major foreign policy issues. One of the Foundation's centres, the Centre for Security and Strategy (CSS), works on issues regarding national security and international relations—interpreting, analysing and generating opinion on issues of national importance.[18] The Observer Research Foundation, founded in the 1990s during the period of India's transition to a new engagement with the international economic order, bringing together leading Indian economists and policymakers to present the agenda for India's economic reforms, is supported by a group of business leaders including Reliance. In short, the Indian foreign policy community to this day remains limited to and revolves around an evolving and shifting informal network where the political leadership controls the policy process. It is their initiatives which, if successful, 'become established national policies'. And, to echo K. Subrahmanyam's thoughts, the absence of a 'permanent establishment' allows the leadership not to concern itself with generating national consensus either on the ends or the means of India's foreign policy.[19] Modi has undoubtedly utilized this lack of a permanent foreign policy establishment to muscle his government's advantage to usher in major shifts in Indian foreign policy.

A paradigm shift clearly implies that, in addition to entailing a dramatic change in goals as opposed to merely routine adjustments to existing policies or policy instruments, the existing status quo has, in effect, been abandoned or 'discredited'. Of course, this kind of dramatic change would not have been possible had Modi not received such a resounding electoral mandate—the constraints of coalition politics would otherwise have ensured that the status quo would prevail. Although, with the strong new mandate at hand, the architecture of Modi's new policy regime was fundamentally conceived on the failure of earlier policies, that does not signify discontinuity with all of the successful past policies nor that the new framework will not be built upon some of them. But the paradigm change clearly points to the lessened weight of past decisions. In addition, unlike Vajpayee who failed to take India's foreign policy in a different direction when the opportunity was offered to him, Modi has not placed a high value on the status quo, sustaining the Nehruvian framework. Instead, his own ideas are at the core of policy change and these ideas appear to be widely shared by both the domestic and foreign constituencies, a fact that contributes significantly towards legitimizing the paradigm shift.

A New Interpretative Framework and Policy Learning

While a paradigm shift clearly points to the irreversibility of the new foreign policy goals and its instruments through the abandonment of the prevailing status quo, the ultimate form it takes will largely depend upon the implementation of the new agenda. Policy learning is an essential element of the implementation process, and it has taken on urgency as the Modi government faces two significant and challenging domestic issues. First, directly connected to the Hindutva nationalists, emboldened by the BJP victory, there has been an alarming increase in religious polarization and intolerance which could have serious negative consequences for Modi's legitimacy, both internally and externally. His problems emanate from the hard-core ideologues in his own party, including the BJP President Amit Shah, the RSS and other organizations in the Sangh Parivar. Similarly, the fragile nature of the PDP–BJP coalition in the state of Jammu and Kashmir could prove disastrous in bringing the paradigm shift to fruition. The BJP has made several mistakes in understanding the peculiarities of the Kashmir state, and its inexperience in state governance has led to deepening the alienation of Kashmir Valley's population and to once more opening up the political space for the secessionist groups. Pakistan's extra-curricular activities—its support of militant groups like Jaish-e-Mohammad who have continued their attacks on Indian military establishments (Pathankot in 2015 and Uri in 2016) and its vocal internationalization of the Kashmir issue, as the Kashmir Valley unrest erupted after Indian security forces killed homegrown Hizbul Mujahideen leader Burhan Wani—have created challenges for the Modi government in the Valley as well as made it difficult to continue on the course of composite bilateral dialogue with Pakistan.

Pakistan has been the best test case for the Modi government in policy learning. After a rough road in 2014–15 and the cancellation of National Security Advisors' talks, the Modi government began to realize the crucial need to engage Pakistan in order to ensure the success of its foreign policy goals, including attracting much needed foreign direct investment. At the December 2015 Heart of Asia Ministerial Conference in Afghanistan, Sushma Swaraj shifted the government's rhetoric on India–Pakistan engagement from 'first talk on terrorism, then everything else' to extending 'our hand to Pakistan'. Speaking as much to the Indian audience as the others, she suggested,

> It is time that we display the maturity and self-confidence to do business with each other and strengthen regional trade and cooperation. The entire world is waiting and rooting for a change. Let us not disappoint

them. For its part, India is prepared to move our cooperation at a pace which Pakistan is comfortable with.[20]

Both countries agreed on several points: to condemn terrorism and to cooperate to eliminate it, to have the National Security Advisors address all issues connected to terrorism, to expedite the early conclusion of the Mumbai trial and most significantly, to start to a Comprehensive Bilateral Dialogue where the Foreign Secretaries are to work out the modalities and schedules of meetings (including on Jammu and Kashmir). Speaking to India's top military commanders at Kochi on 14 December 2015, Modi emphasized the significance of a stable and peaceful neighbourhood, 'Our neighbourhood is most critical for our future and for our place in the world' and by engaging Pakistan, we are trying to

[T]urn the course of history, bring an end to terrorism, build peaceful relations, advance cooperation and promote stability and prosperity in our region. There are many challenges and barriers on the path. But the effort is worth it because the peace dividends are huge.[21]

However, all this was to change after the 18 September 2016 Uri terrorist attack. For the first time, India responded by crossing over the LoC and attacked several of the militants' launching pads. And for the first time, India publicly moved from a policy of strategic constraint to that of a military response of 'surgical strikes'. This could be viewed as a reversal of what Indian foreign policy had observed for almost seven decades, a self-imposed constraint of 'strategic diffidence' and a reluctance to use 'hard power'.

Continuity till 2014: Punctuated Incrementalism at Work

Prior to Modi's arrival on the scene, one can discern three distinct historical foreign policy periods which, to a large extent, share a common normative framework and, during the past three decades, an overall lack of the strategic direction. The Nehruvian era (1947–62) projected India as a soft, non-aligned power; the second period (1962–91) pushed India to explore hard power strategies as a result of the Sino-Indian conflict; and the third period (1991–2014) witnessed a pragmatic approach to foreign policy at the end of the Cold War and with the accelerated pace of globalization. This last phase not only combined hard power and soft power responses (the beginning of a 'smart power' strategy), but also 'Looked East' towards the ASEAN nations to meet the demands of India's new economic liberalization policy within the changed environment of increasing globalization. Despite these changes to India's adaptation to the new global realities, different coalition governments had rendered India's foreign policy rudderless. However, punctuated incrementalism ensured both continuity and stasis in foreign policy. The irrelevance of non-alignment notwithstanding both scholars and policy practitioners continued to adhere to the traditional normative and cognitive script—strategic autonomy.

The observers of Indian foreign policy share our view that, until the arrival of Narendra Modi at the helm of the new government, India's foreign policy, although witnessing some discernible changes, has by and large maintained continuity with its Nehruvian foundational tenets.[22] The 1977 anti-Congress coalition Janata government, with Atal Bihari Vajpayee serving as the foreign minister, had a real opportunity to shift India's foreign policy.[23] But although the coalition partners shared a pro-West and free market ideological agenda, as James Chiriyankandath points out, the government 'did not depart markedly from the polices of its predecessors', an indication of just 'how much the Nehruvian perspective had come to be accepted as meeting Indian needs of the Cold War'.[24] Similarly no attempt was made to reorient foreign policy in two successive Congress governments of Indira Gandhi (1980–84) and Rajiv Gandhi (1984–89). Even, during 1998–2004, the BJP, with its bold nuclear initiatives and pro-US alignment, justified the shifts in foreign policy in reference to the Nehruvian framework. In his case study on the BJP foreign policy vis-á-vis the Nehruvian tradition, Sreeram S. Chaulia suggests that the BJP's self-assertion of implementing an alternative model 'capable of shaking roots of the Congress party's foreign policy' did not hold much water.[25] He concludes that

> [T]he Nehruvian tradition has survived BJP's rhetorical and ideological challenge and that notwithstanding the party's braggadocio about altering the discourse on India's place and attitude towards the world, the standards and benchmarks set by Nehru at the time of freedom continue to inform the present Indian government's foreign policy.[26]

Acknowledging the three most significant initiatives undertaken by the Vajpayee government—the Pokhran II nuclear test, the Pakistan Policy, including 'Bus Diplomacy' and the post–Cold War alignment with the United States—which were a break with the past policy framework, Chaulia suggests that 'there is a classic undying and timeless core in Indian foreign policy bequeathed by Nehru, which even an instinctively anti-Nehruvian political phenomenon like BJP is not able to disregard' and Vajpayee's justification for the nuclear test was largely couched in Indian traditional foreign policy themes of universal disarmament and comprehensive test bans, departing 'little from the idealism, obstinate defiance and independent action of the Nehruvian tradition'.[27] However, while the new approach could be described as, to use Stephen Cohen's phrase, 'militant Nehruvian', the BJP framed its actions within the normative framework of non-alignment. Moreover, Chiriyankandath, tracing India's foreign policy within the new post–Cold War context, points out that even the Vajpayee government's pre-eminent agenda of seeking recognition for India as a major power reflects aspirations that had been longstanding and could scarcely be considered new. The BJP 'has only imparted a fresh urgency to this and, compared with previous governments, the differences, while important, have been of nuance rather than marked by dramatic U-turns'.[28] Similarly, Sumit Ganguly, while acknowledging that the tone of the BJP government was self-confident and the content of its policies was more pragmatic, advised the government that a coherent Indian foreign policy would require a twofold pragmatic shift: first, 'to eschew the verbiage and institutional relics of the Cold War such as the "non-aligned movement"', and second, 'to accept a necessary shrinking of sovereignty'—an imperative of globalization (2009: 33). In 2013, Ganguly further reiterated that Indian policymakers who consider their foremost responsibility to protect India's national sovereignty need 'to change—at least at the regional level, to start—if trust, peace and meaningful cooperation are to be established in South Asia, all of which are in the interests of both India and its neighbors'.[29]

Similarly, Dalmia and Malone characterize Indian foreign policy in the twenty-first century,

> As a marked shift towards pragmatism and a willingness to do business with all, resembling in few of its important specifics that of Indira Gandhi in the mid-1970s, and even less that of her father in the 1950s and 1960s. Running in parallel with elements of real change, however, were strong elements of continuity.[30]

T.A. Keenleyside also asserted in his 1980 study of non-alignment in Indian foreign policy that there was a general agreement among leading scholars such as M.S. Rajan, Sauripada Bhattacharya and A.P. Rana, and Indian politicians/ diplomats like K.P.S. Menon about how through the years, when confronted by changes, non-alignment has remained essentially intact. This meant sometimes stretching the concept of non-alignment and redefining it. New terms were generated to describe different phases of non-alignment, such as 'optimum alignment' (Raj Krishna), 'bi-alignment (equal proximity to superpowers)' (Sauripada Bhattacharya), 'disassociative alignment' (A.P. Rana). All this renaming was 'a device for non-aligned foreign policies in temporarily "suspended" positions of what one can only call tangential alignments'.[31] Keenleyside suggests that

> The widespread belief that this doctrine is rooted in the 'collective unconscious of the Indian people' with their tradition of being 'tolerant

of all views and faiths', together with the 'anxiety to maintain a historic foreign policy for fear of reproach of having deviated from the Nehru heritage', have led to a tendency to reaffirm at moments of foreign policy change that India remains non-aligned, while at the same time explaining away much that was essential to that posture as originally conceived.[32]

Harsh Pant's historical overview also supports the thesis of continuity. He points out that at many critical junctures, for example, after each of the 1962 Indo-China war, the 1971 liberation of Bangladesh and the 1989 ending of the Cold War, India foreign policy remained largely reactive and underwent no real change in terms of the direction. According to Pant, India continued on an ad hoc path, 'responding to foreign policy challenges on a case-by-case basis without any requirement for a long-term strategic policy framework'. On the non-alignment cognitive structure, this is what Pant had to say about pre-Modi foreign policy makers:

> Whatever the merits or otherwise of NAM, it is clear that the Indian foreign policy establishment continues to rigidly hold on the concepts and intellectual frameworks which may have had some utility when they were developed but which have become outmoded in the present strategic context.[33]

Subrata Mitra is of the same opinion. While systematically tracing changes in Indian diplomacy, during the period beginning in the Nehruvian era until the Manmohan Singh-led UPA government, following the end of the Indo-US Agreement on Nuclear Cooperation in 2009, Mitra concludes that, In terms of both tone and content, the 'main framework of non-alignment has remained'.[34] Interestingly, non-alignment as a normative paradigm has also remained the fall-back option for various governments when faced with challenging external relationships. For example, Ramesh Thakur, in tracing India's foreign policy towards Vietnam from 1946 to 1979 through different stages, from engagement to indifference, suggests that the fall-back option for the Janata Party was a return to non-alignment:

> In the first stage, its policy was one of benign neglect of the French war that turned swiftly to active opposition to American objectives

and techniques. In the second, it played a mediatory role in the India-chaired ICC while attempting to preclude great power intervention through an implementation of the Geneva Agreements. In the third, India in effect followed a policy of treating the enemy of its enemy as a friend, as Krishna Menon complained to Michael Brecher. In the fourth period, India obeyed the maxim that discretion was the better part of valour, until dramatic developments globally in 1971 led to the contrary belief in the fifth period that boldness pays better dividends. In the final period, India seems to have reverted to a policy of circumspection towards Indochina in keeping with the professed objective of a return to genuine nonalignment.[35]

Paradigm Shift in the Normative Structure: Non-alignment to Multilevel Alignments

It is indeed surprising that this continuity in foreign policy framework remained virtually unbroken until Modi's arrival on the scene in view of its obviously weak effectiveness and inefficiency. Under Modi's leadership, India is now moving away from this historical consensus and framework whose origins can be traced back to the idealism of the Nehru era, the self-affirmation of post-Independent India and the politics of the Cold War. Indian foreign policy observers are hesitant to acknowledge that Modi's foreign policy world is different and that we are witnessing the emergence of a new world view. What they fail to see is that with a new discursive shift, old concepts are being radically displaced and the historical normative status quo has been abandoned. In Chapter 2, we outline the Nehruvian legacy of policy anomalies leading to policy failures, the very context which Prime Minister Modi inherited when he formed the new national government. Given the deeply entrenched character of the foreign policy norms and framework that we have described, the advent of radical change was quite unexpected, even surprising and consequently fully in need of an explanation.

Modi's foreign policy, although sharing certain continuities with the past, should be viewed as transformative, abandoning the prevailing normative status quo in favour of a new coherent, pragmatic and strategic approach. During the launch of C. Raja Mohan's book in July 2015, India's Foreign Secretary, S. Jaishankar, summarized policy discontinuities with the past: the Modi government's proactive yet nimble, take-charge approach to foreign policy rather than the stodgy reactive approach of the past; a clear set of priorities with an integrated view of the regions and the simultaneous pursuance of multiple relationships; policy instruments of new narratives, a new lexicon and new imagery; the promotion of 'soft power'; inclusion of the Indian diaspora; and, most important, the linking of foreign policy with national development.[36] He aptly pointed out that Modi's foreign policy likely reflects a very novel development, marked by the radical changes in the overarching terms of policy discourse and policy content. While Jaishankar was also correct to acknowledge that some foreign policy decisions under the new foreign policy share certain continuities with the past, what he failed to provide, at that early juncture, was an explanation of why the whole Modi approach should be viewed as transformative. He should have stressed that it is because the prevailing normative status quo has been abandoned in favour of a new paradigm. He should have pushed the point that the new paradigm performs multiple functions: it responds to previous policy anomalies and failures while adjusting and expanding existing lines of policy to the newly articulated goals and simultaneous changes and adjustments of three policy components—the instrument settings, the instruments themselves and the hierarchy of goals behind policy. However, in his keynote address, delivered on 21 November 2016, at an event organized by the Institute for Defence Studies (IDS) in collaboration with the Norwegian Institute of Defence Studies (IFS), he did provide some rationale for the shift in the foreign policy agenda.

As mentioned earlier, a paradigm shift does not signify discontinuity with all of the successful past policies nor that the new framework will not be built upon some of them, but the paradigm change highlights a change in the locus of impact of past decisions. Within this context, the new government has clearly built upon its 'Act Policy' upon Narasimha Rao's 'Look East' policy and his looking beyond the traditional Middle East policy by establishing relations with Israel. Moreover, the present concerns with China's increasing diplomatic and security footprints in the Indian Ocean and beyond are not new, and the many components of India's present maritime security policy, such as the *Mausaum* project and the Trilateral Highway project, connecting Thailand, Myanmar and India, are a continuation of past policies. However, the way in which past decisions matter has changed, both in terms of policy discourse (the language, in particular, and the tone of foreign policy, in general) and the centrality of these policies in relation to the pursuance of multilevel alignment rather than the adherence to the normative framework of non-alignment. The shift is most evident in setting aside the diplomatic brand of Nehru, and in particular, in moving away from the Congress party and the UPA governments' reliance on global idealism and regional appeasement in their approach to Pakistan, China and Tibet. Within the framework of non-alignment, peaceful coexistence and anti-militarism, there has been a traditional reluctance among Modi's predecessors to expand India's diplomatic and military links with non-traditional partners of India, such as Israel, Japan and Vietnam.[37] This reluctance has been replaced by a proactive, integrated view of the regions and the simultaneous pursuance of multiple relationships, within, what Jaishankar has described, as a clear set of priorities.

India's foreign policy has now a new language and a new tone. Through impressive oratory and a powerful command over the Hindi language, Modi delivers the message of change in India and amongst Indians, particularly to the Indian diaspora, of the new dynamics of India's foreign policy. In his uniquely assertive and self-assured, yet not overbearing manner, Modi speaks credibly of a confident India whose global image is reflected in the strength of its own vast population and in its diaspora and which will only work shoulder to shoulder with all powers (eye to eye), small or big. The message, mostly delivered in Hindi, is clear: India, with its 1.2 billion population, is a great country. '*Bharat mahan desh hai, Bharat visahl desh hai, sawa sau crore deshwasi ka desh hai*'. (India is great nation, a richly endowed nation, and it is a nation of 1.25 billion people.) India's engagement with the world is to take place within the context of equal partnership, *brabri* (equality). To the cheering crowd of the Indian diaspora in Singapore, Modi elaborated on these terms: '*Na hum aankh jhukakar ke baat karenge aur na hum aankh dekhakar ke baat karenge; hum duniya se aankh milakar baat karenge*'. (India is neither to meet the world by casting down its eyes, nor it will glare at the world, but India will meet the world 'eye to eye'.) Moreover, 'Neither will we bow down to others, nor we will bully others, but we will work shoulder to shoulder with them.'[38] According to Modi, *brabri* has already produced results, and India is being treated equally by other nations and not being perceived as a mere market for their goods. This *brabri* has found resonance in a Modi–Obama vision statement, '*Chalein Saath Saath*' (Forward Together We Go). The United States government has been more than obliging in response to Modi's initiatives to strengthen their strategic partnership. According to Ashley Tellis,

> Unlike his predecessor, Manmohan Singh, who also ardently sought a strategic partnership with the United States but was prevented from consummating it by pressures from within his own party, Modi neither has the patience for the traditional Indian shibboleths about nonalignment and strategic autonomy nor is he diffident about cementing stronger ties with Washington because of its value for India's vital interests.[39]

Most significantly, within this context of partnership, Modi has put India on the same footing as China, despite China's overwhelming influence in the world economy, by declaring that 'the re-emergence of India and China and their relationship will have a profound impact on the two countries and the course of this century'. During his May 2015 visit to China, Modi's conversations with Chinese leaders have apparently been candid yet friendly, covering all issues, 'including those that trouble smooth development of our relations'. In order to realize the full potential of an India–China partnership, Modi asked China to 'take a strategic and long term view of our relations'.[40] This visit also resulted in the two countries agreeing to work together on climate change in full accordance with the principles of 'equity and common but differentiated responsibilities and respective capabilities, reflecting different historical responsibilities, development stages and national circumstances between developed and developing countries'. During the Paris Climate Change Summit (November 2015), India emerged as a significant strategic stakeholder in terms of its own domestic interests as well as representing the view of developing countries. Along with China, it pushed the 'climate justice' argument. Both countries provided leadership to the developing countries bloc in the G-77 + China group by successfully advocating for the principle of common but differentiated responsibilities, ensuring its inclusion among the different pillars of the agreement. The new narrative of *brabri* was in full operation during the conference. India entered the conference with a commitment to seek an agreement on shared responsibilities so that the burden on the developing world to fight climate change would not be more onerous than that of the developed world. Modi's team was to forcefully reject the US Secretary of State John Kerry's statement that India would be a challenge and rallied the G-77 + China group around the Indian slogan *Singhasan khali karo ki Janata Aati hai* (India and developing countries are arriving, developed nations should vacate the carbon space).[41] Modi was to repeat this message during the Summit:

> Climate change is not of our making. It is the result of global warming that came from the prosperity and progress of an industrial age powered by fossil fuel. But, we in India face its consequences today. We see it in the risks of our farmers, the changes in weather patterns, and the intensity of natural disasters.[42]

Nowhere was the shift in the discourse of foreign policy more evident than in Modi's speech at the Inaugural Ceremony of the

Third India–Africa Forum Summit on 29 October 2015. There was no longer talk of decolonization and the anti-imperialist struggles uniting India and Africa, instead, 'a new promise of a great future for an ancient relationship'. Modi began his speech by acknowledging that India has failed Africa in the past:

> There are times when we have not done as well as you have wanted us to. There have been occasions when we have not been as attentive as we should be. There are commitments we have not fulfilled as quickly as we should have.

New partnership is to revolve around the alignment of India's development priorities and Africa's vision for its future: Africa's Blue Revolution, embedded in its Blue Economy (maritime resources and the whole economy around the maritime industry), development of human capital and institutions, a global trading regime, reforming international institutions like the UN to respond to the new realities of this century and countering terrorism and extremism. It is interesting to note that Modi views the Indian Ocean as the new linkage between India and Africa, including the safety of 'our oceans', 'Our histories have intersected since ages. Once united by geography, we are now linked by the Indian Ocean'. And, of course, putting his distinctive stamp on his remarks, Modi invoked India's heritage consistent with vernacularization of India's foreign policy.

> We will work together: … From the spirit of India's ancient belief: *santa svayam perhite nihitabhiyoga* (great souls are always taking the initiative to do good to others); from the inspiration of Mandela's call to live in a way that respects and enhances the freedom of others.[43]

The following section explains the different components of the new policy paradigm—its priorities, goals and instruments—with its consequent dual impacts of, on the one hand, a radical departure from the historical legacy within which India has been trapped despite changes in the domestic politico-economic-military and in the external geo-political environments, and, on the other hand, redefining India's global identity as one of the world's leading powers.

The Modi Government's Priorities and Goals

Breaking with the past, the Modi government has established two priorities creating a symbiotic relationship between the domestic and foreign policy agendas: the simultaneous pursuance of (a) domestic economic goals (growth, job creation, infrastructure enhancement) and (b) strategic security goals (diplomatic, military and economic relations with external powers). Moving beyond the government's agenda of linking foreign policy largely to its developmental priorities and seeking a global environment conducive to its well-being by generating institutional regional and global institutional capability and capacity, Modi's domestic neoliberal agenda of growth, on the one hand, and the inclusive development goals (*Sabka Sath, Sabka Vikas*), on the other hand, are to be pursued through successes in foreign policy. In explaining the Modi government's proactive foreign policy at the launch of Raja Mohan's book, Indian Foreign Secretary S. Jaishankar made this connection evident. He noted that there was now 'a more explicit link made between diplomacy and national development efforts, with India working hard to leverage its international relationships to bring resources, technology and best practices to further its own development such as through the Make in India initiative'.[44] Domestic programmes such as Make in India, Smart Cities and Energy security can only be possible if the Indian diaspora and the global powers engage economically with India through their financial and technological know-how in the Indian economy. Modi's thinking is not far from, what Pratap Bhanu Mehta noted in 2003, that

> India's prospects as an international player depend on its own internal health, its capacity to project not only economic strength, but the makings of a decent and civilised society. Get your domestic policy and conception of national identity right, and a good foreign policy will follow in its wake.[45]

The discernible difference is that in addition to setting aside, what Rajiv Sikri terms, an ongoing suspicion of the motives of its immediate neighbours and a defensive attitude towards China, Modi has been able to present the two policy agendas—domestic and foreign—as existing in a symbiotic relationship.[46]

With regard to a strategic security agenda, although there is no clear enunciation of what constitutes this agenda, one can readily identify four aspects through the government's various recent pronouncements and actions. These are as follows: (a) maintaining India's territorial integrity and securing its borders; (b) having zero tolerance for export terrorism; (c) recovering both the diplomatic and security space in its own neighbourhood which, over the years, India had voluntarily abandoned to China and (d) intensifying the quest to expand India's diplomatic, economic and strategic space. The last of these objectives is to be achieved by building substantial ties with Japan, Australia, Southeast Asian nations, such as Vietnam and Indonesia, the European powers, especially France, the United Kingdom and Germany, and Russia along with the United States. In addition, the Modi government has articulated a vision of an Indian Ocean community driven by an external balancing strategy against China's influence in the Indian Ocean, as well as India's desire for a greater global role, reflecting among countries around the Indian Ocean littoral. China's push to build its Silk Route network and its push into the South China Sea and the Indian Ocean have been recognized as potentially impacting upon both Indian security and trade. Almost 40 per cent of world trade passed through the Indian Ocean. It does make sense to make the Indian Ocean a part of regional security.

The first two strategic priorities can be subsumed under Modi's slogan, *Ek Bharat Shreshtha Bharat* (One India, Glorious India). However, these are not new strategic priorities for Indian policy makers. It is the third (attention to the neighbourhood) which, in interaction with the first two, gives a new meaning and significance to Modi's strategic security agenda. India's neglect of the neighbourhood in the past has allowed China to acquire a powerful presence in South Asia. The marked increase in size of the Chinese footprint has been met by a concomitant discontinuance of India's strategic influence in South Asia and the Indian Ocean. In acknowledging China as the world's leading economic power and recognizing its overwhelming relevance as India's largest trading partner, the Modi government perceives China to be the most significant yet difficult challenge within its economic and strategic policy agenda. It is also cognizant of the fact that India's problems with Pakistan can be alleviated with China's intervention, particularly in regard to the issues of terrorism and Kashmir. Pakistan remains an essential element in India's security agenda and with the 2015 formation of the PDP–BJP coalition government in the state of Jammu and Kashmir, the domestic and the international aspects of Indian foreign policy have come to be conflated.

Undoubtedly, China and its increasing strategic influence in South Asia and the Indian Ocean have been on India's radar for a while, but the Modi government has been careful not to join Washington in a campaign to confront China militarily. Instead, India is working towards containing it bilaterally in the Himalayas by upgrading its military defences. Meanwhile in the Indian Ocean, it has expanded its commitment to provide new resources for India's naval development. In his one-on-one conversations, Modi has tactfully requested President Xi Jinping to avoid expansionist thinking and to be sensitive about Indian concerns about the development of the China–Pakistan economic and military corridor that links China with Pakistan up to Gwadar and which passes through the Kashmir region. The pattern of Modi–Xi engagement is a far cry from, what Stephan Cohen characterized as 'militant Nehruism'. Nehru had appeased the Chinese leaders on Tibet, and he and his advisers had allowed China to act with impunity on the border issue during mid-1950s to 1962. Nehru and Menon, with their left leanings and anti-militaristic values, had doubted that China would go to war with India. Moreover, the two distrusted the Indian generals to the point that they actually impeded India's military modernization. Modi's China policy, on the other hand, seeks a robust pattern of military containment in the Himalayas and in the Indian Ocean, as well as strong diplomatic and economic engagements.

The fourth component of the strategic security agenda, that is, intensifying the quest to expand India's diplomatic, economic and strategic space by building substantial ties with various global partners, is to be accomplished by creating transactional relationships—balancing India's measured demands (e.g., the need for modern defence equipment) and seeking support for the other side which appeals to their interests and values (e.g., commercial and strategic interests of Japan) in order to present a positive-sum game (mutual benefit of both sides). The strategic security partnership agenda is to be accomplished through building defence relationships, civil nuclear cooperation agreements and infrastructural investments. But, most significantly, this agenda has been carved to accommodate the interests of the partner countries: US–India ties have been referred to as 'a defining partnership of the twenty-first century', a partnership based on shared values and a common interest to fight terrorism.[47] Moreover, through these partnership arrangements, Modi has signalled the abandonment of India's historical concerns of compromising its autonomy and being drawn into a military alliance with the United States. For example, while it may appear that the Logistics Exchange Memorandum of Agreement (LEMOA) signed in August 2016 by the United States and India (like the other two military logistic agreements, apparently agreed to in principle—the Communications Interoperability and Security Memorandum of Agreement and the Basic Exchange and Cooperation Agreement for Geo-Spatial Cooperation), providing access to each other's land, air and naval bases for repair and resupply, is mundane, its significance, however, lies in India's having moved clearly beyond the strategic autonomy concept. Although both governments took great pains to point out that the agreement did not allow for basing US troops in India, thus not undermining Indian autonomy, they do consider this as a deepening of their relationship which undoubtedly is to have a direct impact on Pakistan and China, although there was no mention of either country. The agreement underscored the significance of reinforcing the rule of law, guaranteeing freedom of navigation and countering terror. It stayed true to Modi's foreign policy goal of combating terrorism and his persistent messages to various international fora of India's intention to settle disputes in the South China Sea and the Indian Ocean by adhering to international norms.

Another example of the strategic security partnership agenda is India's relationship with Israel. For the first time, the nature of India's relationship with that country is now in the open. According to C. Raja Mohan, the fact that Israel is the largest external supplier of military equipment to India had been kept under wraps in order not to alienate the Muslim population within and outside India: 'Cynics in Israel would point out that Delhi was treating Tel Aviv like a mistress—engage in private but refuse to be seen with in public. The Modi government is having none of that'.[48]

The Modi Government's Foreign Policy Goals

Three goals, though not mutually exclusive, have been established to realize the simultaneous pursuance of domestic economic and strategic security priorities. They are as follows: (a) re-conceptualizing the neighbourhood, (b) bringing about multilevel alignments and (c) developing the brand India globally.

Re-conceptualizing the Neighbourhood

First, India is to actively engage with its immediate (South Asia) and extended neighbourhoods (East and South East). In June 2014, through the President's address to the Indian Parliament, the Modi government sent a clear signal of its commitment:

> This shows my government's commitment and determination to work towards building a peaceful, stable and economically inter-linked

neighbourhood which is essential for the collective development and prosperity of the South Asian Region. We will further work together with South Asian leaders to revitalise SAARC as an effective instrument for regional cooperation and as a united voice on global issues.[49]

At the UN General Assembly, he reiterated the primacy of India's neighbourhood, explaining that India desired a peaceful and stable environment for its development, 'A nation's destiny is linked to its neighbourhood. That is why my government has placed the highest priority on advancing friendship and cooperation with her neighbours'. While the Prime Minister undertook his first state visits to Bhutan and Nepal, the Minister for External Affairs covered all the South Asia region countries in order to convey the new government's message of regional cooperation. In addition, India has been forthcoming in settling old disputes with its neighbouring countries. During his October 2014 visit to Nepal, Modi gave a virtual blank cheque to Nepal to come up with a proposal to revise or replace the 1950 Treaty of Peace and Friendship between the two countries which has been a long-standing and thorny point of contention for the Nepalese. Party politics was set aside when, in June 2015, the Modi government ensured the passage of the constitutional amendment, resulting in the land boundary agreement between India and Bangladesh, putting an end to the statelessness of more than 51,000 people living in 162 enclaves since 1947.

It should be noted that emphasis on the neighbourhood is not a novelty in Indian foreign policy. I.K. Gujral, first as India's foreign minister (1989–90) and later as the prime minister (1996), had formulated a set of five principles to guide the conduct of foreign relations with India's immediate neighbours. The Gujral doctrine, among other principles, emphasized non-reciprocity (India's readiness to give without expecting anything in return) in its relations with its neighbours with all of whom it had the fundamental objective of recasting its relationships. Atal Bihari Vajpayee in the BJP-led coalition government in 1998 pushed forward the Gujral doctrine, with a conscious strategy to put the neighbours at ease at a time when

India had just successfully conducted a set of nuclear tests. Towards the end of 1998, India concluded the Indo-Sri Lanka Free Trade Agreement. Vajpayee opened communication with Pakistan and made his historic bus journey to Lahore. It would, however, be a mistake to interpret Modi's engagement with the neighbourhood as simply revisiting the Gujral doctrine, if we consider how his neighbourhood first policy is a fully integral part of an overarching strategy, symbiotically to interconnect the domestic and the foreign agendas. Modi is adamant that India's neighbours are crucial for the Indian economy and that only an improved South Asian connectivity can drive stability and growth, on the one hand, and generate strategic security partnerships, on the other. Jaishankar, at the IDS/IFS seminar in November 2016 noted that the lack of connectivity was holding back both India and South Asia as a region; it was imperative that India and the region connect themselves within in the larger connectivity grid in Asia.

Moreover, a neighbourhood that embraces India is also a strategic counter to China. From this perspective, Modi has unabashedly revised the concept of India's strategic and economic neighbourhood and extended it to include the countries in the Indian Ocean area. Modi's approach to the neighbourhood is quite different from Nehru's, who viewed China and India as the two Asian powers. In this view, their countries were bound to gravitate towards one or the other, Japan and Southeast Asian nations were of secondary importance and peaceful coexistence between China and India was necessary if not inevitable. Nehru's global vision was indeed to develop peaceful relationships but without a well-defined strategy to form meaningful relationships at the regional level. Nehru's world in action and rhetoric was to build India as one of the principals of world affairs along with the United States, China and Russia. Modi, in contrast, has framed his policy with the recognition that because of the Sino-Indian rivalry the context is one of competition. Without naming China, India speaks about this context in terms of the growing significance of the maritime space where the future depends upon the littoral countries—land shaping the ocean rather than the ocean shaping the land. There is also a deep recognition that, as Jaishankar has pointed out, there are strategic security implications for the region as a result of fluidity at the great power level. There are general uncertainties at the regional level which get further aggravated by the absence of 'a security architecture' and by sharp regional rivalries. All this requires a different foreign policy approach. At the same time, Modi has given Narasimha Rao's and Manmohan Singh's 'Look East' policy a vigorous 'Act East and West' orientation by taking his diplomacy into China's backyard in Japan and in the South China Sea: the Modi government has strengthened bilateral ties with Vietnam, Mongolia and Central Asian countries; it is actively seeking a place in oil exploration in the disputed South China Sea; and the heightened focus on Africa, where India and Indians have historical, political and commercial links, is part of the dream to create the basics of a stable regional, political, economic, cultural and a strategic infrastructure that connects the Indian Ocean world from Africa to the South China Sea.

Bringing About Multilevel Alignments

Second, there is no longer talk of non-alignment. Quite the contrary, India is set to seek multilevel alignments, pursuing a diversity of interests in diverse settings with diverse powers. This suggests an engagement with 'a multiplicity of actors in a varied range of arenas and try(ing) to straddle what can be contradictory trends in India's foreign policy'. Such an approach towards an engagement with great powers is possible due to 'a more fluid and multi-polar' global system.[50] In this multi-polar environment, the new foreign policy agenda requires India to look for multiple opportunities, allowing it to pursue its agenda in an optimal yet nimble manner. 'Fluidity' is the operative mantra in this multilevel alignment approach. And The 'Look East' policy has been converted into an 'Act East' and 'Link West' policy, signalling the ushering in of a new multilevel alignment strategy. This strategy proposes alignments aimed at avoiding zero-sum outcomes by pursuing a course of integrative bargaining among diverse powers with diverse interests. In integrative bargaining, 'each party works at understanding what the other really needs out of the negotiation', which, in turn, 'depends on being able to question the other party about their interests, or otherwise discover what they really are'.[51] Paradoxically, the more difficult and competing the interests that are brought to the table for discussion, the more likely a positive-sum outcome could be achieved. Such a kind of strategy has allowed India to engage with Japan, the United States, Russia and China without getting cornered in one box—on the one hand, building strategic partnerships, for example, with the United States with whom it shares liberal democratic traditions as well as common strategic interests in the Asia-Pacific and, on the other hand, finding common ground with Russia and China where India's interests diverge from the Western liberal democratic countries.

One could see the beginning of this thinking when Modi spoke at the UN General Assembly:

> While we speak of an interdependent world, have we become more united as nations? Today, we still operate in various Gs with different numbers. India, too, is involved in several. But, how much are we able to work together as G1 or G-All? On the one side, we say that our destinies are inter-linked, on the other hand we still think in terms of zero sum game. If the other benefits, I stand to lose.

Modi has wrapped his multilevel alignment policy around the concept of '*Vasudhaiva-kutumbakam*' (the world is one family). That kind of approach allows Modi, on the one hand, to disagree with his counterparts, just as one might do with another member of the family, and on the other hand, to engage different partners who might be each other's adversary. No wonder then that Modi appeared quite comfortable when, during his China visit in May 2015, he publicly and confidently revealed that during his meeting with the Chinese Premier, Li Keqiang, he had stressed the need for China to reconsider its approach on some of the issues and to take a strategic and long-term view of Indo-Chinese relations that have been holding the two countries back from realizing the full potential of their partnership.

Developing the Brand India Globally

Third, India will actively develop the 'brand India' globally. The key strategy for marketing a confident and a strong India has been through connecting and building enduring links with the Indian diaspora. At the core of the development of the brand India are two objectives: (a) to generate maximum leverage for foreign policy by occupying the mindset of influential Indians abroad and (b) to expect that the policy messages being sent to the diasporic community will drill down to the audience at home, thereby playing 'a symbolic role in the building of a national profile'.[52] In pursuing these objectives, Modi has few qualms about building on Nehru's message, by giving it his own twist, namely that India deserves global recognition because of its historical civilizational accomplishments, sheer size and moral principles pushing for equality and social justice. Not only have Modi's speeches, in cities such as New York, Sydney, Toronto and Vancouver (each event attended by some 20,000 people of Indian origin), helped create a sense of pride among the Indian diasporic communities in their heritage (Indian civilization) and India's accomplishments (its democracy and technological feats such as the Mars mission), but have also constituted a call to all Indians to reconnect with India, contribute to India's growth and help the Modi government realize the agenda of *Swachh Bharat* and 'Make in India'. For example, Modi has characterized Mahatma Gandhi himself as a non-resident Indian (NRI) who returned from South Africa to his country and gave India its Independence from colonial rule. He will often point out to the Indian diaspora that now it is their turn to do something for Gandhi, 'Let's give him a clean India (*Swachh Bharat*)'; and 'whatever we can do, we should do for our country'. Addressing the Indian diaspora in China, he once more invoked Gandhi, calling him '*Yug Purush*' and

'*Vishwa Manav*'. This time he emphasized the significance of Gandhian ideals in tackling the two major global problems of terrorism and global warming.

During his visits to New York and Sydney, Modi invited people of the Indian diaspora to attend the celebrations of 100 years of Mahatma Gandhi's return to India during the 13th *Pravasi Bharatiya Divas* in 2015. Over 3,000 NRIs as well as persons of Indian origin attended the event in January 2015. On this occasion, the Vice-President of India, Mohammad Hamid Ansari, reiterated Modi's message of the need for greater participation by the diaspora to contribute towards building a new India:

> Overseas Indians can play a major role in building a new India, as they are having experience and resources to deal with problems. They have taken initiatives to transform the country in which they are living. We welcome them to replicate those initiatives here.

In all his foreign visits, Modi has stayed on course.

In the development of a global Indian brand, Prime Minister Modi has made cultural connectivity one of the major focuses of his visits abroad, bringing into prominence historical and cultural ties between India and its neighbours. Culture is being used, confidently and unapologetically by Modi, as a soft power tool to push forward India's agenda abroad. While Modi makes it a point to visit religious sites in the neighbouring countries—Buddhist monasteries and Hindu temples—to attract both the Hindu and the Buddhist populations from foreign lands, pilgrimage tourism to India has been identified as one of the major planks of cultural connectivity. The Ministry of Tourism has launched a new scheme called *Swadesh Darshan* for the integrated development of tourist circuits on specific spiritual heritage spots in the states of Arunachal Pradesh, Jammu and Kashmir, Maharashtra, Meghalaya, Mizoram, Nagaland, Uttarakhand, Punjab and Tripura. The Ministry has also planned to launch spiritual circuits across India which would include a Buddhist Circuit, a Jain Circuit and a Sufi Circuit.

Is there a larger underlying motive behind the pursuit of this proactive foreign policy agenda? Jaishankar in his keynote address to the IDS/IFS crowd gave two specific hints in answers to this question. First, India was not a party to the 1945 global architecture which meant that India was deprived of a decision-making role. It is imperative that India, with the second largest population and one of the top 10 largest economies, 'get its place' in the global order. Second, India has now the possibility of advancing its 'own great power prospects'. It knows its own agenda and it is 'prepared to engage the great powers' robustly. All this, at a minimum, clearly reflects a decisive shift in India's foreign policy.

Policy Instruments

All these goals are to be realized through the use of the foreign policy tool of 'smart power'—a nuanced combination of hard or military power, soft power and economic power. Modi calls this a strategy of *shakti* (power/divine energy) and *shanti* (peace). Within this strategy of *shakti* and *shanti*, Sushma Swaraj, Minister of External Affairs, has identified five specific policy instruments to help achieve new goals of foreign policy, which she has labelled the 'Five S Plank': scale up trade and investments, speed up connectivity, build 100 smart cities with focus on urban development and water management, target skill development and develop a state focus to promote engagement with Indian states. The last one, that is, state focus or 'cooperative and competitive federalism', is emerging as one of the most important policy instruments in reshaping Indian federalism. It is intended to create a proactive role for the regional governments in economic diplomacy. The President, in his address to the Indian Parliament in June 2015, laid out his government's plans:

> India is a federal polity. But, over the years, the federal spirit has been diluted. The States and the Centre should function as an organic Team India. In order to actively engage with the States on national issues,

my government will reinvigorate fora like the National Development
Council and the Inter-State Council. The Centre will be an enabler
in the rapid progress of States through Cooperative Federalism. State-
specific development models will be developed taking into account the
special needs and unique problems of Coastal, Hilly and Desert areas.

Accordingly, the Planning Commission, a six-decade-old institution for centralized economic planning, has been dismantled,
and a new think tank, NITI Aayog, has been established in its
place, allowing state governments access to the architecture
of economic growth and development. In February 2015, the
Modi government accepted recommendations of the 14th
Finance Commission for increasing the share of states in central
taxes from 32 per cent to 42 per cent, giving more power to
states in determining how they spend this money. The underlying intent is for the states gradually to become self-sufficient,
an essential requirement for building their capacity to attract
investment. While, through this tool of cooperative federalism,
Modi is in the process of building an 'Organic Team India',
competitive federalism is making Indian sub-nationalist governments stakeholders in India's economic diplomacy. While
some have expressed concern that the richer states will be the
principal beneficiaries in such an inter-state competition, for
the time being it is simply being viewed as a means of creating
a pro-investment policy environment to meet Modi's policy
agenda of Make in India.

Added to these policy instruments is the introduction of the
new modes of communication, namely the vernacularization
and Hinduization of Indian foreign policy. There is increasing
usage of the Hindi language in official communication,
particularly in foreign and multilateral venues, sanskritized
idioms in spoken Hindi and in policy nomenclatures. Modi
and Sushma Swaraj regularly use the Hindi language with
Sanskritized Hindu traditional idioms in the national and
international fora. At the UN General Assembly Session in
September 2014, Prime Minister Modi made his maiden
speech in Hindi. He repeatedly invoked India's Vedic traditions
and emphasized India's philosophy of the globalized world,

Vasudhaiva Kutumbakam (the entire earth is one family), a concept embedded in the Vedic scripture *Maha Upanishad*. The notion of a united, strong and modern India has been captured under the phrase *Ek Bharat Shreshtha Bharat* where it is the duty of all to work collectively towards an inclusive development: *Sabka Saath, Sabka Vikas*. India is the 'Mother India' to whom all Indians have a special responsibility, 'All join our hands to serve our Mother India. Whatever we can do, we should do for our country'. Creating a *Swachh Bharat* is 'making Mother India pristine once again. I have come with the determination that 125 crore Indians will not let Mother India remain dirty'. Invoking India's great indigenous leaders has become part of the mobilization strategy. Gandhi, along with other national leaders such as Sardar Patel, is often invoked, 'We will not leave any stone unturned to fulfil Bapu's (Gandhi's) dreams'. Modi has strategically been balancing nationalist with Hindu heroes. Thus, while Modi, to the great chagrin of the Congress party, has adopted Gandhi, he has often, consistent with his own Hindutva background, invoked Vivekananda, a nineteenth century ascetic who, among other things, helped introduce Hinduism to the United States. In the unveiling of a statue of the Swami in Kuala Lumpur, he credited him with originating the concept of 'One Asia'. As Modi would have it, while Swami Vivekananda represents the identity of the soul of ancient India and personifies the thousands-year-old Indian culture and civilization, he also foresaw how Asia could provide spiritual leadership to the world to deal with its present challenges, like terrorism, climate change and global warming. In addition to Modi's visits to sacred Hindu and Buddhist sites abroad, Hindutva symbols, idioms and heroes have come to be inextricably linked, in one way or another, with almost all of the Modi government's policy agendas. In this regard, Ganguly, as have many others, cautions against the perils of Modi's cultural diplomacy to India's secular fabric. But it is, in fact, this vernacularization of the new foreign policy that seals its fate, so to speak, and makes the paradigm shift complete.

In this chapter, we have established that not only is foreign policy under the Modi administration transformative in both style and content, but also there has been a paradigmatic shift in the cognitive framework. Our discussion has sought to demonstrate that any understanding of Modi's foreign policy is best approached by looking at its foundations in the social norms, networks and beliefs within the foreign policy domain. The institutional norms embedded in Nehruvian non-alignment, with its later iteration as strategic autonomy, were seen to have regulated pre-Modi Indian foreign policy. Although significant policy changes were to take place, particularly after 1991, non-alignment as a cognitive script was to maintain its symbolic presence in Indian foreign policy. Thus, continuity and change could be captured under what we have termed a punctuated incrementalism. The Modi government has made a clear break with the past. Chapters 3–5 describe in detail this break with the past in three different cuts: Modi's re-articulation of neighbourhood (with a completely new set of meanings attached to the concept of neighbourhood) within the broad framework of the strategy of multilevel alignments, India's complex relationship with China and Modi's Pakistan policy.

Notes

1. "Only development can wipe away tears from the eyes of poor, empower youth & women: PM in Singapore." Modi's address in Singapore, 24 November 2015. Available at: http://www.narendramodi.in/pm-s-address-at-indian-community-reception-event-in-singapore-377328 (accessed on 15 May 2017).
2. http://www.bjp.org/images/pdf_2014/full_manifesto_english_07.04.2014.pdf
3. Bharatiya Janata Party, *Manifesto 2014*, 39.
4. Mohan, *Modi's World*, 2.
5. Pant, *Indian Foreign Policy*, 13–14.
6. One other exception to the continuity argument is Sumit Ganguly. Although not as forceful as C. Raja Mohan, he does suggest in one of his recent essays that Modi is 'less hamstring by the weight of the past' and with the discontinuation of the non-alignment rhetoric, there are three

new foreign policy imperatives: an engagement with industrial nations to boost India's economy, China coping strategy and improvement with India's neighbours. See Ganguly, 'Hindu Nationalism and the Foreign Policy of India's Bharatiya Janata Party'.

7. Hall, 'Policy Paradigms, Social Learning, and the State', 279.
8. Pant, *Indian Foreign Policy*, 11–12.
9. See 'Modi Running External Affairs Ministry on Whims', *The Times of India*.
10. There are few works which provide detailed descriptions of the working of the Ministry of External Affairs and its relationship with the political leadership. See Benner, *The Indian Foreign Policy Bureaucracy*; Kamath, 'Need to Correct Some Debilitating Features of Foreign Policy Making in India', 17–30.
11. Anderson, 'The Domestic Roots of Indian Foreign Policy', 48.
12. Some observers have not been complementary in describing the inner circle of the political leadership. For example, Surjit Mansingh in her 1984 book described Indira Gandhi's domination in directing India's external affairs bypassing institutional mechanisms and 'using men of ability almost as errand boys'. See Mansingh, *India's Search for Power*, 43.
13. For a detailed historical description of the role of political institutions and Ministry of External Affairs, see Chapters 3 and 4 in Bandyopadhyaya, *The Making of India's Foreign Policy*.
14. Mohan, 'The Making of Indian Foreign Policy'.
15. Miller, 'India's Feeble Foreign Policy'; Pant, 'Strategic Analysis'.
16 The Muscle Team has brought in financial, business and strategic expertise. Misra has joined Modi's team with a vast experience in the international financial and trade institutions such as the International Monetary Fund (IMF), the World Bank and the World Trade Organization (WTO). Ajit Doval is an internal security specialist and has held views that India should revisit no-first-use nuclear doctrine and not accept Pakistan's offensive, given India's asymmetrical advantage in military and economic power over Pakistan. On Pakistan and India's no-first-use nuclear doctrine, Doval wrote,

> The 26/11 terrorist action at Mumbai depicted a new order of lethality in Pakistan's unabated covert offensive against India. For almost three decades, India has passively accepted such provocations. It has failed to retaliate in a proactive manner that could raise costs for Pakistan and compel it to roll back its anti-India terrorist infrastructure…. India's tolerance threshold should not be unrealistically raised in the backdrop of nuclear blackmail as Pakistan has its own vulnerabilities many times higher than India and in its strategic calculus it cannot ignore the threat that

India can pose should the conflict grow beyond a point. India also needs to revisit its no-first-use nuclear doctrine.

See Doval, 'Internal Security—Need for Course Correction'. Sushma Swaraj is also known for her hawkish military opinions. In 2013, when Indian soldiers were killed by the Pakistani army after infiltrating in Jammu, she proposed that India should get 10 heads for every Indian soldier killed. Arun Jaitley's dual appointment as the Minister of Finance and Defence was seen as the Indian defence modernization programme receiving a priority of the Modi government.

17. The Vivekananda International Foundation describes itself as an 'independent, non-partisan institution that promotes quality research and in-depth studies'. Established in December 2009, though with no formal organizational links with the Rashtriya Swayam Sevak Sangh (RSS) or the Bharatiya Janata Party, it is affiliated to the Vivekananda Kendra, a charitable organization set up by Eknath Ranade, full-time missionary and former General Secretary of the RSS. The staff members at the Vivekananda International Foundation are largely composed of retired bureaucrats and intelligence officials and retired military personnel. The foundation has several centres of study to conduct research in line with its declared mission, including Centre for National Security and Strategic Studies, Centre for International Relations and Diplomacy, Centre for Neighbourhood Studies and Centre for Historical and Civilizational Studies.

18. India Foundation was founded in 2009 and has emerged as one of the most influential think tanks, organizing high-level conferences. Some of its recent events include Bilateral Conference on 'India–Myanmar: Frontiers of New Relationship', July 2015 and Indian Oceans Conference September 2016. With the on-going Kashmir conflict and Pakistan's involvement, it organized a two-day conference on 6–7 September 2016 in collaboration with the Federation of Indian Chambers of Commerce and Industry (FICCI), New Delhi, as a part of FICCI's Homeland Security programme, on 'Smart Border Management' and was inaugurated by Mr N.N. Vohra, Honourable Governor of Jammu and Kashmir, Government of India. For details on Indian Foundation, see their website http://www.indiafoundation.in/#1469885755183-010fbf87-75c1

19. Subrahmanyam, 'Forget the Consensus', quoted in Mohan, 'The Making of Indian Foreign Policy', 4.

20. Roy, 'Derailed Three Years'.

21. 'Talks with Pakistan Is to Try and Turn Course of History', *The New Indian Express*.

22 Although limited, contrary views have been expressed. It has been suggested by some foreign policy studies that the 1962 Sino-Indian War was a watershed moment in India's foreign policy when the political

leadership abandoned the idealistic and doctrinaire postures in favour of a more realistic policy. However, these scholars do support the thesis that non-alignment policy was still being pursued but now as an independent policy, with the goal to maximize national interests (see Misra, *Studies in Indian Foreign Policy*; Rana, 'The Intellectual Dimensions of India's Non-Alignment, 299–312). Similarly, in 2007, some foreign policy scholars predicted 'dramatic shifts' in India's foreign policy. For example, Chenoy and Chenoy point out that India, in the wake of agreements between India and the USA (2004 Bush and Vajpayee's 'Next Step for Strategic Partnership' agreement; 2005 'New Framework for the US–India Defence Relationship'), as witnessing a shift from 'non-alignment to alignment', 'from the goal of creating a multipolar world to endorsing the US concept of a unipolar world', an alteration in the strategic environment 'where military engagement is being privileged' and, most significantly, 'the national consensus that existed around non-alignment has broken down' (see Chenoy and Chenoy, 'India's Foreign Policy Shifts and the Calculus of Power', 3547). However, they also stress that India's foreign policy vision 'officially continues to adhere to non-alignment' (Ibid., 3555).

23. In two separate edited books, most of the contributors agreed that during the Janata government, there was far more continuity than change. See Prasad, *India's Foreign Policy*; Sharma, *Janata's Foreign Policy*.
24. Chiriyankandath, 'Realigning India', 201.
25. Chaulia, 'BJP, India's Foreign Policy and the "Realist Alternative" to the Nehruvian Tradition', 216.
26. Ibid., 215.
27. Ibid., 217, 222.
28. Chiriyankandath, 'Realigning India', 200.
29. Ganguly and Sridharan, 'The End of India's Sovereignty Hawks?'
30. Dalmia and Malone, 'Historical Influences on India's Foreign Policy', 1046. They point to three enduring characteristics in Indian foreign policy: Deference to sovereignty vis-à-vis its neighbours (strategic restraint); attribution to economic factors; and the principle of autonomy.
31. Keenleyside, 'Prelude to Power', 462–63.
32. Ibid., 461.
33. Pant, *Indian Foreign Policy*, 7.
34. Mitra, 'The Reluctant Hegemon'.
35. Thakur, 'India's Vietnam Policy, 1946–1979', 956.
36. Parameswaran, 'A New "Proactive" Indian Foreign Policy under Modi?'
37. The Nehruvian economic policy was fundamentally a socialist economy with central planning and an extensive state control apparatus. This approach, although tied to the imperatives of the Indian left, did remain disconnected from, what proved to be, the driving element of economic modernization to build a country's power and autonomy as in the cases

of the United States, Japan, China and Israel. The Nehruvian rhetoric was aspirational and sought to tie modernization to the welfare of the Indian poor. However, India's socialist economy barely improved the well-being of India's poor but it did create an enormous and a corrupt state apparatus and enhanced the power of the Congress party and the Indian bureaucracy as a result of growing state controls.

38. 'Only development can wipe away tears from the eyes of poor, empower youth and women: PM in Singapore'. Modi's address in Singapore, 24 November 2015. Available at: http://www.narendramodi.in/pm-s-address-at-indian-community-reception-event-in-singapore-377328 (accessed on 15 May 2017).
39. Tellis, 'Back to First Principles'.
40. NDTV.com. 'Full Text of PM Modi's Statement after Meeting Premier Li Keqiang in Beijing'.
41. http://www.firstpost.com/world/india-rebuts-john-kerry-remark-displays-new-appetite-to-take-on-us-at-climate-change-convention-2518128.html (accessed on 15 May 2017).
42. Davenport and Harrison, 'Citing Urgency, World Leaders Converge on France for Climate Talks'.
43. DNA, Full Speech: PM Modi's Address at the Third India–Africa Forum Summit'.
44. Parameswaran, 'A New "Proactive" Indian Foreign Policy under Modi?'
45. Mehta, 'Review: A New Foreign Policy?' 3175.
46. Sikri, *Challenge and Strategy*.
47. Ayres, 'Three Takeaways on US–India Defense Ties'.
48. Cohen and Rabinovitch, 'Under Modi, Israel and India Forge Deeper Business Ties'.
49. http://presidentofindia.nic.in/speeches-detail.htm?293
50. See Jaishankar, 'Keynote Address by Foreign Secretary Dr S. Jaishankar at the IFS-IDSA Seminar'.
51. Chris Honeyman, 'Integrative Bargaining'.
52. Mitra, 'The Reluctant Hegemon', 400.

2

The Nehruvian Legacy: Policy Anomalies and Policy Failure

In this chapter, we trace Nehru's strategic legacy for India, an essential starting point to counterpoise to Modi's new Indian diplomatic rule book. This following discussion points out, in the first instance, that the Nehru era story is that of India's shrinking strategic footprint as a result of foreign aggressiveness and of the failure of Nehru's policies (embedded, as they were, in the non-alignment cognitive framework), which were to invite others to act with impunity against India and to counter which Nehru and his team were unable to build serious defences. Second, we describe how Nehruvian principles—especially the value of non-alignment—were to remain firm in India's diplomatic narrative while an incremental transformation in India's approach to military strategy and economic modernization took place after the Sino Indian War of 1962. India's diplomatic and military strategy continued to show signs of the lingering influence of Nehruvian soft power elements with some acknowledgement of the importance of hard military power.

Prior to the emergence of a Modi-led majority government of the Bharatiya Janata Party (BJP)—a centre-right, nationalistic, pro-business and anti-Congress party and advocate of good governance policies—it had been Jawaharlal Nehru, the Nehru–Gandhi dynasty and the Congress party which, from 1947 to 2014, dominated India's political and public space.[1] Nehruism offered an ideal vision, supported by a rarefied rhetoric, about the importance of world peace, about an end to power politics as the driving force in modern international relations and about building bridges among rival nations, a rhetoric that reflected the importance of global norms rather than 'narrow' national interests.[2] Foreign policy was more concerned with the forces of nationalism, racism and the legacy of colonialism than it was about the inevitability of war as a result of the competition between the communist and non-communist bloc.[3] The rhetoric of the Nehruvian era retarded the development of an Indian process of geo-political engagement with troublesome neighbours—Pakistan and China—and of the major expansionist powers, especially the United States.[4] These countries did not recognize many limits to their ambition and they maintained their right to act with impunity against Indian interests whenever it suited them; and to back up this right, they developed diplomatic and military tools to intervene against India. Intervention is an accepted principle of international relations in a world of unequal powers; in the Indian case, this meant that China, Pakistan and the United States deemed that India was a fit object for their intervention. Pakistan's leaders believed that their legacy came from the Mughal rulers of India in the past. They regarded themselves as the successors of the Mughals and repeatedly told their American and Chinese interlocutors that Pakistanis could not accept Hindu dominance because of the history and the memory of Muslim domination of the 'Indian subcontinent'.[5] China's ambition was to expand its power in the southern zone of the Asian continent. Geography, history and Maoist ideology were on China's side. By 1949, the communists had defeated Japanese, American and Kuomintang (KMT) forces in China and controlled a large landmass between Russia and Japan and up to the Himalayas. From a period of internal weakness and civil war, the Maoists had changed the course of Chinese history and reversed the decline of imperial China's power and of the process of its expansionism. By 1950, the Maoists took Tibet by force and, significantly, Mao made a public declaration about the liberation of Bhutan, Sikkim and India along with Tibet and a few other places.[6] In sum, the distribution of world power was underway by the establishment of American hegemony in the Americas and in Europe by 1945, by the establishment of Bolshevik authority in the vast expanse of the Union of Soviet Socialist Republics (USSR) and by the establishment of Chinese communist authority in China. The Indian subcontinent and Southeast Asia, however, did not have a dominant political centre nor a stable political and an economic system in the wake of the retreat of the European empires in Asia and the winding down of the British Raj in India. Power remained undistributed in the area from Afghanistan to the Philippines and the Indian Ocean area. Into this void came Nehru's non-alignment, anti-military, anti-balance of power and zone of peace stance which earned India's government neither fear nor respect among the major powers.

Without economic and military strength to back its rhetoric, India's international and regional influence was dissipated in the world of competitive powers. In the early 1950s, American practitioners saw India's democratic set-up as an alternative to Chinese communism in Asia, and in the diplomatic sphere they appreciated Nehru's effort to reduce tensions between America and Russia. But as Indian ties deepened with Russia, the 'you are either with us or against us' line gained ground and, in American calculations, placed India on the other side: in the camp of the opposition.[7] Moreover, in US policy thinking, India was less useful as an intermediary as Washington and Moscow opened their bilateral dialogue on arms control (from the mid-1950s), as they learned to manage their crises, for example, the Cuban Missile Crisis (1962), and as Pakistan was deemed to be a reliable partner and a check against Indian 'expansionism' or regional hegemony. So, India emerged as an object of American intervention because of Washington's acceptance of the theory of the desirability of an Indo-Pakistani balance of power in the subcontinent.[8] The British theory of Hindu–Muslim parity in the constitutional affairs of India now had a new translation into the subcontinent's international relations. Having toyed with the idea of peaceful co-existence with India, China within a few years of signing the agreement in 1954 turned its back to the idea and embraced instead the Pakistan–US theory about the importance of an Indo-Pakistani balance of power in the subcontinent. These decisions circumscribed India's importance to the world as an independent voice in Third-World affairs, and furthermore they tied India's position to the quality of its relations with Pakistan, and as US–China sought relations with each other, the importance of India's democracy in Asia lost its salience in American foreign affairs. The trend of dissipation of India's international influence became entrenched as a result of two factors. First, the United States, China and Pakistan based their foreign policies in relation to India on their calculations of their respective national interests and the perceptions of their leaders about Nehru and his policies.[9] Second, the failure of Nehru and Congress party leaders to develop diplomatic and military positions based on geo-political and power calculations revealed Indian policy planners to be weak-minded, reactive and open to persuasion by the major powers by means of pressure, blackmail, intervention and war against India.

India's diplomatic and military trajectory could have developed quite otherwise had Nehru made different choices.

What If ...

1. ...Instead of ordering a ceasefire in Kashmir following the tribal invasion and the introduction of Indian troops in light of the Maharaja's accession to India, and instead of taking the issue to the UN Security Council, India had continued the war and liberated the whole of Kashmir; then Kashmir would have been a non-issue in Indo-Pakistan and Indo-US/UK relations.

2. The second major error was that Nehru quickly accepted in 1950 China's claim to sovereignty in Tibet, disregarding Tibetan and British claims and the historical record that at times Tibet had been independent, at times it had been autonomous

and China had a nominal claim to suzerainty over Tibet as per British policy which was known to China. Nehru's action was a cardinal error. It is standard practice among sovereign nations to apply the principle of quid pro quo or compensation to adjust conflicting claims and to safeguard national interests. China's interest was to secure Tibet as a part of its concern with frontier security. India's interest was to secure the Indo-Tibet border and secure China's formal agreement about the validity of the McMahon Line when the time was ripe in the early 1950s to have such an agreement in the atmosphere of Sino-Indian peaceful co-existence. Nehru not only misread Chinese strategic ambitions as revealed by Mao's statements about the need to liberate Tibet, Bhutan, Sikkim and India from colonial and bourgeoisie influences but also failed to appreciate that without the existence of Tibet as a buffer between China and India; India required strong military defences in its long border with China.

3. The third major error by Nehru and Krishna Menon, Nehru's close adviser and confidant, was not to have recognized the urgency of the need to build India's military strength early on—even as Pakistan had been openly confrontational with India within a few months after it gained Independence, while China had started to get confrontational by the mid-1950s and openly so by 1959. Nehru gave the defence ministry to Menon—who effectively convinced Indians about the importance of disarmament and undermined the Indian military's requests to build up military defences against clear signs of a Chinese military build-up in the Himalayan region.[10] Menon's rationale was that foreign exchange limitations inhibited defence acquisitions and the choice was between guns or butter—defence or economic development. In retrospect, this appeared to be an erroneous choice and a wrong way to frame a national debate. Its spurious character was eventually to become clear when the Government of India found the resources to build its armed forces after the debacle in 1962. The 1963 defence budget outlay was almost three times that of 1962. Given this fact, it was surprising that Nehru–Menon

had used the rationale of insufficient funds to avoid military modernization. The problem, however, was not merely one of budgets and resource allocation for defence purposes. It was above all about a Nehru–Menon attitude that favoured a pro-China, pro-disarmament and international peace policy, and a mistrust of military power and balance of power policies that included a mistrust of Indian military officers and the military machinery.[11] It was ironic that Nehru trusted Mountbatten and he was unable to balance different ideological position of his socialist and left leaning colleagues with those of his other peers in the Cabinet like Vallabhbhai Patel and experienced civil servants like Sir Girija Shankar Bajpai. The latter had counselled Nehru about the danger China represented for India, about not looking at defence simply as a problem of Pakistan and about the need to consider a balance of power policy.[12]

The pro-China policy was facilitated by the inputs from the Indian Intelligence Bureau (IB). Nehru gave the IB to B.N. Mullik, a seasoned intelligence officer, but his analysis was that China would not attack India even if it could. Mullik functioned as the intelligence czar between 1950 and 1965 and his assessment was widely accepted by Nehru, the Ministry of External Affairs (MEA) and the Ministry of Defence (MOD) headed by Menon but not by Army headquarters. But in the Nehru–Menon–Mullik-centric Indian national security policy apparatus, the Army headquarters did not count in an atmosphere where, first, Nehru knew best, and, second, there was the issue of civilian control over military officers. The twin assumptions—that Nehru and his like-minded associates knew best while Nehru's Cabinet colleagues and opposition members such as Manohar Lohia and the Indian military professionals did not—effectively marginalized India in the world of international diplomacy and military power politics.

4. Nehru's approach to Indian economic modernization was defective in that it lacked a clear philosophical and policy rationale (i.e., why should India modernize instead of adopting the Gandhian approach by building village-based autonomous communities?) and the institutional method

adopted had a Nehru-centric, state-centric as well as socialist and anti-capitalist orientation. Baldev Raj Nayar's influential work[13] on Indian modernization points out that the major powers—the United States, China and Japan—sought to modernize because of geo-political reasons; power was essential to secure autonomy in the international sphere. In his public declarations, Nehru spoke of the importance of India's Independence and the right to make decisions on merit as the sign of its sovereignty but at the same time the connection between power/autonomy and modernization was not made explicitly. Rather, Nehru emphasized the importance of moral force and peace policy and rejected power politics and geo-politics. Was Nehru downplaying power politics in his approach to economic and foreign affairs including modernization because he wanted India to have a period of external peace to build India's economy, or was he genuinely confused about the intimate connection between modernization and power politics and the quest for autonomy on the world stage? And/or was Nehru playing the anti-capitalist, pro-Left card to solidify his socialist credentials in the Congress party and in Indian politics, and to gain from an ideological polarization between the Indian Left and the Indian Right?[14] The domestic-ideological motivation merits consideration because Nehru came to power in the Congress party and maintained his power after 1947 by splitting the Left–Right factions of the party and by marginalizing rightist leaders who had an appeal in party ranks because of their administrative experience, such as Subhas Chandra Bose and Vallabhbhai Patel.[15] Some suggest this as an interesting twist in Nehru's personality and the method he used in relation to the development of his primary position in Indian politics and to the development of his approach to Indian diplomacy and military affairs. Indeed Nehru and the Congress party he controlled sought modernization by centrally and state-controlled economic planning and social and political programmes. As the leader of the governing party, Nehru talked about constitutional principles, social reforms, poverty alleviation and public welfare schemes. In this respect, he was in tune with many North American scholars who believed in modernization as a means to increase public welfare.

The Nehruvian and Congress party's narrative was to overemphasize the importance of state planning and controls over the Indian economy, and to underscore the role of the public sector in the quest for Indian modernization. The narrow anti-capitalist view of the private sector under Nehru and the Congress party's state-sponsored socialism was facilitated by the Indian bureaucracy and by the Indian Left who were ideologically and politically aligned with the ruling Congress party. This narrative dominated the public, political and policy space of India from 1947 to the early 1990s. During this period, India's political and bureaucratic elite was arrogant about the role of the public sector even though there was evidence that India's private sector performed better than the public sector in a crucial area like steel production. Nayar's scholarly analysis of the performance of India's public and private sectors in the steel industry firmly supported this conclusion. Liberalization and globalization did not find favour in the Nehruvian era because it was the politics of the Indian Left and socialism that shaped the Government of India's economic decision-making. And the idealist rhetoric about anti-poverty programmes remained aspirational; hundreds of millions of Indians are still poor after almost 50 years of Congress party rule.

What if Nehru had accepted the view drawn from a study of world history that the major powers sought modernization for geo-political reasons and power was a prerequisite to secure autonomy in the international sphere? He could then have placed India on a trajectory of economic and military development that brought Indian capitalism to work with the state to modernize India, and sustained faster economic growth could have created the means to use state resources for military modernization in the early years of India's Independence.

Nehru was a firm believer in constitutional government and his belief in the importance of free elections showed his commitment to democracy. But in the diplomatic and the military spheres, he adopted a Nehru-centric system which relied on a small foreign service whose officers were beholden to Nehru because Panditji knew best.[16] Like many others, Nehru's biographer, Michael Brecher, was to observe the key role played by Nehru by stating that 'in no other state does one man dominate foreign policy as does Nehru in India'.[17] And, moreover, the Indian Armed Forces had no role to play because of their marginal position in Indian defence decision-making. Nehru's diplomatic decision-making system was small and secretive, much like the eighteenth-century European court system, and in the absence of public debates about policies towards China, Tibet, border defences, Kashmir, Pakistan and military modernization, the cross currents of mainstream Indian society were not available to provide inputs into Nehru's decision-making in external affairs. As a result, India's diplomatic and military strategy was not connected and supported by either Indian nationalism or public opinion. Public support of a country's external policy is a core element in a democracy's approach to the outside world but this is not possible in the absence of a consultative government machinery.

In summary: First, what we have been characterizing as Nehru's errors may be seen to have created situations in India's frontier regions which enabled foreign powers to act with impunity against Indian strategic interests and which sharply reduced India's manoeuvrability in the region and in the international sphere with respect to core Indian strategic interests. Second, the Nehru approach of adopting a Nehru-centric, closed and secretive decision-making system relating to Kashmir, Tibet and China affairs can be compared to that of the European court system of the eighteenth century. At that time, decisions about war and peace were in the province of the European sovereign and the population did not have a say since sovereignty rested in the person of the king. At the same time, nationalism in Europe did not play a role in decisions regarding war and peace. The disconnect between the decision-making by the king and the court, on the one hand, and public opinion and nationalism, on the other hand, was evident in Indian diplomatic and military affairs during the 1950s when Nehru held court with his ambassadors who depended on his patronage. The problem with the courtly approach adopted by Nehru was that it was secretive, closed to public scrutiny and it was based on Nehru's intuition about world affairs rather than specialized knowledge and staff work and inputs by diplomatic and military professionals. Third, the Nehru era revealed a profound disconnect from Indian theoretical and philosophical traditions about the importance of power politics and geo-politics in the conduct of statecraft. Not only was there an inconsistency between the prescriptions of *Arthashastra* and Nehru but even the work of Nehru's contemporaries like the erudite K.M. Panikkar who wrote on Himalayan and Indian defence issues and the importance of sea power and the Indian Ocean did not find a way into Nehru's thought process and diplomacy.[18] Finally, the Nehruvian diplomatic and military record revealed a major and a sad truth: Nehru trusted Mountbatten, for example, rather than his own peers (e.g., Vallabhbhai Patel and Sir Girija Shankar Bajpai) and his military officers in matters of statecraft.

Incremental Transformation in India's Approach to Military Strategy and Economic Modernization After 1962

The defeat in the 1962 war with China shook India's self-confidence and basically discredited Nehru's approach to peace and war issues. In his Foreword to the MOD's official report on the 1962 war, the then Defence Secretary of India Mr N.N. Vohra noted: 'the present record of the Sino-Indian Conflict of 1962 highlights various political, strategic and tactical failures on our side'.[19] The process to adjust India's approach to soft and hard power was slow, incremental and prolonged, retarded as it was by endless internal debates. There were many reasons for this pattern of change. Precisely, when the international environment was undergoing a rapid change, the Indian rate of strategic adaptation was slow and subject to internal and external vetoes. Indian leaders lacked the confidence, the conviction and knowledge of policy tools, given their inexperience with the practicalities of statecraft, the character of the world situation and the challenges it presented to Indian strategic interests. Their main preoccupation was with the quest of personal power through victory in elections, but they reacted to external crises with their backs to the wall as Indian public opinion created pressure on them to act to ward off the foreign threat(s). This was the dominant pattern in Indian external and defence affairs during 1947–62. Post-1962, a combination of external threats and domestic public pressure were the two triggers which stimulated the Indian leaders to act in the areas of defence, foreign affairs and internal modernization. Indian politicians suffered from repeated bouts of election fever as their life experiences had no doubt prepared them for political agitation and electioneering rather than international negotiations and war preparation in contending with aggressive regional neighbours. Nehru had relied on soft power to establish India's international presence by his personal East–West, North–South diplomacy. He was successful in the first half of the 1950s because international circumstances favoured his initiatives and Nehru had a small band of Indian practitioners who knew how to mediate and negotiate among great power rivals as in the case of conflicts in Korea, Indo-China, Suez and East–West disarmament.

The key elements in Nehru's tool set of soft power were as follows:

Indian democracy was an alternative to China's communist and authoritarian political model; Indian pluralism and secularism appealed to Western rule and value-based academic and government practitioners when the bipolar system showed rigid animosities and high mistrust between Washington, Moscow and Beijing. The Western powers embraced the Indian narrative about the importance of India's democratic political model in Asia.

Indian diplomatic practitioners showed remarkable skills in reducing the danger of war and in bridging differences among great power rivals in the conflicts in Korea, Indo-China and Suez, and in promoting the case for nuclear disarmament during the early 1950s. These efforts were relevant because of the high mistrust and conflicting interests of the great power rivals, and India's ability to find common ground to reduce the tensions was generally appreciated.[20]

Nehru advocated non-alignment as the preferred path for newly emerging nations following decades of colonialism. For him and fellow Indians, non-alignment meant a rejection of the belief in the inevitability of bipolarity and ideological rivalry between communism and capitalism. Indian non-alignment acknowledged that nationalism was the elemental force in modern international relations rather than communism or American style capitalism; and non-alignment had an aspirational side: it was meant to create a zone of peace that avoided the extension of cold war-based alliances in regions of conflict outside Europe and the Far East. Nehru's appeal to the Non-Aligned Movement (NAM) countries was the opposition of newly emerging and independent states to the alliance politics of the great powers and a fear of war and the need for an anti-war international coalition that checked the expansionism of the Western alliance system in particular and to a lesser extent the Soviet alliance system in Eastern Europe.

These elements of Indian soft power became redundant by the early 1960s as global and regional geo-politics and the great powers' diplomacy gained traction, as the danger of nuclear war receded in the aftermath of the Cuban Missile Crisis and the US–Soviet arms control negotiations, and as regional conflicts in Southeast Asia and the Middle East achieved a stability of sorts with predictable parameters of fighting and negotiating among the rival nations. When the rivals established direct channels of discourse among them the role of third party, mediators like India lost in importance. When regional rivals sought the protection of international allies, the importance of non-alignment also lost its appeal.

Three additional developments elevated China's international position and downgraded India's. First, China's rise as a military force in Asia was confirmed by its performance in the Korean conflict which put a brake against American military expansion in Asia. Second, its victory in the 1962 conflict with India showed that India did not have staying power in Asia and in the 'Indian subcontinent'. Third, China revealed increasingly anti-Soviet attitudes and policy. The combination of these three developments made China appear as the third pole of power in the international system, and thus a potential negotiating partner of the United States and the Western powers who were troubled by Soviet aggressiveness. In this rapidly altered context, NAM remained one scenario of a potential third force but the ascendancy of China was the development to be reckoned with, the reality which was recognized by the major powers in the world. NAM and a zone of peace diplomacy remained an aspiration and an unrealistic possibility because the so-called zone of peace had become the site of numerous local and regional conflicts and non-alignment became an increasingly remote ideal, given the emerging pattern of alignments between members of NAM and their foreign patrons. With changing international circumstances, the appeal of India's soft power diminished. Nehru's appeasement of Pakistan in Kashmir and China in Tibet in the early 1950s was an important manifestation of soft power precisely when the conflicting interests between Pakistan and India, and China and India, would have required a geo-political response with hard military power as the basis of Indian diplomacy.

Between 1962 and the 1990s, India's diplomatic and military strategy showed signs of the lingering influence of Nehruvian soft power elements and some acknowledgement of the importance of hard military power. Nehru's rhetorical principles—especially the value of non-alignment—held firm in India's diplomatic narrative[21] Along with the incremental build-up of India's military capability came episodic applications of military force to settle political controversies, but these instances were inconclusive because they did not lead to a peace settlement with Pakistan or China–India's main geo-political rivals. The first application of Indian military force occurred in the war with Pakistan in 1965.[22] To relieve the pressure in Kashmir as a result of Pakistani military intervention, Prime Minister Lal Bahadur Shastri ordered the Indian Army to cross the international border with Pakistan and threaten key cities—Lahore and Sialkot. This war turned out to be a military stalemate because Indian forces had run out of spare parts in the wake of the embargo on war supplies by the great powers and this led to mediation by Moscow and the agreement at Tashkent to accept a ceasefire. But Shastri's decision to take the fight to Pakistan had a psychological dimension. It crossed the Nehru–Mountbatten red line against war with Pakistan, and it terrified the Pakistani population in the threatened cities. And there was a lesson learned, namely not to start a fight without adequate spare parts as India was subject to great power intervention through embargos and political diplomacy by both Washington and Moscow. Both saw themselves as guardians of the peace in the subcontinent in their roles as members of the Security Council where the Kashmir dispute had long lain on the agenda as a result of Nehru–Mountbatten diplomatic action in 1948.

The second military episode, the 1970–71 war in East Pakistan, led to the formation of Bangladesh as a result of the internal uprising among Bangladesh Muslims in their revolt against West Pakistani domination and thanks to Indian military to help ensure Bangladeshi autonomy and, if necessary, independence.[23] Here, the lesson of 1965 had been learned: India made full military preparations to fight and win the military campaign in a matter of weeks before the great powers gained the time to secure a ceasefire—the preferred norm in the UN culture of the Security Council powers. This episode changed the subcontinent's geo-politics by breaking up Pakistan but it was inconclusive in the sense that India's military victory and the formal surrender of the Pakistani Army in East Pakistan did not lead to a peace settlement between Pakistan and India.

Typically, in world history—for example, in the case of the Second World War—a key consequence of victory by the application of military force against the enemy is to have a peace settlement which is dictated by the victor and which is accepted by the vanquished. This was the norm applied by the Western allies against Germany, and by the United States against Japan. A peace settlement brings closure to a conflict. The Indian government failed to meet this standard in the aftermath of the Bangladesh war because the government's mindset, that is, of political leaders and their bureaucratic advisers, looked at the world of diplomacy and armed strength—the worlds of soft and hard power—as two separated silos. Neither the Indian political leaders of the time nor the civilian bureaucracy seemed to understand the relevance of the concept of coercive diplomacy for India's relationship with Pakistan. Mostly, Indian political leaders have been interested in the years since 1947 with their electoral fortunes and gains in their personal power rather than the formation of an integrated political-military strategy to engage the threats in a hostile external environment.

Nehru's foreign policy prescriptions were ill-equipped to deal with the military requirements to counter hostile neighbours and to form a diplomatic strategy to counter the expansionist activities of Pakistan, the United States and China in relation to India during the 1950s and the 1960s. Missing from the Nehru narrative was the idea of Indian national security in relation to Indian defences in the Himalayan region. Missing also from the Nehru/Congress party narrative was the link between the modernization imperative and power politics until the post-Nehru era ushered in a subtle and a significant transformative process: first to build Indian military strength (1963); then to apply Indian military power in Pakistan (1965) in a defensive–offensive military operation; then to use Indian military power to break up Pakistan (1971), followed by the signalling of the presence of Indian capacity to test a nuclear device (1974); and eventually to open up the process of economic liberalization (1991 onwards). Note that the changes were incremental and guarded: they were mostly reactions to perceived impending dangers and they did not arise from a process that was driven by planning for the future. The sequence of Indian actions in the military and economic spheres amounted to slowly, if ineluctably, chipping away the Nehruvian prescriptions against liberalization and capitalism, against the development of a modern military machine and against the use of force against Pakistan itself as had been the Nehru–Mountbatten policy.

The failure to convert the Indian military victory over Pakistani Armed Forces and over a hostile USA–China–Pakistan coalition in the Bangladesh war into a peace settlement with Pakistan in 1972 clearly indicated that the Government of India did not believe in an integrated political/diplomatic-military strategy as a means of bringing an end to the conflict with Pakistan. As a result, India's military victory in 1971 did not alter the balance of power in South Asia and in Asia in general. One of the main reasons being that there were no limits placed on the ability of China and the United States to rebuild defeated Pakistan's military strength and its diplomatic self-confidence. It is important to note that precisely when India adopted a programme to secure its military and economic modernization, it was the time that China transferred sensitive nuclear and missile capacity to Pakistan to balance Indian nuclear power, and the United States and Saudi Arabia continued to finance Pakistan's military modernization as a counter-balance to India. This proved to be an unstable balance between, on the one hand, an irredentist power (Pakistan) that was fully armed, with its external and domestic policies controlled by its military since the 1950s, and, on the other hand, India that was a democratic and a territorially satisfied country but lacking the key elements of a major power.

The 1971 war did not settle the Indian debate about the danger to Indian interests presented by Western, Chinese and Pakistani policies which emphasized the desirability and importance of an Indo-Pakistani military and diplomatic balance. Indeed, the official articulation that India faced an existential threat to its security from Pakistan and China came only with the 1998 nuclear tests and the declaration that India was henceforth a nuclear weapon state. Until then the 1965 and 1971 wars had been little more than episodes in the larger process of India's slow military and economic modernization and had done nothing to settle the escalating pattern of the rivalries with Pakistan and China. And it was only the 1998 nuclear tests that set the stage for stabilizing Indian diplomatic and military relations with those two countries. They effectively limited the ability of China, Pakistan and the United States to act with impunity against Indian interests. Indeed, the May 1998 Pokhran-II nuclear tests, as they were referred to proudly by the Indian government, showed several important changes: that India fully intended to stay in the nuclear game despite the opposition of the United States, China, Pakistan and US allies; that Indian nuclear weapons were now a part of India's diplomatic and military strategy; that Nehru's and the Congress party's peace and nuclear disarmament diplomacy did not serve Indian strategic interests and that India now saw itself as a participant in the balance of power in Asia with China clearly identified as a rival power.[24] Despite hand-wringing and feeble efforts by some members of the world community to portray India as an outlaw state because of its refusal to accept 'global' anti-proliferation norms and rules, President G.W. Bush basically took India out of the penalty box. He declared that India was a responsible nuclear power, made an agreement to negotiate an end to the sanctions against India and opened a strategic dialogue between India and the United States. Other nations, mainly the Europeans, Japan, Canada, Australia and the Southeast Asians followed suit because now they had the cover of US diplomacy in their nuclear dealings with India.

The Pokhran-II tests and their consequences formed the first transformative stage in the establishment of an integrated military and diplomatic strategy that was invulnerable to being rolled back by external interventions or by Indian coalition politics. The tests expanded India's diplomatic and military horizons by enabling India to strengthen its ties with traditional (the United States, Europeans, Canada, Iran and Southeast Asians) and non-traditional (Israel, Japan, Australia and the BRICS nations) strategic partners. The new, post-1998 Indian strategic tilts were a far cry from Nehru's sphere of diplomacy which had been limited to the Soviet Union, Pakistan, China and the NAM countries, at the UN, to protect India's case on Kashmir and had entailed participation in international peacekeeping and the promotion of the cause of nuclear disarmament. Even though by his actions in Kashmir, Tibet and China in the early 1950s, Nehru and his Congress party successors had shrunk India's room to manoeuvre on the world stage; BJP Prime Minister A.B. Vajpayee, while heading a minority government, succeeded in widening it. This was accomplished by the Indian Army engaging Chinese forces in the Himalayas in probing episodes by the People's Liberation Army (PLA), by offering resistance to violations in the Line of Control (LoC) in Kashmir and by announcing a 'Look East' policy that expanded India's diplomatic and economic horizon in Asian affairs. But periodic terrorist attacks on Indian targets outside Kashmir were prevented neither by the BJP government nor by successive Congress party governments following Vajpayee's defeat in elections in 2004. Moreover, since the early 1980s, internal security problems had mushroomed: the insurgency in Jammu and Kashmir intensified, a new independence movement emerged in Indian Punjab (Khalistan), while insurgencies in India's Northeast and Central provinces up to Andhra Pradesh gained ground and created a belt of domestic instability. These developments related to ISI-inspired activities in India's neighbourhood as well as grievances among Kashmiri Muslim population against the Indian State and among Indian tribals who feared the takeover of their lands and livelihood by corporations and state governments (though the insurgencies in India's northeast, however, had histories going back to the 1940s).

The replacement in 2004 of the BJP-minority Vajpayee government by two minority governments led by Prime Minister

Manmohan Singh was an aberration in Indian politics and government. It produced something like a government with two heads: front man, Prime Minister Manmohan Singh and President Sonia Gandhi. It is with the latter and the important lieutenants of Congress party that the real power resided and it was they who controlled government appointments and policy initiatives. This bizarre arrangement impeded the efforts towards military and economic modernization because the government's initiatives had to pass scrutiny by a core group of coalition partners. The coalition was dominated by people who were beholden to Sonia Gandhi because she was the real centre of power, and this core group was influenced predominantly by Indian socialists and the Left who were opposed to India's nuclearization and military development and who did not believe in economic liberalization and globalization. Moreover, the socialists had influence in Indian politics and government beyond the size of their Parliamentary representation because they could influence the politics of the core group of the Congress party's coalition. Much like Nehru's small coterie, this group also functioned in a closed and secretive fashion and its decisions lacked transparency.

In sum, the period from 1947 to 2014, barring the few episodes and transformative actions noted in this chapter, showed idealistic and reified Nehruvian rhetoric, retarded geo-political engagements because geo politics and power politics did not inform the Indian political and bureaucratic mindsets. India's strategic footprint shrank within the 'Indian' subcontinent and in the world as a result of decisions taken in the early 1950s relating to Pakistan, Kashmir, Tibet and China, and as a result of failure by Nehru and his admirers to encourage Indian military and economic modernization and to seek mid-course correction of Nehru's approach to diplomacy and strategy. External events forced the changes in Indian thinking because India's political culture reacts to threats rather than seeks preventive and deterrent actions which convey red lines to friend and foe.

Notes

1. There is a large scholarly material available on Nehru's foreign policy and his conceptualization of non-alignment. Some important works include Gopal, *Jawaharlal Nehru: Biography, 1947–1956*; Brecher, *Nehru: A Political Biography*; Mullik, *My Years with Nehru*; Rana, *The Imperatives of Nonalignment*; Stein, *India and the Soviet Union*.
2. Kundra, *Indian Foreign Policy, 1947–54* gives Nehru's worldviews. Rajkumar, *The Background of Indian Foreign Policy* is a useful source of primary materials. Nehru was the primary framer of Congress party resolutions on foreign affairs since the 1930s. Nehru emphasized Indianness, Asianism, idealism and the importance of the Asiatic federation involving China and India and a few other Asian states, and these ideas were projected by Nehru after 1947. Gopal, *Jawaharlal Nehru* gives a balanced assessment of Nehru's idealism as well as his naiveté about China and his bad relationship with the USA and the tilt towards Moscow in the early 1950s. Nehru thought that the US leadership was immature in foreign affairs, see page 60, and for the USA's negative view of Nehru, see pages 109–10.
3. K.P. Karunakaran, who, in his 1958 volume, was to provide an account of the main international problems which engaged the attention of Indian statesmen during the period February 1950–December 1953, points to the contradictory response of the Nehru team's approach to global issues. For example, he points out that when the UN was confronted with issues of the Great Power rivalry, India spoke the language of means, and with regard to colonial issues, India used the language of ends. See Karunakaran, *'India in World Affairs 1950–53*.
4. Scholarly opinions do differ with regard to Nehru's contributions. For example, Michael Brecher points out that B.R. Nanda in his 1976 book on Nehru years gives an effusive tribute to

> Nehru's achievements: architect of the new Commonwealth; moderating influence on Soviet behaviour during the dispute over Austria's independence and the Berlin crisis of 1961; prophet of changes in the Soviet Union, the potential for Indo-Soviet cooperation, the probability of a Sino-Soviet split, and the certainty of detente between the US and USSR; and prescience concerning the danger of Great Power involvement in the Indo-China wars. Only with respect to China was Nehru faulted: '... he tragically misjudged Chinese intentions and policies towards India ...' but, by and large, his policies 'have stood the test of time'.

See Brecher, 'Nehru's Foreign Policy and the China–India Conflict Revisited', 99.

5. For example, Pakistan's foreign secretary Sultan M. Khan saw India's victory in 1971 as a military and a psychological blow because Muslims had ruled the subcontinent over the Hindus for hundreds of years. See Amb. Bush telegram to State Department, 10 December 1971, in Aijazuddin, *The White House and Pakistan*, 473.

6. Mao's speech on radio on New Year 1950 outlined the plan to liberate these areas. See Peisel, *The Secret War in Tibet*, 14.

7. Escott Reid notes that during 'most' of the period from 1952 to 1957, the relations between India and the USA were bad. See Reid, *Envoy to Nehru*, preface. For the US bias in favour of Pakistan because of its strategic importance, see the memorandum by the Chiefs of Staff, 24 March 1949, Washington, DC, which noted that South Asia was of marginal importance except for Pakistan and the main danger was the fear of Soviet domination of the area. See Arif, *American-Pakistan Relations*, 15–17.

8. See Aijazuddin, 'US government labelled Indian military action in 1971 as "aggression" at the UN in December 1971', 442.

9. Even countries like Australia, which did not occupy much global significance during this period, also operated within the Anglo-American framework. Not only did Australia's Prime Minister Menzies distrust Nehru's non-alignment policy, but he was also to assert, during his visit to India and Pakistan en route to the Prime Ministers' Conference in 1951 (to play a mediating role between Indian and Pakistan on Kashmir issue),

   > This Kashmir business dominates all political thinking in Pakistan and a good deal of it in India. Unless it is settled we can cancel out the whole Indian subcontinent from any real democratic strategic planning, and will be grievously weakened in the Middle East in the event of a great war.

   See Gurry, 'Leadership and Bilateral Relations', 517

10. Nehru and Krishna Menon were anti-military power and anti-military alliances and were obsessed with the policy of nuclear disarmament. Both were close to each other personally and ideologically. See Kutty, 'V.K. Krishna Menon', Chapters 11–12. B.N. Mullik, *The Chinese Betrayal*, notes the lack of Indian strategic planning and leadership in the Himalayan region.

11. Neville Maxwell, reporting on the 1963 Henderson Brooks Report on the border war with China, points to the struggle between different factions in the army as a result of "the strains placed on the Army by the government's contradictory and hypocritical policies—on the one hand proclaiming China an eternal friend against whom it was unnecessary to arm, on the other using armed force to seize territory it knew China

regarded as its own." See Maxwell, 'Henderson Brooks Report: An Introduction.'

12. G.S. Bajpai, one time head of India's foreign office, noted that it was a mistake to assume that the military threat to India came only from Pakistan. He urged Nehru that military strength was needed for an independent policy, and that India was a stabilizing element for peace in Asia. See Bajpai, 'India and the Balance of Power', 1–8; Vallabhbhai Patel's warning to Nehru about China's malign intentions was in a letter dated 7 November 1950, describing China a potential enemy of India. This letter was printed in full in Mullik, *My Years with Nehru*, 115–22. Nehru ignored both warnings.

13. Nayar. *The Modernization Imperative and Indian Planning.* This is the pioneering study that brought into focus the relationship between economic reforms and geo-politics, and between economic liberalization and strategic autonomy which had been the basic motivation in the development of the USA and Japan.

14. Spear, *A History of India*, 239 and 245. This notes Nehru's links with Indian leftists, making him a symbol of the Congress party's left-wing supporters.

15. Similar ideological rift could also be found in the Indian Civil Service, particularly the ones handling foreign policy. Submil Dutt, who held the position of foreign secretary under Nehru, in his 1977 book on the Nehru era recalls that some members of the Civil Service who were socialist looked to Nehru for sustenance, while the conservatives looked to Patel, causing major irritants between the Civil Service and the political leadership. See Dutt, *With Nehru in the Foreign Office.*

16. Mehta, 'Panditji Knows Best: The Abdication of Advice and Dissent by the Bureaucracy', makes a compelling case.

17. Brecher, *Nehru: A Political Biography*, 564.

18. K.M. Panikkar's major work, *Asia and Western Dominance*, made the case for the importance of guarding against Western imperialism. Tanham, 'India's Strategic Thought', notes India's defensive strategic orientation and land-oriented basis, and the absence of strategic thinking. He noted that the Government of India did not articulate a coherent strategic vision and it was passive in military affairs. This judgement was made years after the China debacle.

19. See Prasad et al. *History of the Conflict with China, 1962.*

20. This is acknowledged by Escott Reid and S. Gopal concerning India's mediatory roles in the Korean and Suez crises.

21. All leaders following Nehru made a point to assert Nehruvian framework of non-alignment both at home and abroad. In its 1981 issue, the *Economic and Political Weekly*, reporting on Indira Gandhi's trip to East Europe, suggested that Mrs Gandhi was trying to recuperate the dwindling credibility of India's policy of non-alignment.

Increasingly, Indira Gandhi is trying to cast herself more and more in the image of her father, emphasising not merely the continuity of the Nehru foreign policy, but also legitimising herself as Nehru's heir—and not merely in a physical sense either. These anxieties to establish the legitimacy of the Nehru heritage in her own person and her policies are of course linked with her anxiety about the future. In other words, while repeatedly looking back to Nehru (and the 'family') in recent times, she is also looking forward to the future to ensure that these same 'traditions' would continue along the same lines.

See *Economic and Political Weekly*, 'Going Places', 1878.

22. Singh, *War Despatches*. It is the most detailed account.
23. See Jacob, *Surrender at Dacca*. It is one of several insider accounts.
24. Kapur, *Pokhran and Beyond*. It is the most detailed history of India's nuclear diplomacy.

3

Extended Neighbourhood and Multilevel Alignments

Narendra Modi's message of regional cooperation to the South Asian leaders at the 18th SAARC summit held in Kathmandu at the end of November 2014 was straightforward and clear— 'when we join our hands and walk in step, the path becomes easier, the journey quicker and the destination closer'. What was perhaps more important is what he said in Hindi to characterize his neighbourhood first policy (indeed, the only Hindi sentence in a speech delivered in English): *paas hone se saath hone ki taaqat zyaada hai* (being near each other is not important, it is being together that counts). In this one sentence, Modi had reconstructed the concept of neighbourhood from one based primarily on geographical territory and boundaries into one that placed the emphasis on working together across boundaries. A message was being sent to Pakistan, and Modi's neighbourhood policy was beginning to take shape within the larger framework of a multilevel alignment normative structure. This was Modi's second meeting with the region's leaders, held in a chilly environment between India and Pakistan, the first meeting having been at his swearing-in ceremony. In August 2014, India had shelved the bilateral talks at the foreign secretary level—its prompt response to a meeting that took place between the Pakistani high commissioner in India and the Kashmiri separatist group leaders of the Hurriyat Conference. This was a marked change from the previous practice of allowing Pakistani representatives to engage with the separatist leadership. The Modi government's message was clear: the talks were to be solely bilateral and there was no place for third parties. The euphoria and optimism built during and after the attendance of all South Asian regional leaders, including Pakistan's Prime Minister Nawaz Sharif, at Modi's swearing-in ceremony in New Delhi, had evaporated and doubts were now raised as to whether it was feasible for Modi to implement his 'neighbourhood first' commitment. After the September 2016 Uri attack and India's withdrawal from the SAARC summit which was to be held in Islamabad in November, the Modi government was beginning to sharpen its neighbourhood policy within the larger framework of an extended neighbourhood through regional forums such as the Bay of Bengal Initiative for Multi-sectoral Technical and Economic Cooperation (BIMSTEC) and BRICS.

The discussion in this chapter is divided into four parts. We begin by giving a broad description of India's neighbourhood and a brief historical overview of Indian foreign policy in the region and the legacy of policy successes and failures which the Modi government has inherited. In the second section, we discuss the shift in Modi's policy towards the neighbourhood, discussing in detail the reconceptualization of the neighbourhood as the immediate and extended neighbourhood such that different and distinct strategies are to be pursued for each; there is a sense in which the local and the global are not distinct in Modi's world—we use Roland Robertson's convenient term 'Glocal' to capture this phenomenon. The third section discusses how the Modi government has provided consistency to its policy goals and instruments by reconciling its neighbourhood strategy to its multilevel alignment strategy in the full glocal sense. The foreign policy goals, such as combating terrorism, entailing a muscular policy towards Pakistan or poking at China's policy without thereby wrecking the Sino-Indian relationship, are being pursued at multiple levels—within and outside the neighbourhood. The fourth section takes stock of Modi's neighbourhood policy through the end of 2016. It is not our intention, for obvious reasons, to pass judgement on the merits, feasibility or prospects of any of the numerous policy conceptualizations and initiatives discussed in the sequel, but rather to describe, analyse and help place in perspective a series of foreign policy developments, many of profoundly innovative character and potentially immense import to India's prospects in the coming decades.

India's Messy Neighbourhood

Modi has certainly inherited a messy, even chaotic state of affairs in the South Asian neighbourhood. Territorial issues have remained a constant source of tension between India and China, with India claiming about 15,000 square miles of Chinese-controlled territory in Aksai Chin, while China claims India's Arunachal Pradesh (about 34,000 square miles) as 'Southern Tibet'. India's relationship with Pakistan continues to be fragile, particularly in light of continuing Line of Control (LoC) violations and terrorist attacks onto Indian territory. The region of Kashmir has remained a flashpoint between India and Pakistan for more than 60 years, and two other major irritants in India and Pakistan relations are the latter's support of Islamic militant groups like Lashkar-e-Taiba (LeT) and its unwillingness to prosecute Hafiz Muhammad Saeed, the Mumbai attacks' mastermind and head of Jamaat-ud-Dawa. In addition, the Pakistan army- and Inter-Services Intelligence (ISI)-supported Jaish-e-Mohammad (JeM) terrorist group has been implicated in the Pathankot and Uri attacks on the Indian side of the LoC. For its part, Pakistan blames India for supporting the Baluchistan separatist movement and, in particular, accuses India's intelligence agency, the Research and Analysis Wing (RAW), of providing financial assistance to the militant groups. While Nepal and Sri Lanka appear to be on the path of recovery from long periods of political instability, terrorism and violence, that cannot be said about India, Pakistan or Afghanistan where terrorism remains a major threat. But it is China's increasing strategic influence in India's backyard in the Maldives, Pakistan, Nepal, Bangladesh and Sri Lanka, along with its unswerving support of Pakistan, that remains for a foreseeable future India's most important and difficult foreign policy challenge. Nepal's neglect by New Delhi during the past two decades gave China the opportunity to strategically penetrate Nepal with military and infrastructural assistance. It is yet to be seen whether Sri Lanka, with its strategic military and economic ties with China, will pursue a more balanced approach towards India and China as proposed by Sri Lanka's new president, Sirisena. Since establishing ties with Bangladesh in 1976 and signing a Defence Cooperation Agreement in 2002, China has developed a strong military relationship with that country. China is now Bangladesh's largest supplier of military equipment. New Ming-class submarines, ordered in 2013, were expected to join the Bangladeshi fleet in 2016. The Bangladesh–China–India–Myanmar corridor and the Maritime Silk Road feature prominently as an important components of China's 'One Road, One Belt' policy, both through land and sea. No wonder then that Bangladesh has been a big supporter of China becoming a full member of SAARC. India has been working through difficult policy choices in Afghanistan after the Western forces pull-out in 2014. Pakistan–China relations, which started on a positive note with the 1966 military assistance pact and the 1972 strategic alliance pact, have been on an uninterrupted upward trajectory, culminating recently with the conclusion of the $46 billion China–Pakistan Economic Corridor (CPEC). Afghanistan's Ashraf Ghani is facing a difficult time in implementing his vision of a self-reliant and peaceful Afghanistan after the withdrawal of foreign troops. In addition, the region is the least integrated in terms of commerce and trade, with intra-SAARC trade continuing at less than 5 per cent of the region's total trade. Perhaps even more than has been the case with his predecessors, Modi's work is cut out for him—to say the least.

The neighbourhood has long figured prominently in India's foreign policy. Under Nehru's leadership, India did establish generally good and friendly relations with its neighbours.

Even with troubled relations which had begun over the issue of Kashmir in 1947, India was able to work collaboratively with Pakistan on rehabilitating some 10 million partition refugees living in camps. Unable to receive any assistance from the United Nations (UN), India and Pakistan entered into bilateral treaties, the so-called Inter-dominion Conference Agreements (1948–51), which allowed the two countries to establish across their borders effective legal norms and administrative structures for standardizing reciprocal processes for resettlement programmes, property administration and other relief arrangements. Again, in 1960, with the assistance of the World Bank, the two countries signed the Indus Waters Treaty in order to share the water of the Indus River system. Between 1949 and 1954, India signed individual treaties of Friendship with Bhutan (1949), Nepal (1950) and Burma (1951). At Nehru's instance, in 1950, a treaty was signed with Sikkim, giving it the status of an Indian protectorate. In 1954, India and China signed a treaty in order to promote trade between the Tibet Region of China and India and to facilitate pilgrimage and travel by the region's people. This agreement, with India ceding its British-inherited extraterritorial rights, effectively implied Chinese sovereignty over Tibet.[1] Both countries agreed to conduct their relations on Panchsheel principles: mutual respect for each other's territorial integrity and sovereignty, mutual non-aggression, mutual non-interference in each other's internal affairs, equality and mutual benefit, and peaceful co-existence. In addition to these principles, for the conduct of their mutual affairs, India agreed: to withdraw completely within six months the military escorts stationed at Yatung and Gyantse in Tibet; to hand over to China at a reasonable price the postal, telegraph and public telephone services operated by India in Tibet; and to return to the Government of China all lands used or occupied by India other than the lands within its Trade Agency compound walls at Yatung. In 1955, these principles (to which five more were added) were endorsed by the Asian-African Conference in Bandung, Indonesia, and were later to become the basis of the Non-aligned Movement (NAM), established in Belgrade in 1961. The Panchsheel principles turned into the Panchsheel doctrine which to this day has been religiously adhered to by the Indian leadership and by the foreign policy establishment in China's and India's neighbourhood.[2] However, as one commentator has pointed out, Panchsheel was respected 'more in breach rather than observance'. On the surface, however, there has been an almost religious adherence to this empty doctrine as when, in July 2014, the two countries celebrated the 60th anniversary of the Panchsheel Agreement, with Indian Vice President Hamid Ansari making a special trip to Beijing.

Indira Doctrine: The 1962 Sino-Indian War sets the stage for a shift in the neighbourhood policy from Panchsheel-based engagement to the pursuance of regional hegemony through the so-called Indira Doctrine. Indira Gandhi, when she succeeded Lal Bahadur Shastri in 1966, had inherited a different world (the India–Pakistan war, Pakistan's engagement with China and the US military alliance with Pakistan). During her two terms as prime minister, Henry Kissinger's 1971 visit to China with Pakistan's help, Sri Lanka's Civil War and the Tamil exodus to India in 1983 with Sri Lanka seeking support from powers other than India, and Nepal's increasing engagement with China were some of the developments in the region which contributed to creating a far from congenial regional environment for India. In order to keep the United States and China out of the region, the Indira Doctrine clearly articulated that the subcontinent was to be India's exclusive sphere of influence, and foreign intervention in South Asia would be perceived as anti-India's interests. Moreover, 'no South Asian government should ask for outside assistance from any country; if a South Asian nation genuinely needs external assistance, it should seek from India. A failure to do so will be considered anti-Indian'.[3] Without abandoning her father's ideal of non-alignment, she proposed what she considered to be a pragmatic answer to India's dealing with its neighbourhood—not merely to be guided 'by idealism, not merely by sentimentalism, but by very clear thinking and hard-headed analysis of the situation'.[4] Indira was to abandon the post-1962 Sino-Indian conflict defensive foreign policy approach and develop a new rationale for guiding India's relationship with the neighbours—India, the regional hegemon. This doctrine remained the hallmark of first Indira and later Rajiv Gandhi's governments' neighbourhood policy until the 1990s, and the consequences of this strategy—a mistrust of India and a growing uneasiness amongst her neighbours—are being felt to this day. The Indira Doctrine of regional security which clearly defined India's relationship with its neighbours and 'represented a tough and uncompromising attitude toward the neighbours, large and small' reinforced the image of India as a bully, generating increasing mistrust of the big and dominant power.[5] The doctrine had fundamental limitations. As Surjit Mansingh has maintained, Indira Gandhi, its chief architect, found herself unable to resolve a basic dilemma of power, that is, how to handle major powers in preserving India's autonomy and national interests and yet not appear so powerful as to frighten its small neighbours. This was evident during the 1971 India–Pakistan war when India had the opportunity to resolve the Kashmir issue. Indian military superiority vis-à-vis Pakistan was obvious as it helped to liberate Bangladesh. But, as Harsh Pant points out,

> India appeared not to have the total defeat of Pakistan as a strategic objective. The threat of external involvement from China never materialized as a result of the pact that India had signed with Russia. The Chinese may in the past have been content to involve themselves militarily against India alone, but were more hesitant when confronted with Russia. Similarly, the Russian influence did not develop militarily following the United States deterrent posture (sending its carrier battle group to the Bay of Bengal).[6]

Despite a convincing military victory over Pakistan, India engaged in diplomatic negotiations with Pakistan in 1971 that led to the signing of the Simla Peace Agreement, whereby the two countries resolved to settle their differences by peaceful means through bilateral negotiations and not to interfere with the other country's internal matters, invoking as a basis their mutual respect for peace, security, territorial sovereignty, mutual friendship and equality. These were significant exceptions to the regional hegemonic foreign policy strategy.

Re-engaging the Neighbourhood: In the early 1990s, faced with the collapse of the Soviet Union and a worsening domestic economic situation, Prime Minister Narasimha Rao initiated India's Look East policy. India's leadership's emphasis on the immediate neighbourhood can also be traced back to when Inder Kumar Gujral was the minister of external affairs in V.P. Singh's National Front government (1989–90) and later in H.D. Deve Gowda's United Front government (1996–97). Responding to a changed global geo-political environment at the end of the Cold War and to India's slow but steady shift towards the liberalization of its economy, the Gujral Doctrine set out five principles to guide the conduct of India's foreign relations with its neighbours: first, non-reciprocity with its neighbours and accommodation in good faith and trust; second, no usage of its territory by any South Asian country against the interest of another country of the region; third, non-interference in the internal affairs of another; fourth, mutual respect for each other's territorial integrity and sovereignty; and, finally, the settlement of all disputes through peaceful bilateral negotiations. The fundamental thinking behind these principles was that they would create a climate of cooperation in the region.

Although hailed in South Asia as a fresh approach to generating cooperation (particularly in order to deal with Pakistan and the Kashmir issue), the Gujral Doctrine lacked weight and momentum, largely because of India's comparatively slow economic growth. The significance of India's neighbourhood was not lost on each successive government. Prime Minister Manmohan Singh (2004–14) consistently asserted during his term, 'India cannot prosper and progress without its neighbouring countries also prospering, and progressing, in equal measure'. This emphasis on the neighbourhood, however, was directionless and suffered from what most scholars have described as India's three-decade-old 'feeble foreign policy' lacking 'an insightful strategic formulation'. Ganguly and Pardesi were to conclude in their 2009 study, tracing India's foreign policy and its changes over time, that 'New Delhi needs to proactively shape its regional environment in tandem with its neighbours'.[7]

The Indira Doctrine has left a stubbornly lasting legacy. Prime Minister Modi faces a difficult and challenging road ahead. Conciliating the neighbourhood and convincing neighbours, both large and small, of India's intentions to have a crisis-free, geo-politically stable and economically inter-linked neighbourhood are directly connected to Modi's team successfully erasing the memory of the Indira Doctrine and pursuing in its place a regional hegemonic strategy. How well Modi succeeds in his ambitions to turn India into a leading global power depends importantly on his government's successful implementation of its neighbourhood strategy. Modi is fully aware that he has inherited a messy neighbourhood and that the strategy devised to conciliate the immediate neighbourhood cannot be simplistic. Modi's response to the complexity of the immediate neighbourhood has been twofold: (a) free the concept of neighbourhood from its geographical boundaries (he intends to have his cake and eat it too) and (b) intimately connect neighbourhood priorities to a global foreign policy agenda of multilevel alignments.

Modi Shifts the Policy Agenda

The primacy of the neighbourhood figures prominently in Modi government's ambitious, pragmatic and active foreign policy agenda. It is axiomatic in Modi's thinking that becoming a credible leading global power means becoming a credible regional power. It is for India as the dominant regional power to exercise its responsibility to ensure and deliver the collective development and prosperity of the whole South Asian region. And that is only possible if there is a crisis-free, geo-politically stable and economically inter-linked neighbourhood. This has meant undertaking a wide range of initiatives: cooperation for all countries in the SAARC region; economic partnership with China and Japan; the 'Act East policy' (expanding on the Look East policy); Look East–Link West and the proactive pursuance of high diplomacy through foreign visits. Within that policy context, India has adopted an increasingly positive attitude towards SAARC, though not much success has been achieved due to the continuing chilly India–Pakistan relations. With regard to the neighbourhood, Modi has borrowed from Gujral's foreign policy book: during his visit to Nepal in August 2014, he clearly outlined India's desire to take its relations with its neighbours to a higher plane and articulated his government's core principles, virtually in Gujral Doctrine terms, namely respect for sovereignty, equality in partnership regardless of asymmetry in size, non-interference in internal affairs and the promotion of meaningful cooperation guided by trust and friendship. Modi's ambition for the SAARC countries, with India as leader and by far the dominant member, is to see the regional organization attain its own stature in the world and to emerge as a 'power' in its own right. One of India's primary foci for Modi to see India emerging as a leader of South Asia as a precondition to pursuing its dream of becoming a superpower.

However, becoming a credible leading power also means convincing other global powers, particularly China and the United States, that India can fill such a role. There is no doubt that Modi's proactive foreign agenda and his undisputed clout as a leader coming from his strong electoral mandate have obliged these two great powers to view India in a different light and, indeed, both have been actively engaging India since Modi's arrival on the Indian national scene. China was the first country to reach out to Modi after his election with Premier Li Keqiang's phone call to India's new prime minister. Chinese Foreign Minister Wang Yi visited India in June, followed by the BRICS interaction in July and President Xi Jinping's visit to India in September. During Xi Jinping's visit, Modi's firm stance on India's borders was taken note of by both domestic and foreign audiences. Modi told the media that 'a climate of mutual trust and confidence; respect for each other's sensitivities and concerns; and, peace and stability in our relations and along our borders are essential for us to realize the enormous potential in our relations'.[8] Earlier, President Obama had telephoned Modi on 19 May, the eve of his swearing-in as India's next prime minister, inviting him to pay an official visit to the United States. The Obama White House made it a point to consistently point out that the US president deeply valued his relationship with the Indian prime minister and that the two leaders had a strong partnership, specifically on expanding economic opportunities. With such types of endorsement from global leaders such as Obama and Xi Jinping, India was on its way to establish itself as a credible leading power.

It was at the East Asia Summit and the ASEAN–India Summit held in Myanmar in November 2014 that Modi began to outline the contours of India's ambitious regional agenda and referred explicitly to the East Asian countries as India's neighbours. In his opening statement at the ASEAN–India Summit, Modi maintained that 'The ASEAN community is India's neighbour. We have ancient relations of trade, religion, culture, art and traditions. We have enriched each other through our interaction. This constitutes a strong foundation of a modern relationship'. The message was clear and unambiguous that India desired a greater global role in which the 'Look East' policy was to be recast as the 'Act East' policy—an action-oriented policy towards ASEAN specifically and East Asia more generally, which is to be based on practical partnerships with Japan, Vietnam, Australia and ASEAN. Moreover, in this closer engagement with Asia-Pacific, security and stability in the South China Sea figure prominently as Indian priorities. Modi was laying claim to India's assuming a more active and prominent strategic role in the Asia-Pacific region. This is exemplified by an enhanced defence diplomacy in East and Southeast Asia. Modi himself drew to his audiences' attention at the 2015 East Asia Summit and the ASEAN–India Summit that since his government came to power 18 months earlier, no region had seen greater engagement from India than the Asia-Pacific and the Indian Ocean.

What exactly is the Modi government's neighbourhood first policy? Although there are no official documents on this particular subject, one can discern the policy's major parameters through the prime minister's public strategic statements, both at home and abroad. Three things are obvious: an extension of the concept of 'neighbourhood'; the promotion of different strategies for each of the two—immediate and extended—neighbourhoods; and the choice of whether to take the bilateral or multilateral route depending upon the context and the strategic interests involved so as to keep within the framework of multilevel alignments.

Modi's New Neighbourhood—'Glocal': Reconceptualization, Underlying Motives and Strategies

Modi has been unabashed in his revising the concept of India's strategic and economic neighbourhood and has extended it to encompass countries in and beyond the Indian Ocean areas, to include the Pacific Ocean and to look East as well as West, particularly to include Iran. The immediate neighbourhood is now the extended neighbourhood, allowing the Modi government to break away from India's historical preoccupation to be seen as the 'consensual hegemon' by other South Asian countries and, as Bhabani Sen Gupta suggested years ago, to move away from the 'claustrophobic confines of the region'.[9] In this respect, the neighbourhood first policy cannot be seen in isolation from the Modi government's overarching foreign policy goal of multilevel alignment. It is clear what lies behind this: Modi is adamant that India's immediate and extended neighbourhoods are of crucial importance for the Indian economy. He sees it as imperative that this neighbourhood embrace India and, even if not necessarily as a strategic counterweight to China, that it be at a minimum interconnected with India's security and economic goals so that India can secure its sphere of influence in and around the Indian Ocean. While both China and India are coming to terms with each other there—China with its 'Maritime Silk Road' and Asia-Pacific Free Trade Area and India with its 'Make in India', 'Act East' and Modi's 'Bharat Mala' and 'Sagar Mala'—Modi's government is pursuing systemically and strategically its agenda, on the one hand, of maintaining positive relationships with its neighbours without compromising India's national security, and, on the other hand, of pursuing a larger global role for India through a proactive economic and strategic engagement with East and Southeast Asian countries and Western powers.

Within the context of a diverse array of energy, economic and security interests which, one could say, are implicitly connected in one way or another with 'balancing' China, the Modi government is pushing forward with an ambitious twofold agenda. First, to focus internally on developing a seamless connectivity through road, railway and port-led development through coastal economic zones in order that India can actively and fully take the lead in driving the economic development of a wider region; and second, to commit to an external active and decisive trade and investment engagement with its extended neighbours, and to provide selective strategic infrastructural support to countries in the Indian Ocean. But these goals of connectivity are inter-linked with the Modi government's proactive attempts to shape and increase India's naval footprint in and around the Indian Ocean and to develop diplomatic and defence relationships with the littoral countries.

The Indian Ocean which is home to four waterways and chokepoints (the Suez Canal; the Bab-el-Mandeb connecting the Indian Ocean with the Red Sea by way of Gulf of Aden; the Strait of Hormuz connecting the oil fields of the Persian Gulf, the Gulf of Oman and the Indian Ocean; and the Strait of Malacca which lies between Malaysia, Singapore and Indonesia and connects the Indian Ocean with the South China Sea and the Pacific Ocean) has always been perceived as important in all recent Indian foreign policy thinking due to its unique strategic location and its rich endowment of natural resources. The Modi government has not only amply recognized its strategic significance but has also taken a number of relevant steps. Under his government, the ocean and the littoral states have been paid exponentially increasing attention as China vies for control over the oceans and access to the littoral states. At stake are two-thirds of the world's oil and one-third of the world's gas reserves. Nearly 90 per cent of world trade in commodities and goods continues to flow by those seas and the growing resurgence of Islamic militancy has caused global concerns about the stability of the Indian Ocean's trade and energy security. During the past few years, maritime drug crime, human trafficking and increasing migration have added to India's maritime concerns, thus making it imperative for India to look deeply at its own naval capacities and seek new kinds of security cooperation with other regional and extra-regional powers.

During his very first business trip outside the capital after assuming office, a visit to the Indian Navy's newest aircraft carrier INS Vikramaditya off Goa, the new prime minister emphasized that India's sea lanes of communication depended on the security of maritime trade which the Indian Navy must guarantee. And this was followed by an active engagement with the United States and other major and middle powers that are beginning to see India as a natural balancer against China's rise. In March 2015, making a new push to seal in its partnerships around the Indian Ocean, Modi undertook a tour of the region which included visits to Sri Lanka, Mauritius and Seychelles. In Seychelles, he launched the first of the planned 32 coastal surveillance radar (CSR) stations in the Indian Ocean. While the original intent behind setting up the CSR stations had been to prevent any further Mumbai-type attacks from originating via the sea, China and maritime security figure prominently in the India–Seychelles relationship. During his visit, Modi asserted,

> We regard Seychelles as a vital partner in our Indian Ocean neighborhood. Our relationship is unique and special. It is founded on a deep sense of mutual trust and confidence. Our security partnership

is strong and has enabled us to fulfill our shared responsibility to advance maritime security in the region.[10]

Modi added that he hoped that 'Seychelles will soon be a full partner in the maritime security cooperation between India, Maldives, and Sri Lanka'.

After years of geostrategic neglect, the Andaman and Nicobar Islands which occupy a strategically important zone, being only 22 nautical miles from Myanmar and 90 nautical miles from Indonesia, have finally entered within India's security radar. Although established in 2001 to put land, sea and air military forces under one command (India's first unified and only theatre command), the Andaman and Nicobar Command (ANC) has remained ineffective due to a lack of resources, environmental clearances and to ongoing turf wars among the Indian Army, Navy and Air Force. In May 2015, Navy Chief Admiral Robin Dhowan announced that there was 'a very big plan' underway and all three services were involved. The ANC was to be better equipped and that had been given top priority by the Ministry of Defence. In early 2016, India opened the door to collaborating with Japan on developing and upgrading civilian infrastructure on the islands. Although a modest project, Japan is to build a 15-megawatt diesel power plant on South Andaman Island, it points to a major shift in India's historical policy stance of not allowing foreign investment on the strategically important islands.

At the end of 2015, the Indian Navy released its third Maritime Security Strategy document, 'Ensuring Secure Seas', considered as one of the most comprehensive policy and strategy documents since 1998. While it picks up on the themes of the previous strategy documents, combining the themes of fulfilling national economic needs and pursuing security interests by dealing with the threats at sea, the new document takes on a different significance. It has outlined the Modi government's bold assertions about India's strategic stakes in the Indian Ocean region. The maritime strategy is conceived as a basically holistic and seamless approach—a constructive way of dealing with maritime security through both multilateral and regional maritime engagements. And without specifically mentioning China, in line with the government's view of positive-sum game, it asserts that the maritime neighbourhood is to be engaged through strategic military assistance, local capacity building, technical cooperation and strategic communications. On 15 December 2015 at the Indian Navy's first ever Combined Commanders' Conference (Air Force, Army and Navy), on board the INS Vikramaditya, while speaking about India's actions in extending its reach in the Indian Ocean region and for the first time articulating a clear strategy for its maritime region, the prime minister was careful in what he had to say about China. Modi said,

> We are also pursuing closer relations with China to harness the full potential of our economic partnership. We will aim to address outstanding issues, maintain stability on the border, and develop greater mutual understanding and trust in our overlapping neighbourhood. I believe that India and China can engage constructively across the complexity of their relationship as two self-assured and confident nations, aware of their interests and responsibilities. We will continue to strengthen our defence capabilities and infrastructure, engage our neighbours more closely and strengthen our regional and global partnerships, including in maritime security.[11]

Some connectivity projects are building upon former UPA government initiatives, such as moving forward on the multi-modal transport connectivity under the proposed Bangladesh–China–India–Myanmar (BCIM) economic corridor (but with the new promise of connecting all northeast state capitals to the rail network by 2020). But the two foundational projects of Modi's internal connectivity strategy are Sagar Mala and Bharat Mala (India's plans to connect the entire Himalayan belt of Indian states through a network of rail and roads)—the integrated development of India's maritime sector and, within the context of cooperative federalism where the central and the state governments would work collaboratively, the setting up of 10 coastal economic regions.

While the Sagar Mala project is envisioned to set in motion wide-ranging infrastructural development, its other goals include an exploration of short-sea shipping, ship-building and the specializing of ports in certain economic activities such as energy, coal, chemicals and agro-products. Recently dubbed the 'Blue Revolution—Sagar Mala project', it has been unveiled by Minister for Road Transport and Highways Nitin Gadkari in an ambitious blueprint for coastline development. A National Perspective Plan for the entire coastline was announced in April 2016 which identified coastal economic zones, plans for the upgrading and modernization of about 200 ports as well as for new railway connectivity. Moreover, the government plans to submit new legislation to nationalize 101 internal waterways for cheap transportation and granting infrastructure status to ship-building in Kochi and Kandla. In emphasizing a cooperative maritime security in the Indian Ocean, Modi has couched India's role as facilitating the growth and security for all, reminiscent of and consistent with his domestic slogan *Sabka Saath, Sabka Vikas* which, in the Indian Ocean context, becomes SAGAR—Security and Growth for All in the Region. Speaking in Mauritius on the commissioning of the Coast ship Barracuda in March 2015, Modi pointed to the significance of the Indian Ocean, India's responsibility to shape its future and the shared commitment and responsibility in ensuring that the seas are safe and free for all. He noted,

> Today the world speaks of 21st century driven by dynamism and the energy of Asia and the Pacific. But, its course will be determined by the tides of the Indian Ocean. That's why Indian Ocean is at the centre of global attention…. We seek future for Indian Ocean that lives up the name SAGAR—Security and Growth for all in the Region.[12]

Acknowledging that other countries (but without mentioning either China or the United States by name) have strong interests and stakes in the region, Modi laid India's claim to the ocean, and, based on shared values, he sought strategic convergence of the Indian Ocean neighbours on issues where different parties have legitimate interests and concerns: 'Those who live in this region have the primary responsibility for peace, stability and prosperity in the Indian Ocean. Yet, the engagement with others who hold strong interests and stakes in the Indian Ocean (obviously the reference here is to China and the United States) will have to be done collaboratively and cooperatively, through dialogue, capacity-building and economic partnership'. Modi carefully connected his SAGAR approach to his multilevel alignment foreign policy strategy, which suggests inter-linkages, aimed at avoiding zero-sum outcomes by pursuing a course of integrative bargaining with diverse powers with diverse interests.[13]

In the spirit of positive-sum outcomes, in June 2014, India's Ministry of Culture launched Project Mausam (weather) at the 38th World Heritage Session at Doha, Qatar, to share knowledge, traditions, technologies and ideas along maritime routes that link different parts of the Indian Ocean littoral as well as those that connect the coastal centres to their hinterlands. The project is driven by the belief that, historically, Indian sailors, through their knowledge about weather-related phenomena, particularly Monsoon Rivers, had been able to forge relations amongst nations and groups linked by the Indian Ocean, allowing them successfully to conduct the ancient Indian maritime trade. Project 'Mausam', a response to China's Maritime Silk Road, conceptualizes a new world along the littoral of the Indian Ocean as stretching from East Africa, along the Arabian Peninsula, past southern Iran to the major countries of South Asia and thence to Sri Lanka and Southeast. But India is carefully adhering to the use of cooperative language so that the project, like Sagar Mala or the Blue Revolution, is not seen as 'balancing China'. Through this project, the ministry aims to accomplish two goals: first, at the macro level, to re-connect and re-establish communications between countries of the Indian Ocean world, which would lead to an enhanced understanding of cultural values and concerns; and, second, at the micro level, to understand national cultures in their regional maritime milieu. Interestingly, China is also making it a point to formulate its strategic maritime goals in the language of cooperation. During Prime Minister Modi's visit in April 2015, China expressed its readiness to work with India to link its ambitious Maritime Silk Route plans with India's 'Mausam' project in a bid to address New Delhi's strategic concerns and derive 'common benefits'.

Despite its cooperative language, Modi's government continues to generate influence along the strategic maritime route where China's presence has been growing for the past decade or so. The decision is to ensure an active defence and security engagement with East and Southeast Asia, rather than assuming the posture of a 'hesitant defence partner'; Modi's 2015 visits to Mauritius, Sri Lanka and Seychelles where he became the first Indian prime minister to travel to Seychelles in 33 years and to Sri Lanka in 28 years are a case in point. During his visit to island nations in the Indian Ocean, Modi was successful in reaching an agreement with Mauritius and Seychelles to promote India's economic and security connectivity in the region. While receiving the rights to develop Agalega Island in Mauritius and Assumption Island in Seychelles, India signed an agreement with Mauritius to upgrade existing and set up new infrastructure at the outer island of Mauritius. India also signed a memorandum of understanding for creating a framework for cooperation in the field of ocean economy. These agreements were followed by Prime Minister Modi's 2016 announcement of a new $500 million line of credit for Vietnam to boost defence ties. Note that India had already committed in its October 2014 agreement to sell new naval vessels to Vietnam with India providing a $100 million line of credit—the first significant military hardware supply transaction between India and Vietnam. These vessels are to be used by Vietnam for surveillance of its coast and around its military bases in the Spratly Island chain in the South China Sea where China is locked in a bitter dispute with Vietnam and other nations. The 2014 agreement was just four months after Modi's ascendency on the national scene, whereby India and Vietnam agreed to expand cooperation in oil and gas exploration and production in contested waters of the South China Sea, despite previous objections from China. While India had vibrant ties with Vietnam going back to Nehru days, these remained diplomatic alignments, largely as a result of opposition to American policies in Vietnam and Southeast Asia. But now the bilateral relationship has been elevated to the status of military and economic cooperation.

Careful not to take a dig at China as he had in his September visit to Japan (referring to China as following the path of expansionism and for which he received criticism), Modi, in a nimble learning mode, subsequently adopted a lexicon, carefully stocked with terms such as 'restraint', 'shared interests in maritime security' and 'peaceful settlement of maritime disputes in accordance with international law' when referring to maritime security and India's interests. At the 2015 ASEAN–India Summit, connectivity, both physical and digital, was the centrepiece of Modi's address. India unveiled a $1 billion line of credit to boost projects that enhance connectivity with ASEAN nations. Although inherited from the UPA government's 2012 plan of 3,200-km trilateral highway project connecting India with Myanmar and Thailand, Modi announced that the highway project is 'making good progress and should be completed by 2018' (later revised to 2020) and that, in order to ensure that the proposed highway serves as an east–west economic corridor, it should be extended to Laos, Cambodia and Vietnam. Since Myanmar is India's land bridge to Southeast Asia, this highway will be the first overland link between India and Southeast Asia. Also in the making is the Kaladan Multi-modal Transit Transport Project, which aims to connect Kolkata with Sittwe Port in Myanmar, thereby linking India to the ASEAN countries. In another initiative, at the October 2016 summit meeting of BIMSTEC, leaders discussed speeding up the process of building multi-modal connectivity physically in the area. Also, both Bangladesh and Myanmar are emerging as significant actors in the Bay of Bengal connectivity projects. In addition to establishing strategic links in the region, the Modi government is eying the possibility of extending port connectivity from the Bay of Bengal to the currently landlocked northeastern states through transit facilities offered by Bangladesh.

On 15 June 2015, the Bangladesh–Bhutan–India–Nepal (BBIN) Motor Vehicles Agreement was signed, enhancing land, rail and maritime connectivity. While 50 per cent of the funding is to come from the Asian Development Bank (under whose auspices both China and India have initiated projects to improve connectivity that will ultimately enhance trade), India approved $1.08 billion for construction and the upgrade of a 600-km-long road connecting Bangladesh, Nepal and Bhutan. In August 2016, a railway link was established connecting Agartala in Tripura, India, and Akhaura in Bangladesh. Speaking, in early January 2016, at the 3rd India–CLMV (Cambodia, Laos, Myanmar and Vietnam) Business Conclave in Chennai, Commerce and Industry Minister Nirmala Sitharaman summarized the Indian plans for connectivity in this region,

> We are not just looking at trilateral highways, but understanding how the port connectivity can be improved.... We are very keen to open up our ports so that the traditional link between the sea ports can be improved rather than going through a circuited manner.[14]

Being late in the game, India does face challenges. Its investment, for example, of $224 million in Myanmar infrastructural connectivity projects, is a fraction of that of China's $3.3 billion during the year 2015–16. In addition to the financial constraints, Khriezo Yhome, a research fellow at the Observer Research Foundation's Neighbourhood Regional Studies Initiative, points out further challenges for India—poor bureaucratic coordination, insufficient monitoring, difficult terrain and roads linking India with Myanmar which 'run through insurgency-wracked regions, creating problems for smooth implementation of projects'.[15] The delays in completing these projects detract from the credibility of India's commitment to its goals, and the region might begin to question whether India, unlike China, has the capacity or political will to deliver these projects.

Although partnership with countries in the extended neighbourhood such as Australia, Singapore and Japan, on the one hand, and ASEAN members, on the other, is premised on decisive trade, investment and energy security goals, China and its increasing strategic influence in the region frame the background for many agreements. With the goal of expanding India's strategic footprint in the ASEAN region, some of the agreements signed with Singapore included expanding cooperation in maritime security (the sharing of White-Shipping information between the two navies and greater bilateral coastal guard cooperation), collaboration in defence technology and the continuation of joint military exercises and training between their armies. During Japan's Prime Minister Shinzo Abe's visit to India in December 2015, the two countries signed several agreements including a memorandum of understanding on the peaceful use of nuclear energy and the introduction of Japan's high speed train, the Shinkansen, on the Mumbai–Ahmedabad route. Prime Minister Modi remarked,

> Today, we have also taken two more decisive steps in our security cooperation. MoU on civil nuclear energy co-operation isn't just about commerce & clean energy but symbolic of mutual confidence & partnership for a secure world. I also appreciate Prime Minister Abe Shinzo's support for India's membership of the APEC.[16]

However, it is the agreement on defence cooperation which stands out, for although China is not mentioned, the issue of its containment looms large in the background. The Indo-Japanese defence cooperation is to take three routes: first, enhancing defence and security cooperation by making available to each other defence equipment and technology necessary to implement joint research, development and/or production projects; second, regularization of Japan's participation in the India–US Malabar exercises on a regular basis; and third, the beginning of Air Force–Air Force staff talks. Without any doubt, it was for the benefit of China that the Abe–Modi joint statement specifically referred to concerns about the unilateral action in the South China Sea and to the establishment of a code of conduct by consensus to achieve peace and stability in the region.

> In view of critical importance of the sea lanes of communications in the South China Sea for regional energy security and trade and commerce

which underpins continued peace and prosperity of the Indo-Pacific, the two Prime Ministers noting the developments in the South China Sea called upon all States to avoid unilateral actions that could lead to tensions in the region. They were of the view that full and effective implementation of the 2002 Declaration on the Conduct of Parties in the South China Sea and early conclusion of the negotiations to establish a Code of Conduct in the South China Sea by consensus will contribute to peace and stability of the region. They decided to hold regular close consultations on the issues related to maritime safety and security of sea lanes of communication.[17]

In a direct challenge to Beijing, a long-standing military and political partner of Islamabad, the Indian Navy is in the midst of accelerated modernization. Russia, France, Britain and the United States have been asked by the Indian Navy to participate in a tender and compete for a contract to develop a new aircraft carrier. This, second indigenous aircraft carrier (IAC-2), INS Vishal is expected to launch fighters, radar surveillance aircraft, and tactical tanker aircraft. During President Obama's Republic-day visit in January 2015, the United States offered to India to build such a carrier, with the objective to considerably alter the naval balance of power in Asia. During the year 2016, the two countries, having established a Joint Working Group on Aircraft Carrier Technology Cooperation (JWGACTC), held meetings to discuss their ongoing cooperation on aircraft carrier technology.

A Triangulation Strategy: An evident common theme connecting all these initiatives is that India is consciously beefing up strategic partnerships with other countries, such as Australia, Afghanistan, Iran, Japan, Central Asian and Southeast countries as well as Russia, all within a global strategic calculus, in order to contain China's growing presence in the region and, more specifically, to counter to China–Pakistan axis. In relation to realizing these objectives, one of the policy instruments being pursued by the Modi government is to use what is sometimes called a triangulation strategy—by analogy with the surveying technique of fixing a common point by approaching it simultaneously from alternative directions. This has resulted in recent agreements with Iran, Afghanistan and Japan. The Chabahar agreement creates a strategic partnership with Iran, giving India a trade, investment and maritime foothold in the region and brings into play the triad of Afghanistan, Iran and India to offset Pakistan. India is taking advantage of the opportunities opened for itself as a result of the landmark nuclear deal reached between Iran and the P5+1 group of countries. Having kept on importing oil from Iran (though in much smaller quantities than before and paying Iran in rupees), India sees various possibilities of collaboration between itself and Iran. In addition to increasing oil imports from Iran, discussions have been taking place between the two countries about the construction of a subsea pipeline. The National Iranian Gas Export Company (NIGEC) and India's South Asia Gas Enterprise (SAGE) have been considering building an undersea pipeline intended to bypass Pakistan's exclusive economic zone (EEZ).

India is also aware that while it is courting Iran, China is not sitting idle. The latter's new initiative, the China–Iran corridor (the first freight train from Yiwu, Zhejiang province, in eastern China to Tehran, doing a 14-day journey, made a historic trip in January 2016) is an attempt to revive the ancient Silk Route between China and Iran. Moreover, during the visit of Chinese President Xi Jinping to Iran in January 2106, the two countries agreed to increase trade to $600 billion in the coming decade trade from $53 billion in 2013. India knows that it is undertaking a lengthy journey and that it must pursue a long-term strategy to build links with Iran—the new power in the Middle East. It is also a counter to the Arab countries which have done little for Indian interests in Kashmir and virtually nothing to soften Islamic militancy. This triangulation approach complements the Doval Doctrine guiding Modi government's Pakistan strategy—retaliate hard against Pakistan in response to its attacks on the LoC and its support to terrorist activities in Kashmir.

Similarly, the recent nuclear deal with Japan is significant as a major follow-up to the 2005–08 deal with President

Bush (the United States concluded a similar deal with India in 2005). The November 2016 agreement is the first of its kind that Japan has undertaken with a non-signatory to the Non-Proliferation Treaty, effectively putting aside its historical condemnation of Indian nuclear weapons policy. Japan, a major player in the nuclear energy market, would export nuclear technology to India, including fuel and equipment in addition to technologies for nuclear power production, as India looks to atomic energy to sustain its rapid economic growth. This agreement comes with a caveat and a fair condition: nuclear cooperation will cease if India tests again. Without any mention of China, the agreement (although in the making for the past six years) is couched in terms of clean energy partnership and climate change, though both parties emphasized the rising importance of the Indo-Pacific region as a key driver for prosperity in the world. But the new agreement does have China looming in the background as was evident in the 2015 memorandum of understanding between the two countries on the peaceful use of nuclear energy. India and Japan referred to the South China Sea issue despite China's warning to India. This dovetails neatly into the continuing maritime exercises which India and the United States have been conducting to advance multinational maritime relationships and mutual security issue and which crucially was expanded in 2016 from a bilateral United States to a trilateral exercise to include Japan. This annual exercise took place in Malabar in June 2016 near Okinawa Island, about 400 km from the contested Senkaku Islands. And anti-submarine warfare was one of the elements of the Malabar exercises—the simulated exercise being to hunt down Chinese submarines. India's involvement in maritime training exercises in Asia-Pacific was clearly meant as a signal to China that its expansionist policy is drawing resistance and the network of opposition—India along with its partners—is willing to take concrete actions, make agreements where actions go beyond rhetorical declarations and create red lines which might be hard to reverse the longer China takes to tame its behaviour with its neighbours. In addition, consistent with

Modi's priority to create a symbiotic relationship between his domestic and foreign policy agendas, the agreement brings together commerce and military policy. To bolster bilateral ties, India received commitments for Japanese investment in infrastructure, railways and for cooperation in space and agriculture. Along with the US strategic and economic leadership in Asia, India and Japan are now in the game and they do not intend to leave the field of power politics exclusively to China and the United States. This effective triangulation strategy complicates China's dream to create a G-2 world.

In another trilateral dialogue, India, Japan and Australia held their first-ever meeting in New Delhi in 2015, attended by the Indian Foreign Secretary Jaishankar, Japanese Vice Foreign Minister Akitaka Saiki and Australian Secretary of Foreign Affairs and Trade Peter Varghese. The main item on the agenda was maritime security, the South China Sea and trilateral maritime cooperation in the Indian and Pacific Oceans. This initiative was to gain prominence in light of the first-ever joint maritime exercise between the Indian Navy and Royal Australian Navy, to be followed by the Malabar bilateral exercises between the United States and India where Japan was invited to participate. India had wanted Australia to be included in the exercises. While that did not materialize, there was certainly an appetite in the United States to rework the rules of the game for the Malabar exercises. Prashanth Parameswaran noted in his column in *The Diplomat*,

> Robert Scher, the assistant secretary of defense for the Office of Strategy, Plans and Capabilities, told an audience at a Washington, D.C.-based think tank on July 13 that the United States and India should consider permanently expanding the exercise to include these partners instead of doing so on an ad hoc basis. Scher said that expanding the exercise would be one tangible demonstration of Washington and New Delhi working together on maritime security in the Indian Ocean.[18]

It would appear that the Modi government has succeeded in making India a part of a new framework for security cooperation that includes maritime security cooperation and regular maritime exercises.

In each such triangular activity, the Modi government is exercising restraint despite the fact that the policy changes are tangible and they have an escalatory potential against China should the latter not exercise restraint and evince mutual respect of Indian interests. India is also participating in China-led economic and trade initiatives. Although it is speculated that the China-backed Asian Infrastructure Investment Bank (AIIB) would be financing infrastructure projects along the 'Silk Road Economic Belt' and the 'China's Maritime Silk Road', India is one of the 20 founding members of the bank to aid the infrastructure development in the Asian region and reduce the dependence on the Western-dominated World Bank and IMF. India is also an active participant in the regional initiative, where China is a major player, of 16 countries' (ASEAN members, China, Japan, South Korea and New Zealand) Regional Comprehensive Economic Partnership (RCEP). In the works for several years, if it eventually manages to become operational, RCEP would become the largest trading bloc, covering almost half of the world's population and 40 per cent of global trade. Most observers view it as competing with the Trans-Pacific Partnership (TPP) from which China has been obviously excluded. However, India's interests in the RCEP are obvious. In the first place, the new proposed trading bloc fits in with its Act Asia policy and it would allow India to complement its existing free trade agreements (FTAs) with ASEAN countries as well with South Korea and Japan, as India is not a party to either of the other major regional FTA blocs: TPP and the Asia-Pacific Economic Cooperation (APEC). But most significantly, RCEP has the potential to determine the global balance of economic power for coming years. India does not want to be left behind and give the opportunity to China to further enhance its global influence. RCEP is being viewed by Indian leaders as an opportunity to elevate the country's strategic and economic status in the Asia-Pacific region. In addition, India would like to ensure that its trade deficit in goods, which presently sits at

$52.7 billion, does not grow larger. Despite the worries that China may use RCEP to gain more market access in India, India has shown flexibility in the negotiations. In September 2016, it withdrew its proposal for a three-tier tariff system (based on whether it has an FTA with the country or not and which would have resulted in tariff liberalization ranging from 80 per cent to the first tier, 65 per cent to the second tier and 42.5 per cent to the third tier countries) in favour of a single-tier system.

This kind of restraint was evident when, in April 2016, Russia, India and China (RIC) issued a joint communique outlining areas of trilateral agreement between three countries which for the first time included the mention of the South China dispute. The RIC trilateral has been meeting annually since 2002 to discuss regional and global issues and has been partially responsible for the creation of the BRICS block. The communique read:

> Russia, India and China are committed to maintaining a legal order for the seas and oceans based on the principles of international law, as reflected notably in the UN Convention on the Law of the Sea (UNCLOS). All related disputes should be addressed through negotiations and agreements between the parties concerned. In this regard the Ministers called for full respect of all provisions of UNCLOS, as well as the Declaration on the Conduct of Parties in the South China Sea (DOC) and the Guidelines for the implementation of the DOC.[19]

This communique could be perceived as India, without abandoning its stance on the South China Sea, staying quiet on the international rules-based regime to resolve disputes. All this notwithstanding, conciliating China has remained problematic for India. During the 2016 BRICS Summit in Goa, where Modi placed the issue of terrorism first and foremost on the agenda (referring to Pakistan as the 'mothership of terrorism'), China blocked India's attempts to include the names of terrorist groups such as JeM and LeT in the BRICS declaration and declared openly that 'it is against linking any country or religion with terror and asked the world community to acknowledge Pakistan's great sacrifices'.[20]

Two Strategies for Two Neighbourhoods Within a Seamless Framework of Foreign Policy Goals

The emphasis on regional engagement is in keeping with the election manifesto of the Bharatiya Janata Party (BJP) which highlighted the need for India to strengthen relations with its neighbours. Within this context, the Modi government has continued the rapprochement work that had begun under Manmohan Singh's leadership, including the maritime security dialogue with Maldives and Sri Lanka and the pursuit of the Teesta River water-sharing and land boundary agreements with Bangladesh. This foreign policy continuity is also obvious in the revitalizing of the Look East policy which has shaped India's engagement with Asia-Pacific for over more than past two decades. However, the Look East–Act East policy conversion 'is more than just a rebranding' as Danielle Rajendram correctly observed as early as December 2014, six months after Modi's government assumed power. In order to move away from the historical neglect of a clear articulation of its strategic ambition in East and Southeast Asia, Rajendram cautions that 'India will need to move quickly to outline a clear agenda for deepening economic, institutional and defence links with the region that go beyond what has been pledged by the previous government'.[21] Has Modi's government been able to present a clear articulation of its agenda for the extended neighbourhood? From its actions and statements, one can deduce that the Modi government's agenda for the immediate and the extended neighbourhoods is a proactive, well-conceived one and that the starting point of that agenda is to engage the two neighbourhoods differently.

While, on the one hand, India is to engage the extended neighbourhood within the framework of multilevel alignment— pursuing a diversity of interests in diverse settings with diverse powers, in its immediate neighbourhood—on the other hand, it is to promote a developmental and growth policy agenda similar to that which the Indian government is pursuing at home—the extension of the 'domestic' to the South Asian region. Modi sees the region as facing many of the same challenges as India faces at home and as, therefore, requiring similar solutions. In his speech at the 18th SAARC summit held in November 2014, he elaborated upon his goals for the SAARC neighbourhood. He made the point that India's vision 'for the region rests on five pillars—trade, investment, assistance, cooperation in every area, contacts between our people—and all through seamless connectivity'. In his view, only an improved South Asian connectivity will be able to drive stability and growth for all nations. And while this is nothing new, as others before him have pursued this line of thinking and have taken action towards the accomplishment of the same goal, the difference is how Modi has reframed the SAARC countries' development and economic agenda in virtually the same terms as his own domestic priorities of inclusive development, employment for the youth, development of infrastructure and providing electricity to every village and town. In this 'domestification' of the South region prosperity agenda, he pointed out,

> [T]he future I wish for India is the future I wish for our entire region … we speak of ease of doing business in India. Let's extend this to our region. I promise to ensure that our facilities at the border will speed up, not slow down, trade. Let's all make our procedures simple, our facilities better, our standards common and our paper work less burdensome.[22]

However, what followed in this speech was more revealing of his neighbourhood first policy. He extended application of the criteria of his well-publicized domestic 'Make in India' programme to the South Asian region.

> [Modi encouraged his counterparts] to attract Indian investments to produce for the Indian market and create jobs for [our] youth. [He] also [looked] to a future when [our] companies can easily raise funds in India for investments at home; and, when we have cross-border industrial corridors, so that we can take advantage of the natural synergies and connected lives in our Border States.[23]

This is in contrast to his message both to India's newly found wider neighbourhood, the larger Asia-Pacific region, as well as other industrialized countries. Addressing the ASEAN Business and Investment Summit in the Malaysian capital in November 2015, Modi emphasized that India was open for business. The Indian economy was, he said, performing better at a time when the global economy '[was] not exactly doing well'. Enumerating the achievements of his government in bringing about structural economic reforms, Modi remained focused on the agenda of attracting FDI and promoting the 'Make in India' programme. A similar message was given to an audience of 18,000 Indian expatriates in Singapore, which included business representatives from over 300 companies. In his typical advocacy of the new brand India (his government's reforms have 'successfully restored the credibility of India in the eyes of global players'), he also gave a new meaning to FDI, telling his Indian audience in Singapore that, for him, the acronym stands for 'First Develop India'. And, most significantly, in his Singapore lecture, Modi declared that ASEAN is the anchor of India's Act East policy.

> We are linked by geography and history, united against many common challenges and bound by many shared aspirations. With each ASEAN member, we have deepening political, security, defence and economic ties. And, as the ASEAN Community leads the way to regional integration we look forward to a more dynamic partnership between India and ASEAN that holds rich potential for our 1.9 billion people.[24]

Three developments are worth noting. First, an action plan: the ASEAN–India foreign ministers, in their meeting held in August 2015, outlined a new plan of action (2016–20) to further enhance ASEAN–India cooperation along the three verticals of politico-security, economic and socio-cultural relations. This plan was subsequently endorsed by the ASEAN leaders in their November 2015 meeting. Second, further integration: the RCEP—an FTA between ASEAN and its 6 FTA partners, namely Australia, China, India, Japan, Korea and New Zealand—strongly supported by India, represents India's policy shift from cooperation to integration. In light of the recently signed 12-country agreement on the TPO, both ASEAN and India will have to accelerate the pace of their economic reform processes in order to effectively participate in and benefit from the trade creation possibilities under RCEP. Third, behavioural norms: in outlining his government's Act East policy set against the backdrop of a resurgent domestic economy, Modi pointed out that the most critical need in Asia was to uphold and strengthen rules and norms of collective behaviour built not on the strength of a few but on the consent of all.

> India will work with countries in the region and beyond, including the United States and Russia, to ensure that our commons—ocean, space and cyber—remain avenues of shared prosperity, and not become new theatres of contests.[25]

Irrespective of these two divergent paths, what is common to Modi government's strategies towards the immediate and extended neighbourhood is, as mentioned earlier, the active pursuance of a physical connectivity agenda between India and other countries as a catalyst for deeper engagement and cooperation. Of course, it is difficult to disentangle the strategic and security dimensions from connectivity. China has already proven what connectivity can accomplish for the successful promotion of the country's security and trade interests abroad. While Modi was unable to push forward the connectivity agenda at the SAARC summit, subsequently, during his June 2015 visit to Bangladesh, Modi and Sheikh Hasina decided to connect each other's countries through road, rail and sea. This included, as we have noted in our preceding discussion, a motor vehicle agreement between Bangladesh, Bhutan, Nepal and India to facilitate the movement of cargo between all four countries, and the opening of two bus routes and train service connecting the northeastern states of India with Bangladesh. Similarly, at the 2015 ASEAN–India Summit, as previously mentioned, connectivity, both physical and digital, was the centrepiece of Modi's address. This was followed up, as pointed out earlier in this chapter, with the establishment of a railway link in August 2016 connecting Agartala in Tripura, India, and Akhaura in Bangladesh. Other plans include establishing integrated customs ports and improved land customs stations at key border points with Bangladesh, Nepal and Bhutan to ease the movement of goods and people within the sub-region. With the support of the Asian Development Bank, India is also undertaking two priority road corridor projects. The first road corridor is to connect India with Bangladesh, Nepal and Bhutan through North Bengal; the second is to establish India–Myanmar connectivity in Manipur.

Bilateral and Multilateral Negotiations Within the Multilevel Alignment Strategy

Modi's neighbourhood first policy is an integral part of an overarching strategy of interconnecting the domestic and the foreign policy agendas in a symbiotic relationship. Within that policy context, both bilateral and multilateral negotiations have emerged as relevant for the Modi government. In the immediate South Asian neighbourhood, the government's preference is to pursue both strategies, without getting into the trap of opting for one as advantageous over the other, although, for the time being, bilateralism is triumphing over regionalism. In the view of the Modi government, no South Asian country, if it wishes to overcome its development gap, has much choice but to move forward on an integrated economic agenda, whether or not that happens via SAARC. As Modi outlined in his speech at the SAARC summit, 'there is a new awakening in South Asia; a new recognition of inter-linked destinies; and, a new belief in shared opportunities. The bonds will grow. Through SAARC or outside it. Among us all or some of us'.[26] His government is coming to realize that regional integration might not be an end in itself. This is becoming more evident in light of India's challenging relationship with Pakistan and recently with Nepal over the proclamation of its new federal constitution. But what matters is the stability of the region. And this could be accomplished, on the one hand, through bilateral arrangements, such as the Land Boundary Agreement between India and Bangladesh, and, on the other hand, by engaging world powers and getting their convergence on issues important to India in its neighbourhood.

Modi has made India's concerns about the export of terrorism, particularly from Pakistan, a significant global agenda item in both the multilateral and bilateral contexts. Without mentioning Pakistan, Modi has been able to get several global powers (such as the United States, the United Kingdom, Australia, China, Russia, Japan, Malaysia and Singapore) to agree to combating terrorism as one of the major areas of cooperation between India and other countries.[27] For example, Obama's and Modi's two joint statements in September 2014 and January 2015 expressed the two leaders' shared deep concern over the continued threat posed by terrorism and stressed the need for joint and concerted efforts, including the dismantling of safe havens for terrorist and criminal networks, the disruption of all financial and tactical support for networks such as Al-Qaeda, LeT, JeM, the Dawood Ibrahim's D-Company (a criminal syndicate, based in Karachi, of 5,000 members with strategic alliance with the ISI, LeT and Al-Qaeda) and the Haqqanis. In July 2015, Modi's first visit to the Central Asian region had counter-terrorism and energy at the top of the agenda. In October 2015, China and India concluded a joint anti-terrorism training in Kunming, capital of southwest China's Yunnan province, followed by counter-terrorism consultations between the two countries on 4 November, in New Delhi. Against the backdrop of growing extremism and violence in Africa and India, Modi sought the support of African countries for the Comprehensive Convention on International Terrorism during the third India–Africa Forum Summit, held in New Delhi, in October 2015. 'When terror snuffs out life on the streets and beaches, and in malls and schools of Africa, we feel your pain as our own. And, we see the links that unite us against this threat'. At the summit, India and Africa decided to bolster their cooperation in combatting terror through intelligence sharing and counter-terrorism measures. Similarly, during Modi's November 2015 visit to the United Kingdom, he and David Cameron 'reiterated their call for Pakistan to bring the perpetrators of the November 2008 terrorist attack in Mumbai to justice'. In April 2016, during his two-day visit to Saudi Arabia, Modi and King Salman bin Abdulaziz Al Saud issued a joint statement

> [expressing] strong condemnation of the phenomenon of terrorism in all its forms and manifestations, irrespective of who the perpetrators were and of their motivations, [calling on] all states to reject the use of terrorism against other countries; dismantle terrorism infrastructures where they happen to exist and to cut off any kind of support and financing to the terrorists operating and perpetrating terrorism from their territories against other states; and bring perpetrators of acts of terrorism to justice [agreeing] to work together towards the adoption of India's proposed Comprehensive Convention on International Terrorism in the United Nations [and] agreeing to enhance cooperation in counter-terrorism operations, intelligence sharing and capacity-building and to strengthen cooperation in law enforcement, anti-money laundering, drug-trafficking and other transnational crimes.[28]

At the Hangzhou G-20 Summit, organized by China in September 2016, Modi's speech sent a stern message on terrorism, clearly pointing a finger at Pakistan, though without mentioning it by name, for fomenting terror in South Asia. Of course, the ongoing unrest in the Kashmir Valley after killing of the local Hizbul leader Burhan Wani two months earlier had made the context for Modi's remarks all the more significant. India had openly blamed the Pakistan government for supporting the stone-pelting youth protests which did not seem to abate.

> The growing forces of violence and terror pose a fundamental challenge. There are some nations that use it as an instrument of state policy. India has a policy of zero tolerance to terrorism. Because anything less than that is not enough. For us a terrorist is a terrorist.[29]

At the informal meeting of BRICS on the sidelines of the G-20, Modi was to repeat his message about Pakistan's support of

> [The terrorist groups who] in South Asia and for that matter anywhere do not own banks and factories.... Clearly someone funds and arms

them and the BRICS must intensify its joint efforts not only to fight terror, but to coordinate actions to isolate those who are supporters and sponsors of terror.[30]

While, during the 2016 BRICS Summit, in the immediate aftermath of the September Uri attack and India's surgical strike, and despite China's intransigence to not directly link Pakistan with terrorism, Modi managed to push forward the agenda of combating terrorism. At a plenary session of the summit, Modi spoke about the global reach of terrorism and called for deeper engagement between the national security advisers (NSAs) of the five member nations—Brazil, India, China, Russia and South Africa. The summit declaration, mentioning terrorism at least 24 times, asserted:

> We strongly condemn terrorism in all its forms and manifestations and agree to strengthen cooperation in combating international terrorism both at the bilateral level and at international fora.... We call upon all nations to adopt a comprehensive approach in combating terrorism, which should include countering violent extremism as and when conducive to terrorism, radicalisation, recruitment, movement of terrorists.[31]

In short, all this can be easily translated as being Modi government's strategic multilevel alignment approach to tame its immediate and challenging neighbour, Pakistan. It is intended to leave Pakistan with limited choices when India's agenda has become co terminal with heightened global concerns, whether about the Boko Haram or Al Shabab in Africa or the ISIL terrorism in the Middle East or the terrorist attacks in Paris.

Tracking Modi's Neighbourhood Policy

Inviting the SAARC leaders to his swearing-in ceremony which was accompanied by India's commitment to its immediate neighbourhood, Narendra Modi built a huge set of expectations both at home and abroad about India proactively putting the messy South Asian neighbourhood on a track of peace, stability and cooperation. There has been much concern that the neighbourhood first policy has yet to deliver and has so far failed to live up to its expectations. Indeed, India's relationship with Nepal soured during the last few months of 2015. The Madhesis, who are unhappy with Nepal's new Constitution which they perceive as discriminatory against them, set up an unofficial blockade along the border with India, blocking shipments of essential goods from India for several months. However, India's non-intervention in the matter was viewed by Nepal as amounting to a state-backed endorsement of the blockade. With the election of new Prime Minister Pushpa Kamal Dahal (popularly known as Prachanda), the relationship began to move more in a positive direction. The cordiality between the two countries was evident during Prachanda's three-day visit to India in September 2016 which resulted in a 25-point joint statement—considered by many a huge accomplishment, given the earlier failure of the two governments to issue any statement during its predecessor P.K. Oli's visit in early 2016. In another positive move, from 31 October to 13 November in 2016, India and Nepal conducted their 10th iteration of military training exercises, which are held annually, alternating between the two countries. Recent internal troubles in the Maldives have generated discomfort in India, with no clear response to the emergency actions by the Maldives government to imprison/prosecute/remove several of its leaders. The Modi government having supported the country's ousted first democratically elected president, Mohamed Nasheed, and having called for the preservation of democracy in the Maldives, is currently walking a tight rope with the new President Abdulla Yameen. India, along with other powers interested in the Indian Ocean and China, is carefully keeping tabs on Maldives as the domestic politics of this island nation continue to remain uncertain. On the other hand, relations with Afghanistan have turned around, once more in India's favour.

Most importantly, however, India's relations with Pakistan continue to remain tense and rocky. A huge amount of policy learning by the Modi government has taken place in a relatively brief period of time with respect to implementing its policy goals. Over the first two and a half years of the Modi government, policy instruments were to evolve within the broader framework of policy goals of zero tolerance for terrorism, enhancing connectivity and trade relations and continuing engagement to resolve the contentious issue. In late 2015, the Modi government worked out a strategy to accommodate the hybrid military/civilian regime in Pakistan, basically a new Track 2 version (described in detail in chapter 5). However, this was put on hold after the Uri attack in September 2016. While, for the first time, the Indian government was to cross over the border and carry out a surgical strike against the launching pads of the terrorist groups based in Azad Kashmir, India took pains not to mention Pakistan as the aggressor. No doubt, the mood of euphoria and hope that had prevailed during Modi's swearing-in ceremony has dissipated and Prime Minister Modi is very far from delivering on his promise that 'a stable, economically strong Pakistan is surely in India's interest'. Without a doubt, given on-again, off-again talks with Pakistan from August 2014 to the end of 2015 accompanied by the challenges faced by the coalition government in the state of Jammu and Kashmir (particularly after the killing of Hizbul leader Burhan Wani in July 2016) and the reinvigoration of the Kashmir issue by Pakistan, the general impression left by the Modi government has been that it has an incoherent Pakistan policy.

However, as we show in our chapter on Pakistan, the Modi government has not abandoned its Pakistan policy. Once things get back on track with Pakistan, this policy should be able to bring some sort of reconciliation between the two countries. Modi government's Pakistan policy consists of a dual process—operation to operation talks and comprehensive bilateral dialogue (CBD). This new process of conflict resolution and conflict prevention is a shift from the simultaneous pursuance of Track 1 (official discussions focusing on cease-fires, peace talks, and treaties and other agreements) and more comprehensive and fluid Track 2 diplomacy (unofficial policy-oriented discussions and problem-solving activities on items close to governmental agendas and which is aimed at building relationships and encouraging new thinking that can inform the official process).[32]

From the get-go, the Modi government has insisted on two things: first that there is a zero tolerance for terrorism and second that India–Pakistan dialogue must be bilateral (no third party including the secessionist groups in the Kashmir Valley) and the talks must deal with the issue of terrorism before any other item can be discussed (the well-publicized surgical strikes against the militants based in Pakistan's Azad Kashmir in response to the Uri attacks and successful strategy of isolating Pakistan diplomatically must be viewed in this context). A joint statement released after the Bangkok meeting of 6 December 2015, followed by Minister of External Affairs Sushma Swaraj's statements in Islamabad during the Heart of Asia meeting gave us some indication of the Modi government's Pakistan policy and the new approach it intended to adopt keeping in mind the structural constraints of a hybrid regime in Pakistan. Under, what we have termed as the new Track 2, India and Pakistan engagement is to be divided into two processes. Within the framework of bilateral talks, at the operation level, the two NSAs, outside the media glare, are to address all issues connected to terrorism, including the expedition by Pakistan of the early conclusion of the Mumbai trial. These NSA talks are to be complemented by a comprehensive bilateral dialogue. This bilateral dialogue, to be conducted at the political level, would include a discussion of matters relating to peace and security, confidence-building measures, Jammu and Kashmir, Siachen, Sir Creek, the Wullar Barrage/Tulbul Navigation Project, economic and commercial cooperation, counter-terrorism, narcotics control, humanitarian issues, people–people exchanges and religious tourism. In short, the real work would be done behind the scenes at the NSA level where Pakistan is represented by the army and Kashmir's separatist groups have been denied an official space. This strategy, however unfortunately, has been set aside in light of the Uri attack by JeM and India's response of surgical strikes and India's withdrawal from the SAARC summit at Islamabad, resulting in its cancellation. We see the reactivation of the Track 2 process once India determines that the time is right to move forward. We will be discussing in detail later in Chapter 5 which deals exclusively with Pakistan on Modi's Pakistan policy and its interface with the domestic politics in Kashmir.

The basic foundation for the relationship between India and Myanmar was laid by previous governments (starting with Rajiv Gandhi's visit to Myanmar in 1987 through the signing of a trade agreement in 1994 and up to Manmohan Singh's visit in 2012, building road connectivity and other projects). Accordingly, during his visit to Myanmar in November 2014, Modi reinforced the idea that his neighbourhood first policy was effectively a further enrichment of the previous policy—culture, commerce and connectivity between what Modi and Myanmar's President Thein Sein called 'brother countries'. However, the Indian Army's June 2015 counter-insurgency strike along the Indo-Myanmar border against the Naga insurgents (the National Socialist Council of Nagalim-Khaplang, NSCN-K), destroying 2 militant camps and killing 20 militants, has caused some controversy between the two countries. The Indian Army's retaliation was in response to the killing of 18 soldiers by the NSCN-K in Manipur's Chandel district. While the Myanmar government has denied that any Indian operation took place on its soil, the director of the president's office noted on his Facebook post, 'Myanmar will not accept any foreigner who attacks neighboring countries in the back and creates problems by using our own territory'.[33] As many have noted in India, there was a clear message to Pakistan that India is not prepared to tolerate any proxy war; if any doubts remained as to India's firmness in that regard, they dissipated rapidly after India's aggressive surgical response to the Uri attack. However, India is carefully cultivating Myanmar through its ongoing commitments to see through connectivity projects. In September 2016, Myanmar President

Htin Kyaw visited India. It was the first ever by the head of a civilian government in Myanmar in over five decades. And the conversations largely focused on improving connectivity and counter-insurgency cooperation.

On the positive side, in June 2015, India and Bangladesh signed a historic Land Boundary Agreement, exchanging territories, with 111 enclaves being transferred to Bangladesh and 51 to India. This gives citizenship to more than 50,000 people who had until then remained stateless. It was a dispute that dates back to colonial times and has been a contentious issue since India's Independence. Although there had been two previous attempts to bring this matter to closure, agreement between the two countries remained elusive due to domestic opposition in India, including by the BJP, and in the four affected states of Assam, West Bengal, Tripura and Meghalaya. Sheikh Mujibur Rahman and Indira Gandhi agreed in 1974 to exchange the enclaves of land that both countries had within each other's territory. Bangladesh's Parliament ratified the agreement but India did not. In 2011, Manmohan Singh and Sheikh Hasina signed the current agreement but it was opposed by the BJP and regional parties such as the Trinamool Congress, Asom Gana Parishad and the Assam BJP unit. But Modi was able to secure multiparty support for the agreement's ratification which received unanimous approval in the Indian Parliament. Although the Teesta River Agreement for sharing water is yet to be settled, the resolution of the continuous enclave issue has opened venues for further collaboration between the two neighbours, particularly for transit facilities through Bangladesh to India's landlocked Northeast—crucial for developing India's vast insurgency-ridden region.[34]

In Sri Lanka, the electoral victory of President Sirisena is being considered a game changer for India's relationship with that country. Since 2009, China had been building its base of influence there and has partnered with Sri Lanka in a $1.5 billion port project in the southern coastal town of Hambantota, as a part of its Maritime Silk Road project. It provided huge loans at liberal terms to the Rajapaksa government, enabling it to boost its growing services sector by investing in infrastructure projects such as highways, public amenities and ports. The timing was important for the Sri Lankan government as it had become the object of global protests over alleged human rights violations against the Tamils during its bloody crackdown against the Liberation Tigers of Tamil Eelam (LTTE) and Beijing had loyally stood by Colombo. Immediately after coming into power, President Sirisena announced that Sri Lanka would pursue a balanced foreign policy towards India and China, and in particular, of strengthening ties with India. Modi, during his visit to Colombo—the first stand-alone visit by an Indian prime minister since 1987—in his speech to the Parliament, laid out a new narrative for India's relationship with Sri Lanka. He pointed out the significance of neighbours in determining the future of any country. Modi said, 'The future I dream for India is also a future that I want for our neighbours. The world sees India as the new frontier of economic opportunity, but our neighbours should have the first claim on India'. In accord with the 'Buddhism diplomacy' of India's engagement with its neighbourhood, Modi reached out to the country's large Buddhist populations and acknowledged their history. He offered *dāna* (giving of material things) to the Buddhist monks at the Mahabodhi Society in Colombo. But he also took the opportunity to visit the Tamil-dominated war-ravaged town of Jaffna and called for equitable development and respect for all citizens in Sri Lanka. Although the visit was seen as symbolic, his call to the majority-Sinhalese government to fully implement the 13th amendment, a 1987 constitutional provision on greater autonomy, was to receive domestic support amongst the Indian Tamils.

With the withdrawal of foreign forces from Afghanistan, President Ghani, the leader of the National Unity government, whose elections were contested, has been under pressure to conclude a peace process with the Taliban so that he can obtain some improvement in the Afghan economy, whose annual growth rate has declined from 9 per cent during the past decade to under 2 per cent. Aware of Pakistan's ability to play the role of 'spoiler', he decided to start on a clean slate with Pakistan. Breaking all protocol, in 2014, Ghani made it a point to call on General Raheel Sharif at General Headquarters in Rawalpindi. Ghani also decided to send Afghan cadets to Pakistan for military training and to coordinate and authorize joint military operations between Afghanistan and Pakistan. President Ghani's decision to place Afghanistan's arms-aid request from India on hold was done precisely to create goodwill with Pakistan. Ghani declared that his government is to reconsider Karzai's request for helicopters for Afghanistan's fledgling military which had been badly hit after the Pentagon terminated contracts of Russian-made MiG-17s. Although initially resisting the request in order to avoid becoming more directly involved in the conflict in Afghanistan and fearing that it would antagonize Pakistan, India did finally agree to supply two Cheetah light helicopters, which were to have been delivered in May 2014 but have not yet arrived. Afghanistan also began to lean on China to use its influence on Pakistan to stop its military support for the Afghan Taliban and instead bring them to the negotiating table. Beijing is of the view that reconciliation between Pakistan and Afghanistan is a key to stability in the region and to mitigating extremist militancy.

India has contributed over $2 billion to Afghanistan's reconstruction efforts. And cooperation between the countries has been at both the strategic and security levels. India and Afghanistan have shared intelligence. India has assisted Afghanistan in moving forward its education and commerce agenda. Hamid M. Saboory was to note the impact of all this on Indo-Pak relations.

> As a long-standing Afghan ally, India has legitimate concerns over the sudden shift in Ghani's foreign policy toward Pakistan. Improved relations between Afghanistan and Pakistan will allow the latter to implement its policy of 'bleeding India through a thousand cuts' by moving troops from the Afghan border to the Line of Control with India. These Pakistani troops will be a distraction for Indian forces, reducing their ability to prevent insurgents from crossing the border. In addition, thousands of Indian citizens are currently involved in development projects across Afghanistan. The safety of those citizens will become a major concern for New Delhi.[35]

However, Afghanistan's honeymoon with Pakistan proved short-lived. Faced with domestic opposition towards his gestures of appeasement towards Pakistan as well as the breakdown of Pakistan-sponsored peace talks with the Taliban after the public announcement of Taliban leader Omar's death, Ghani has reverted to the Karzai position on Pakistan. The April 2016 bombing of an elite Afghan intelligence unit in Kabul by the Taliban, which killed 28 and wounded over 300, was to bring back Afghanistan's pivot towards India. In May 2015, Ghani wrote a letter to the Pakistan government, demanding harsh action against the Taliban leadership based in that country, the placement of the Taliban leadership in Peshawar and Quetta under house arrest and the mounting of an offensive against the Taliban-affiliated Haqqani network. Meanwhile, India has been continuing to support development projects in Afghanistan. In late 2015, investing $100 million, India completed the construction of the Afghani Parliament building which began about five years earlier. The building, which houses the Wolesi Jirga (Lower House) and Jirga (Upper House), is being considered as India's symbolic gift for democracy in Afghanistan. In August 2016, Afghan Army Chief of Staff General Qadam Shah Shaheem made a general request to the Ministry of Defence of India for more technical and military assistance from Delhi. Around this time, Afghanistan also reached an agreement with India to airlift trade commodities as tensions remained persistent between Afghanistan and Pakistan along the Durand Line (the main land transit route remained blocked for several days along Durand Line located near Chaman after the Pakistani officials claimed that some of the Afghan demonstrators had attacked the check post at Friendship Gate and set the Pakistani flag on fire).While Afghanistan is in a difficult position today and is trying to walk a tightrope between India and Pakistan, India's interests in Afghanistan remain clear—containing and neutralizing Pakistani influence. A new regional dynamics is beginning to take shape in South Asia. It may well be the case that India and China will have no choice but to participate in something like integrative bargaining, whereby paradoxically, the more difficult and competing the interests brought to the table for discussion, the more likely the emergence of a positive-sum outcome.

At the regional level, SAARC has remained ineffective. SAARC's perennial challenge has been getting its two largest members, India and Pakistan, to cooperate for the benefit of the other member states. Modi's articulation of the neighbourhood first policy had given a sense of hope that he might move SAARC beyond its traditional lacklustre image, reflecting its limited accomplishments. Although it has adopted some important agreements over the years (such as the SAARC Social Charter; the establishment of SAARC University; Conventions on the Suppression of Terrorism, Narcotic Drugs and Psychotropic Substances, Trafficking of Women and Children, and Child Welfare in South Asia; an Agreement on Food Security Reserve; the South Asian Preferential Trading Arrangement [SAPTA]; the South Asian Free Trade Area [SAFTA]; and more recently the SAARC Agreement on Trade in Services [SATIS]), progress on the full-scale implementation of some of these initiatives has been rather slow. The Modi government's earlier foreign policy objective of bringing 'prosperity, peace and stability' to the South Asian region and SAARC being an important vehicle has fallen off the agenda. In June 2014, through the president's address to the Indian Parliament,

> [The Modi government had signalled its] commitment and determination to work towards building a peaceful, stable and economically inter-linked neighborhood which is essential for the collective development and prosperity of the South Asian Region. [It] will further work together with South Asian leaders to revitalize SAARC as an effective instrument for regional cooperation and as a united voice on global issues.[36]

In the event, however, the November 2014 18th SAARC summit was a disastrous affair in so far as Modi's new foreign policy agenda was concerned. Despite the fanfare and pre-discussion about the SAARC agenda where India had taken the lead in defining it, the summit did not accomplish much due to the chilly relations between India and Pakistan over the

Kashmir issue. A handshake at the end of the summit by the two prime ministers, Modi and Nawaz Sharif, was considered to be the meagre saving grace of the fruitless discussions by eight countries. And after the Uri attack in September 2016, one of Modi's key initiatives was to isolate Pakistan: India withdrew from attending the 19th SAARC summit to be held in Islamabad in November and the meeting was cancelled as other SAARC countries followed the suit. Instead, India has been working with its regional neighbours to bypass Pakistan in forwarding the trade and connectivity agenda through other regional networks such as BIMSTEC and BCIM, the details of which were discussed earlier in this chapter.

To conclude, despite several hits and misses, the Modi government has conducted its foreign policy with exceptional finesse. It remains on track with its new normative framework of multilevel alignments, with a consistent articulation of its foreign policy goals of combating terrorism, enhancing connectivity and a clear nexus between the country's foreign policy and its domestic transformation. Within this framework, the Modi government has been able to expand relations with ASEAN and East Asia and several great powers. It has managed to isolate Pakistan globally and has succeeded in getting most countries (with China as a major exception) on board with its foreign policy goal of zero tolerance for terrorism as well as for the countries which provide support to the terrorist groups. While China continues to be a challenge, India has managed to slowly poke, bit-by-bit, at its 'One Road, One Belt' policy without on the one hand alienating China, and, on the other hand, continuing along a positive trajectory.

Notes

1. Secretariat of the United Nations, 'Treaties and International Agreements Registered or Filed and Recorded with the Secretariat of the United Nations', 57–82.
2. Mohan, 'Panchsheel Myths'.
3. Hagerty, 'India's Regional Security Doctrine', 352.

4. Appadorai, *Select Documents on India's Foreign Policy and Relations*, 62.

5. Cohen, *India: Emerging Power*, 137.

6. Pant, *Indian Foreign Policy*, 84.

7. Ganguly and Pardesi, 'Explaining Sixty Years of India's Foreign Policy', 16.

8. Kondapalli, 'Five Big Takeaways from Xi Jinping's Visit to India'.

9. Sengupta, 'India in the 21st Century', 309.

10. *India Today*, 'India, Seychelles Sign 4 Pacts to Boost Security Cooperation'.

11. Press Information Bureau. 'PM Chairs Combined Commanders Conference on Board INS Vikramaditya at Sea'.

12. 'Text of the PM's Remarks on the Commissioning of the Coast ship Barracuda', 12 March 2015. Available at: http://www.narendramodi.in/text-of-the-pms-remarks-on-the-commissioning-of-coast-ship-barracuda-2954 (accessed on 15 May 2017).

13. Shyam Saran, a former foreign secretary, reinforces this view when he points out that India's maritime security policy cannot be seen as the containment of China but

    > [As] far as India is concerned, the network of security arrangements that we have established with various friendly countries in the region is not directed against China or any other country. We have all along expressed our preference for a regional security architecture in the Asia-Pacific which is open, inclusive, transparent and balanced. It should be based on the acknowledgement that all stakeholders in the region have legitimate security concerns and interests which should be reconciled through mutual reassurance and confidence-building rather than through the unilateral buildup of military capabilities and the assertion of narrowly conceived national interests.

    See Saran, 'India and Australia'.

14. Parameswaran, 'India Eyes Stronger Trade Ties with ASEAN States'.

15. Quoted in Ramachandran, 'The Trouble with India's Projects in Myanmar'.

16. Modi, 'No Partner Has Played Such a Decisive Role in India's Economic Transformation as Japan: PM Narendra Modi'.

17. Parashar, 'Modi, Abe Send Message to Beijing on South China Sea'.

18. Parameswaran, 'US Official Calls for Permanent Expansion'.

19. Ministry of Foreign Affairs of the People's Republic of China, 'Joint Communiqué of the 14th Meeting of the Foreign Ministers of the Russian Federation, the Republic of India and the People's Republic of China'.

20. Pant, 'India and Russia Struggle to Regain the Past Glow'.

21. Rajendram, 'India's New Asia-Pacific Strategy', 15.
22. *The Times of India*, 'Text of Modi Speech at SAARC Summit'.
23. Ibid.
24. PMINDIA, 'Text of PM's 37th Singapore Lecture "India's Singapore Story" During Visit to Singapore'.
25. Ministry of External Affairs, '37th Singapore Lecture'.
26. http://www.dailyo.in/politics/prime-minister-narendra-modis-speech-at-the-18th-saarc-summit/story/1/801.html
27. Defence and security cooperation, energy security and civil nuclear cooperation are the other focal points of convergence between India and other global powers. In November 2015, India and Australia finalized their civil nuclear agreement, signed last September to supply uranium to India to meet India's growing energy needs. Australia is home to 40 per cent of the world's uranium, the largest international supplier of uranium. Modi hailed the agreement as 'a milestone and source of trust and confidence'. Similarly, during Modi's visit to the UK in October, the two countries agreed on increasing bilateral cooperation on civil nuclear cooperation and putting final touches to a 2010 bilateral agreement. During Angela Markel's visit to New Delhi in October, India and Germany signed two separate agreements on security cooperation: one on the exchange of information, expertise, best practices and technology on security issues and the other establishing cooperation between the two countries for the carriage of in-flight security officers aboard international flights between two countries.
28. Ministry of External Affairs, 'India–Saudi Arabia Joint Statement'.
29. Rediff News, 'One Nation Is Spreading Terror in South Asia: PM Modi at G20'.
30. See *The Hindu*, 'One Nation in South Asia is Spreading Terror in the Region'.
31. See note 29.
32. There has been a general acknowledgment in both India and Pakistan that despite some of the limitations of the fluid Track 2 diplomacy (e.g., the dominance of quasi-governmental officials dominating the process), further exacerbation of a worsening India–Pakistan relationship was prevented through Track 2 diplomacy (such as several dialogues after the Kargil war and the 2008 Mumbai terror attacks when there was a complete suspension of official diplomatic relations).
33. Iyengar, 'India is Using Its Military Incursions into Burma to Send a Message to Other Countries'.
34. The Teesta River, which originates in Sikkim, flows through the northern part of West Bengal before entering Bangladesh and joining the Brahmaputra River. Its flow is crucial for Bangladesh in the dry period from December to March when the water flow often falls to less than

1,000 cusecs. Water being a state subject, the Centre cannot hope to conclude a deal on sharing Teesta water without getting West Bengal Chief Minister Mamata Banerjee on board. As per an agreement of 2011, which was not signed due to opposition from Banerjee, the two sides had agreed to share the river's water 50:50, the same as the 1996 Ganges water-sharing pact between the neighbours. But in her February meeting, Banerjee assured Sheikh Hasina that a solution would be worked out that protects the interests of both West Bengal and Bangladesh.

35. Saboory, 'President Ghani: Stuck Between India and Pakistan'.
36. Roche, 'President Lays Down Road Map for Foreign Strategy, Security'.

4

Modi and Xi Jinping's Slow Dance Towards Cooperation

In this chapter, we trace the story of the changing dynamics of the asymmetries in the power of China and India and show how a convergence has begun to emerge in their diplomatic discourse in public diplomacy. The chapter provides an overview of both the pace and scope of change in India and China relations prior to and post Modi's arrival on the world scene. We point to a slow-but-steady diplomatic engagement emerging in the 1980s and the 1990s that produced some very concrete results. Tracing this engagement from 1990 onwards, we look at the Modi government's specific effort to strengthen the military infrastructure on the Indian side of the Himalayas, at an expansion of investments in India's commercial and naval activities in the Indian Ocean, and at working towards creating an Indo-Pacific community, but with restraint with regard to the South China Sea. We conclude that India, as well as other Asian nations, appears to be locked in a process of long-term engagement with China and that, as a result, India can no more leave China alone than can China ignore its neighbours. However, Modi's message is clear: China cannot act with impunity in relation to Indian interests.[1]

Mainstream international observers now view China and India as Asian in terms of their material and diplomatic capacities in international relations; even in economic terms, India is now much less the odd man out among the region's other big economies—China and Japan—than it was, say, a decade ago. But the Chinese economy, by any measure, remains much larger than that of India with a massively stronger industrial infrastructure and a much larger middle and affluent class. But here again, India is catching up as, over the past few decades, China's GDP growth has trended downward, while India's has trended strongly upward, and for the past year or so, even given the uncertain reliability of both Chinese and Indian official data, India's growth could finally be outpacing China's with stronger prospects continuing into the future. Still, the asymmetries between the two countries in the economic sphere remain very substantial and are likely to persist for the foreseeable future.[2] This, of course, reflects India's 10-year lag (an understatement, given its snail-paced freeing up its markets) behind China's rapid leap into the capitalist mode. India's current economic performance has seen annual growth rates in the range of 6–7 per cent, a sharp contrast with the anaemic growth rate of about 2–3 per cent of the 1950s–70s in the Nehru era's socialist economy. Generally, the Congress governments and coalition governments were slow to shed the principles of state control over the economy, weaken the dominant position of India's vast and entrenched bureaucracy or accept the importance of private sector-led economic modernization. It was not until the government of Prime Minister Narasimha Rao in 1991 embarked on a process of ad hoc reforms that, continuing under subsequent governments, gradually strengthened India' position in the global economy, made it a reasonably attractive destination for foreign capital and technology, and improved the size and prosperity of the middle class. The communist People's Republic of China (PRC) adopted (with enthusiasm) the capitalist road about 10 years before India began (more cautiously) to do so. Furthermore, Congress-led minority governments between 2004 and 2014, up to the election of the majority Modi government, were slowed down in their progress: Congress had to depend on its coalition of left and centre-left parties, considered by some a traditional bastion of the Nehru political base, along with regional political parties, and decision-making was often a product of compromises among the coalition partners. This resulted in delays in implementation of economic reforms and hesitant decision-making in strategic affairs. As a result of seriously delayed economic development and, in foreign policy, because of internal weaknesses and an attachment to Congress party culture of peace, non-alignment and an unwillingness to accept or to come to terms with the value of power politics in diplomacy and military action, serious asymmetries emerged between the power of China and India.

Even now, asymmetries exist between Chinese and Indian military capacities in the Himalayas but the PRC does not command a dominant position in relation to India, and India continues to expand its capabilities to respond to China's expansion. History tells the story about the changing dynamics. Nehru, the prime maker of Indian diplomacy and defence policy (1947–62), believed in peaceful co-existence as the way to make China and India the two Asian principals. But Mao Tse-tung and Zhou Enlai had different ideas. They did not accept India as a co-equal of China in the world of powers and dismissed Nehru and Gandhi as weak-minded leaders who were allied to Anglo-US imperial circles. Nehru's peace policy could not have contrasted more sharply with Mao's belief that power came from the barrel of the gun. Nehru, instead believed in India as a moral force in the world and he certainly did not believe in guns because he did not believe in power politics: he did not trust his own generals and he had, for example, shunned the use of force to liberate Pakistan-held Kashmir despite the advice of his generals. Instead, he was to order a ceasefire and take the matter to the UN, following Mountbatten's advice.[3]

At the international level, India no doubt had influence because the great powers initially used India as a mediator and made use of Indian draftsmanship in shaping international agreements between the Cold War participants, but they did so in the early 1950s when it suited them. But as the basis of a détente began to take shape in the mid-1950s, Western/ NATO practitioners were deeply disappointed, if not surprised, with Nehru's non-committal position in the Soviet invasion of Hungary 1956 and started to argue that Indian diplomacy lacked the intellectual and diplomatic capital to change international and Asian thinking and great power policies as well as those of India's neighbours.[4] They also believed that Nehru and later Krishna Menon had a policy to starve the Indian armed forces of the military equipment to build their strength and to modernize. The Western powers, however, took India seriously in one strategic area. Nehru had laid the foundation of India's nuclear programme for 'peaceful uses', but Nehru's policy articulations and official publications sponsored by the 'father' of the nuclear programme, Homi J. Bhabha, showed that the Indian programme had a defence potential. The United States saw that as a potential problem for the international control of atomic energy because India has vast reserves of thorium, a potential alternative nuclear fuel for power generation (albeit without weapons applications). India rejected international controls over its strategic reserves and did not recognize the principle of great powers' monopoly over atomic energy in which a country like India became the object of international controls.[5]

The PRC developed nuclear weapons capability in the early 1960s and, after joining the UN Security Council in 1971, it created a full asymmetry in the nuclear field between the two countries. It meant that China had the tool to escalate its conflict with India at a time and place of its choosing, and it had the right to do so but India had neither the ability to do so nor, after the Treaty on the Non-proliferation of Nuclear Weapons (NPT) came into force in 1970, the right to do so. This anomaly was corrected in May 1998 when India successfully conducted the Pokhran-II nuclear tests and Prime Minister A.B. Vajpayee declared that India was henceforth a full-fledged nuclear state. In doing so, Vajpayee noted that India had taken this action because of the growing danger of nuclear developments in Pakistan and China, and China's growing nuclear and missile aid to Pakistan. Vajpayee's public declaration concerning China raised diplomatic tensions between China and India. China resented to be placed in the 'enemy' category.

In this background, India's main advantage in world affairs during the 1950s was that it was a functioning democracy and it was a pluralist nation—two major qualities of Indian soft power. But soft power is not a substitute for hard power and, as Joseph Nye—the concept's originator—points out, soft and hard powers have to work together. It took the Indian diplomatic and political establishment time and effort to learn this lesson. This was a slow process largely because of their faith, almost fixation, in Nehruvian diplomacy and Indian reliance on its cultural diplomacy.

The Rate and Scope of Change in India–China Relations, 1947–62

The relationship between the two nations has undergone massive restructuring since the late 1940s. Following India's Independence in 1947 and China's revolution in 1949, Nehru singled out China as a partner for peace in Asia, building on the theme of anti-colonialism and Indian non-alignment as the way to deal with East–West conflicts. Nehru emphasized Sino-Indian civilizational links and a shared anti-colonial history and also emphasized that China, like India, needed a period of peace for its internal development. He urged the Western powers not to isolate China in the international sphere and instead to bring it into the global mainstream by accepting it into the UN. India's mediatory role in the Korean War was meant to confirm its peace credentials and diplomatic skill in an area of significant conflict between American, Chinese and Russian interests. Nehru had accepted that Tibet was a part of China and this was meant in Nehru's view to build trust with the Chinese government and to mute the criticism that Indians were the 'running dogs of imperialism'. Nehru believed that

China's leaders valued Indian friendship, and his advocacy in the international fora that China was a peaceful nation was meant to induce Sino-Indian cooperation and acceptance of India as a co-equal of China.[6]

Nehru's diplomatic rhetoric about China's importance was an assertion, not an argument. It, as pointed by some, was not based on historical facts and it reflected Nehru's idealism and a romantic view of China which he had apparently gained from his travels. Nehru had written about world history but he did not have a sound understanding of Chinese imperial history and the implication of its view that China was the Middle Kingdom—a superior civilization—while the rest of the Asian world including India was inferior to it. Nehru did not realize that the communist leaders were following the Maoist playbook and that their rules required only a token nod to peaceful co-existence and, in the 1950s, the PRC was to use the Third-World nations to form the anti-imperialist front under Chinese leadership following the Sino-Soviet split.[7] Mao's military writings had laid down the principles of war and strategy in dealing with enemy formations. These principles gave prominence to deception, surprise attacks, building third-party links to attack and isolate the enemy from its flanks, the use of propaganda to demoralize the enemy and so on. Zhou Enlai's writings also brought out the reality that China's leaders operated on the basis of cold-blooded calculations and not on sentiments. Its actions revealed an obsession with frontier security and China's international prestige as shown by its actions in Tibet in 1950, Korea in 1950–53 and by promoting the Sino-Soviet split in 1960. China's actions had enormous consequences. By taking over Tibet, it eliminated the geographical buffer between India and China. By sending its forces into Korea, it brought the American advances in Korea to a halt and showed that a motivated force despite its technological weakness could halt the advance of a superior force. The United States had won the Pacific War against Japan but China placed a limit on America never to fight it again or challenge China in East Asia militarily in a direct confrontation.

China's playbook highlighted the importance of ideological and diplomatic propaganda and policy manoeuvres. It created options to manoeuvre when and where it chose: to use charm diplomacy as in the 1955 Bandung Conference, or to fight as with India in 1962 or to provide moral and material support to friendly countries as with Vietnam during its war with the United States and later to arm Pakistan. At the same time, Mao had made it clear that China could not pursue its interests unaided; it needed allies and to form such alliances, whether they were temporary or long term, it needed to exploit 'contradictions' in the enemy camp. This approach required constant attention to changing world conditions and changing alignments. China used this strategy of manoeuvres to negotiate or to fight India as it suited its interests.[8]

Chinese and Indian manoeuvres in the early 1950s revealed a pattern of Indian concessions and Chinese evasiveness in dealing with Indian interests. Nehru accepted China's position on Tibet without Chinese acceptance of the validity of the McMahon Line and without acknowledgement that India had major interests in Tibet. Nehru had urged the Dalai Lama to make peace with the Chinese but Nehru's advocacy demoralized the Tibetans and India gained nothing from its advocacy.[9] The agreements Nehru signed with the PRC accepted the principle of peaceful co-existence with China but did not contribute anything substantial to Indian security.[10] China formed a pattern of evasiveness in dealing with Nehru but Nehru did not have any leverage over Zhou Enlai. Despite Nehru's pleas to settle the border issue in the early 1950s, Zhou delayed the discussion because 'the time was not ripe for settlement'.[11] The point of this manoeuvre became clear later when it was disclosed that China was building a road through an area which it considered of strategic importance in Aksai Chin; it was started in 1955 and completed by 1957. Another Chinese manoeuvre was to start patrolling the border areas which led to clashes with Indian forces. These clashes led to heightened tensions, diplomatic protests and increased mistrust between the leaders on both sides.

Nehru's diplomatic language did not help the discourse. He claimed that the McMahon Line was the accepted boundary according to history and custom; China argued that it was an imperial construction. Zhou argued that in the interest of good relations between the two countries, the two sides should negotiate a settlement and made various proposals but Nehru made a subtle distinction showing a willingness to 'talk' but not to negotiate as there was nothing to negotiate.[12] No doubt Nehru took steps to strengthen ties with Nepal, Bhutan and Sikkim, beefed up India's administrative presence in the border areas and instructed the Intelligence Bureau to patrol the border areas in order to gain intelligence about Chinese activities.[13] But even with mounting evidence of China's military build-up in the Himalayas, from 1955 onwards, Nehru and Krishna Menon did not take China's potential military threat seriously and kept the Indian armed forces starved of modern equipment and funds, claiming that India lacked foreign exchange. The underlying Nehruvian belief was that China valued Indian friendship and even if China could attack India, it would not do so for the fear of bringing the great powers into a war situation. So, in these circumstances, another asymmetrical situation may be said to have emerged: China gained the option to negotiate or to fight or to take evasive manoeuvres, but India did not have the option to fight and it had cut off the option to negotiate a border settlement. There were two other complicating factors. First, the Indian generals did not have the tools to fight China and Nehru's pacifist beliefs and his mistrust of the generals meant that going to war was not a realistic option for India. Second, the Indian Ministry of External Affairs did not know for sure where the coordinates of the McMahon Line lay and it was in the late 1950s that the ministry first started its research on the subject. In sum, China could act with impunity against Indian interests—which it did—but India had neither the philosophy nor a policy to do so and the approach to either escalate (other than the forward policy) or to negotiate did not exist in the Nehruvian mindset.

Chinese Activism and Indian Learning 1962–90

The 1962 war was explained as a brief border conflict but it appears that it had long-term and psychological aims. First, it was intended to demoralize the Indian government and its people. Second, China's overt action was meant to cut down Nehru to size. Third, by defeating India, China hoped to gain international prestige—that China could take India on its own and by its own efforts. This, moreover, reflected China's belief that power and prestige is taken, not given. The attack on India was calculated. In 'Secret Instructions to the Chinese Army (April 25, 1961)', the General Political Department of the Chinese People's Liberation Army noted: 'We must unite the progressive forces, strive to get at the intermediate forces and isolate imperialism, try to establish friendly relations with all countries, isolate the bloc including Nehru in India and Tito in Yugoslavia and oppose American imperialism'.[14] This war, while it ended Nehru's approach towards China and finished Menon's career, set India on a reformist path, albeit incrementally.

The 1962 war had a tremendous domestic effect in forming a strong identification by the Indian public with the importance of national security and the sense that China was a major long-term rival of India. Pakistan had occupied that position in mainstream Indian thinking as a result of the history of Partition and wars in Kashmir but the war with China brought China's 'betrayal' and Nehru's 'naiveté' into sharp focus along with the public's awareness that China and Pakistan had to be bracketed as India's enemies as a result of their growing military and economic cooperation. Lacking confidence, the Indian government did not articulate this linkage but Indian public opinion was ahead of the government's cautious stance on this point. Clearly, wars and external danger had the effect of forming a political tsunami which the Indian government could not ignore in its policy deliberations. For China, however, it was important as the United States also put China and Pakistan in the same bracket; the Indian government lacked the means and the political will to alter this bracketing with Pakistan in the 1960s. In other words, the seed for the new line in Indian political and social thought was planted as a result of the defeat by China in 1962.

The pattern of Chinese activism gave a strong pay-off with limited risks and many rewards because India did not have much leverage against China. This can be summarized under four points: First, the Chinese takeover of Tibet in 1950 and the consolidation of its position in Xinjiang transformed the strategic architecture in the Himalayas. The absence of a buffer between China and India pressured India to deal with the reality of Chinese animosity and the concomitantly higher costs of Indian defence building. The change in the region's architecture also made China a pole of attraction for India's neighbours who railed against India's big brother attitude and now had an option to respond to Chinese economic and political overtures. The build-up of China–Pakistan relations occurred after 1962. Nehru and his successors had no strong response and, indeed, the strategic initiative had passed into the hands of the Chinese leaders.[15]

Second, in the aftermath of the 1962 war, China unleased a diplomatic campaign against 'Indian expansionism and Soviet imperialism'. Recall that this formula had been the basis of M.A. Jinnah's approach to the US government in May 1947[16] and now it became the basis of China's narrative as well. This narrative appealed to India's neighbours and it was actively promoted by the US government and NATO countries in addition to Pakistan. The likening of India's purported expansionism to the Soviet Union's ambitions shaped the lens though which Richard Nixon, Henry Kissinger, Mao Tse-tung and Zhou Enlai saw India and formed their approach to it. It was not until the latter 1990s, years after the Cold War had ended, that the Western world began to adjust its view about Indian expansionism.

Third, the debacle of the 1962 Sino-Indian War shattered Nehru's prestige. In 1954, Winston Churchill had described

Nehru as the 'shining light of Asia'.[17] As Nehru's vision began to lose credibility, both domestically and globally, after the Sino-Indian War in 1962, the theory of moralism and pacifism as a valid basis for Indian diplomacy crashed on the hard rock of a territorial dispute and a civilizational clash between China and India, and a fight for the leadership of Asia began. The post-Nehru government was to begin to shift its military gears slowly. Having opposed expenditures for Indian military modernization in the past, it raised its defence budget in 1963 and thereafter and launched an assessment of the reasons for Indian failures. Various Ministry of Defence reports placed the blame on Nehru and Menon at the policy-making level, and the military establishment at the level of military tactics and planning. The assessments revealed that the decision-making process was badly flawed: it relied excessively on summitry between Indian and Chinese leaders, and there was lack of coordination between the Ministries of External Affairs and Defence, Army headquarters and the Intelligence Bureau. Each unit functioned as a silo with a narrow vision about China's interests, ambitions and capabilities. Above all, government departments had accepted the policy parameters laid out by Nehru and Menon, and the warnings that V.B. Patel and Girja Shanker Bajpai had issued in the early 1950s were early on dismissed out of hand.[18]

Fourth, a succession of weak governments, weak domestic politics, a weak economy and slow military modernization meant that India was not in a position to engage China at the diplomatic level. The official chill in Sino-Indian relations which set in after the 1962 war began rapidly to thaw when, at the 1970 May Day celebrations in Beijing, Mao signalled to Indian chargé d'affaires, Brijesh Mishra, that it was time for the two countries to engage each other. Mao's nod to the Indian envoy signalled that India was back in the China–India game, although it was not going to be until the late-1970s that diplomatic relations would be formalized by the mutual accrediting of ambassadors. Still, the time was ripe until then; clearly India could not be left alone.[19]

Post-1962, India moved to build its defence capabilities and to be ready to fight. The 1965 war with Pakistan was to be the first test for Indian leaders which had a China angle. Their Pakistani counterparts believed that India's new prime minister, Lal Bahadur Shastri, was weak and inexperienced and they were testing him by sending armed infiltrators to Kashmir thinking that the locals were ready to rise against Indian rule. This did not happen and in a surprising move, Shastri ordered the Indian Army to cross over Pakistan's international border and threaten Lahore and Sialkot, the heart of Pakistan's commercial and political establishments. The Shastri decision, so contrary to the old Nehruvian approach, unnerved the Pakistani population but the great powers intervened through the UN as the Indian forces got close to the two cities, and this resulted in a military stalemate and the Tashkent agreement under Soviet auspices. Still, the Indian action was a psychological blow to the Pakistanis because it broke the Nehru–Mountbatten rule to avoid general war. Indian military planners also learned two lessons from this war: that the superpowers were not interested in a regional war for fear that it could widen the fight and create regional instability and that even though China had threatened India with military action in defence of Pakistan, in the moment of crisis, it revealed itself as risk-averse—it would not fight when the outcome was unpredictable. Intense diplomatic manoeuvrings at the UN became the trademark of Chinese diplomacy, that is, speak loudly but carry a small stick. This experience was repeated in the 1971 Indo-Pakistan war. Indian leaders learned that with cautious risk-taking and diplomatic and military preparations that assessed Chinese intentions and interests and its compulsions, India could deal with China in a war situation. China was preoccupied with the Cultural Revolution during the war and China feared that if it attacked India, the USSR could assist India in the light of the India–USSR friendship treaty. In other words, sober calculations and detachment rather than knee-jerk anti-Indianism defined China's strategic calculus in crisis situations.

Indian war experiences no doubt constituted a learning curve for Indian leaders and pointed to the growing role of Indian nationalism. Nehru had after all built his prestige in India as the leader of the nationalist movement against Western colonialism. Indian public opinion did not play a role in the first Kashmir war in 1947 as the events of the tribal invasion, the Instrument of Accession and the reference of Kashmir dispute to the UN came in quick succession and in the immediate aftermath of Partition, it was hard for Indian public opinion to grasp the significance of the events. Mountbatten had been Nehru's mentor in the first Kashmir war.[20] In contrast, in the 1965 and 1971 wars, Indian practitioners learned to navigate the pressure points and threats from the world system and to mobilize Indian public opinion and support in these wars. They learned to interact with the world leaders in a crisis and to respond to the expectations of Indian public opinion. They learned that both sides were signalling an interest to stabilize and widen the relationship. It was not enough for Indian politicians to win elections and to make speeches; but they also had to soil their hands in the messy business of war and crisis diplomacy, and to use all the tools of statecraft to win. The 1971 war was a major confidence builder for India and it established in the Indian mind that diplomacy and military strategy were essential aspects of foreign policy and that they were two sides of statecraft; both were necessary. Still, after 1971, China did not acknowledge India as an Asian power During the 1970s and 1980s, China stuck to its policy of treating India and Pakistan as peers, and the propaganda that India sought hegemony was maintained in China's dealings with India's neighbours. But at the same time China's leaders began to hedge their bets on India, they sought a low-level diplomatic dialogue, kept open border talks and maintained its pinpricks through periodic border incursions as did India because neither side knew the border coordinates on the ground and held on to their views of each country's legal rights.

After two difficult decades, a slow diplomatic dance emerged in the 1980s and the 1990s between India and China and led to concrete results. While the various border agreements sidelined the border issue as a legacy of history, the claims and counter-claims stayed on the table. But, most significantly, both countries agreed to maintain peace and tranquillity along the Himalayan border, to develop protocols to manage border tensions and to develop economic and cultural exchanges.[21]

1990s: China and India Engage Each Other

From the 1960s, China's main approach towards South Asia was to build its military and economic ties with Pakistan and, following its border agreement with Pakistan, to create a geographical bridge that went from Tibet to Gwadar Port in Pakistan. This created a line of permanent pressure against India because the corridor passed through Pakistan-occupied Kashmir which India claimed for itself.[22] But Indian military interventions in 1965 and 1971 against Pakistan meant that the Indian behaviour required Chinese responses. The pattern of those responses was revealing. In 1965, China railed against Indian aggression and threatened to support military action against India but it did not confirm Z.A. Bhutto's claim that Pakistan enjoyed China's military support. There was an element of bluff in Chinese declarations as well as a comical side. It threatened military action in the Himalayas because Indian sheep had strayed across the border! The Chinese government was outraged by Indian actions in the 1971 war and made their views known to the Nixon administration but here another pattern emerged. As has been pointed out, China thought that the United States would help Pakistan and that Kissinger would urge China to attack India but neither of these things occurred, and both China and the United States lost face with the Pakistanis and the world. This was a sign to Indian planners that China was unlikely to act militarily unless it was assured of military success and that there were limits to its support for Pakistan.

At this time, China assumed a pose of indifference towards Indian security concerns about Chinese military aid to Pakistan. China's apparent nonchalance with respect to such a major item of contention was possible for several reasons: the United States and the United Kingdom had a firm policy to maintain the balance of power between India and Pakistan; Indian diplomacy was being conducted with the Nehruvian framework, lacking the will to participate in shaping the Asian balance of power; India was politically unstable with a series of minority governments, and its economic performance was sub-standard compared to China's; even the 1974 nuclear test did not give India any mileage because Mrs Gandhi called it a peaceful test and claimed to be devoted to nuclear disarmament; and, finally, Western policy gave China the assurance that India's nuclear option could be contained by Western sanctions and as a result there was no imminent threat to China's position as the sole Asian nuclear weapons state in Asia and the sole Asian member of the UN Security Council. In this setting, China felt free to act with impunity against Indian interests vis-à-vis Pakistan, including through intrusions in the border areas.

However, the Chinese policy was not one of blanket indifference. When China and India restored ambassador-level relations in the late 1970s, there followed agreements for ongoing border talks and cooperation in economic and environmental areas. A pose of normalcy was created but without any expectation that a border agreement was in the offing. The value of this approach was to create a basket of issues for the two sides to stay in touch and to minimize the pressures in their relations. Now what 'progress' consisted of would be defined by ongoing talks; most importantly, the dialogue for the first time acquired an institutional basis. This contrasted markedly with Nehru's preference for personal summitry that did not involve other branches of the Indian government at the diplomatic table with China. The discourse had shed its mythic/romantic trappings and was no longer accompanied by the euphoric narrative that China and India had common interests or a shared sense of 'Asianness'. Instead, a much more realistic measure of progress was that an existence of manageable instability in the border areas was now the standard, the new rule in the playbook.

Changing Dynamics

The shift in the tone and direction of Sino-Indian relations took shape under three Indian prime ministers. Rajiv Gandhi firmed up the recently re-established ambassador-level relations and improved the tone of the relationship and its visibility in the public view. Narasimha Rao initiated Indian economic reforms in 1991 which launched the slow process of converting Nehru's socialist economy into a semi-capitalist one, and economic modernization gave a stimulus to military modernization as well. He opened the door to relations with Israel and this move created a pathway to Indo-Israeli defence cooperation.[23] These game changers took shape in a slow, incremental way. But then A.B. Vajpayee literally threw a bombshell. With the 1998 nuclear tests came two declarations: India was a nuclear weapons state and India had taken the step because of the nuclear and missile build-up by Pakistan and China which threatened Indian security. China, of course, had a problem with this view and it fought hard not to let India gain international acceptance of its claim. But China failed to prevail, and as the Bush administration accepted India as a responsible member of the nuclear community, China lost face. The lesson was not lost on the Indian leadership: China feared international isolation and loss of face—so situations had to be created to corner it to accommodate Indian interests. The fear of losing international face if it becomes isolated is real for China, despite its big power status in the world today.

This episode was very costly to China because it laid to rest the almost four-decade-old narrative that India was expansionist, aggressive and a threat to regional peace. Clearly, the United States and Indian strategy had worked and the rewards came to India via the opening of strategic dialogues between India and the major powers. It also revealed that Chinese impassivity vis-à-vis Indian foreign policy concerns is not invincible and that China was likely to take India seriously if India could create a new strategic situation that resulted in a dilemma for China's foreign policy. China could continue to act with impunity or to engage in evasive bargaining and manoeuvres or else it could undertake to negotiate seriously and work with India. With Nehru, the Chinese leaders had resorted to an evasive dialogue, but when eventually India acted in a way which questioned Chinese sincerity and challenged its policy, the pattern of China's behaviour changed.

Geopolitical considerations are no doubt the most salient dimensions of foreign policy formation and diplomacy, but there are institutional and cultural constraints as well that must be taken into account. In the case of China, the nature and speed of longer term policy change will be determined by several considerations. China has a slow learning curve because it has a large party and governmental apparatus and it needs to find consensus to change its policy. It is these internal institutional constraints rather than any absence of perspicacity by its leadership that explains China's at times plodding pace of adjustment. It is up to India to create situations in a non-critical and/or critical manner so that the weight of the reform-minded branches in the Chinese government and party circles can be brought to secure policy change in relation to India. This is a major challenge for the Chinese leaders because China has a proud Han culture and a deep-rooted cultural faith that it is the main Asian power and others are either 'barbarians' or inferior. China still sees itself as the Middle Kingdom—the term it employs to communicate internally and among the Chinese, whereas the secular PRC designation is relegated for use outside its borders, in international relations with the non-Chinese world. It is this proud view of its self which gives such a salience to the prospects of losing face in any encounter. With such an institutional and cultural background reality, it is a tall order for China to change its self-image and worldview quickly, but the China–India case shows that the process to do so has been under way.

The Opening Up of India and the Broadening of the Dialogue with China

Prime Minister Narasimha Rao is widely recognized as the father of Indian economic reforms and the author of India's 'Look East' policy and the opening up of substantive ties with Israel.[24] The former move changed India's orientation away from the Nehruvian socialist economic model and the latter move sought to bring India into the global mainstream in the post-Soviet, post–Cold War international environment. A shrewd practitioner, Rao maintained a low-key manner as he had at all times to keep the Congress party in hand while keeping in check the ambitions of the Nehru–Gandhi family. He sought to widen the range of Indian diplomacy by making it turn towards the East, a signal to China that India was thinking beyond their territorial dispute and that it sought to build its Asian links. Rao had wanted to conduct nuclear weapons tests as early as 1995, but his plans were detected and exposed by the United States and India came under tremendous international pressure; still his thinking showed a willingness to exercise the nuclear weapons option. But the roots of his reforms remained tentative and weak and his diplomatic actions could not escape the standard Congress party injunctions about non-alignment.

Rao, although cast in the Congress party mould, had been innovative in the economic and diplomatic spheres. He also paved the way for Prime Minister A.B. Vajpayee to conduct the 1998 nuclear tests. Vajpayee claimed at the time that China and Pakistan constituted a nuclear threat to India and brought India and China into a public controversy over the issue. Rao has an important place in our narrative because the process he started represents an essential context for Modi's economic and diplomatic policies. 'Look East' was to become 'Act East' in the Modi calculus and a subject of a vigorous international efforts and breakthrough agreements in the diplomatic and military spheres with Western and Asian governments. Modi's economic reforms are mired in opposition parties' politics but the process initiated by Rao has moved forwards and is still aimed at India's modernization. Of course, Modi has gone beyond Rao's actions, for instance, in his robust build-up of the military infrastructure in the Himalayas and in his firm rejection of the Congress party's political and reactive culture and its reliance on dynastic politics. But it seems fair and accurate to recognize Rao as the father of Indian reforms and the leader who first set about to neutralize the most deleterious aspects of the Nehru–Gandhi legacy in Indian foreign policy.

The UPA 2 government of Manmohan Singh was responsible for an important page in the new playbook for a vigorous China policy which we have been describing.[25] By 2008, China's assertiveness in the world and its militant nationalism gained ground with the ascendency of President Xi Jinping. Friction in the Sino-Indian border area had been an old story and a manageable irritant in Sino-Indian relations. With an un-demarcated boundary, both countries often strayed across areas which the other side claimed. Blocking the applications of sanctions at the UN against Pakistan-based jihadi groups was also a recurring pattern in Sino-Pakistani behaviour, and it was an annoyance which India resented but it also emerged as a point of pressure against China because India sought to isolate China on the issue in the world sphere and China was not immune to losing face the longer it took to resolve its position on the critical issue of terrorism. China also claimed that India's northeastern state Arunachal Pradesh was 'Southern Tibet' which India rejected and pointed to the large Indian population which lived in the area; this was also an old Chinese annoyance which did not change the realities on the ground. But then China appeared to have made a mistake. It denied a visa to a senior Indian military officer because he had served in Jammu and Kashmir. The UPA 2 government's reaction was swift. In December 2010, during the visit of the Chinese premier to Delhi, India refused to acknowledge the One China policy by declining to accept that Tibet was a part of China and insisted that China accept Indian sovereignty over Jammu and Kashmir and Arunachal Pradesh as a sign of its acceptance of One India, that is, there had to be a symmetry between the Indian and Chinese policies, a sign of the sensitivity of both sides to each other's interests.[26]

Prime Minister Modi reiterated the new position by omitting the reference to Tibet as a part of China in 2014.[27] This was done by the Indian foreign minister in September 2014 before President Xi Jinping's visit to India when he came to visit Modi in Delhi. However, Chinese references to Arunachal Pradesh as 'Southern Tibet' have continued but not without a response from India and other states: the Indian President hosted the Dalai Lama at the Rashtrapati Bhawan, the US ambassador visited Arunachal Pradesh and dignitaries from Taiwan visited India in 2012 and 2014. There is a continuity in India's China policy between the UPA 2 and Modi governments but Modi's positions have shown an escalatory potential because of India's involvement in a measured way in China's backyard through building economic and military ties with Japan, and with Southeast Asian states, in particular Vietnam, the Prime Minister's comments on the development of a rule-based system in the South China Sea. A major difference between the policy of UPA 2 and China policy of Modi is that the latter has launched a major effort to strengthen the military infrastructure on the Indian side of the Himalayas which indicates a lack of trust about Chinese intentions and the expectation that the dispute is likely to last for a long time. More broadly, China continues to invest heavily in South Asia and the Modi government has expanded its investments in its commercial, industrial and naval activities in the Indian Ocean and there is a move to bring Southeast Asian nations and Australia into an Indo-Pacific community. Despite Beijing's warnings to India to avoid involvement in the South China Sea controversy, India has made measured reference to the issues in a non-provocative way. From the current pattern of competing interests, it appears that China and India as well as other Asian nations are locked in a process of long-term engagement: they cannot leave China alone and neither can China ignore its neighbours.[28] The euphoria by Martin Jacques in his celebrated book about China ruling the world and the decline of the West may be wishful thinking because China itself is beset and hemmed in by dilemmas with its neighbours.[29]

Even though Modi and Xi are not on the same page on many policy issues, there are efforts to narrow the differences and at the very least to seek a convergence in their diplomatic discourse in public diplomacy.[30] The conceptual markers which have been laid down differ sharply from the ones between Nehru and the Chinese leaders of that time. The 15 May 2015 Joint Statement of bilateral talks between India and China, during Modi's three-day visit to Beijing, contains significant points—India and China are two major powers in the region and in the world (note: the bracketing of China with Pakistan is gone); the two are major poles in the global architecture; there is now an opportunity to realize the Asian century; there is no mention of the Chinese century.[31] Earlier, in September 2014, during Xi's visit to India, many agreements were signed which showed that China sought a large number of trade and investment opportunities in India as did India with China but it remains to be seen if these aspirations will be implemented and at what pace. Clearly, China wants to access the Indian market for its high-technology goods and to build trains and nuclear plants in India. These declarations have rhetorical value but it is noteworthy that the various 'peace and tranquillity' agreements which China signed have been adhered to and border peace has been kept between the two countries. If the situation on the ground in the border areas is satisfactory on both sides, then the absence of a formal demarcation line or border agreement matters less; this arrangement helps both sides to keep face and the competing claims are then consigned to history and China can rhetorically blame the border tension on the imperialists!

Prime Minister Modi has embarked on a firm military modernization programme and has also committed research for India's naval development in the Indian Ocean. The list of his foreign visits and the commitments he has secured show a pattern to build links with China's neighbours—mainly Japan, Southeast Asian nations, Mongolia and Central Asian states—and to build India's presence in Afghanistan, Iran and the Gulf region for trade, investment and infrastructure development. His foreign visits show a geo-political design to ensure that China cannot act with impunity in relation to Indian interests. Even though China's economic strength substantially exceeds India's, world powers have taken note of India's rise and have seen that India is a swing element in contemporary international relations. That is why China recognizes that the two Asian powers should stay engaged with each other and practise give-and-take diplomacy. As we have seen, a pattern of engagement along these lines is taking shape and if this is sustained, it points to the rise of a cooperative relationship between China and India in the coming years.

Notes

1. Our discussion does not engage with the three different streams of the Indian strategic thought (as categorized by Kanti Bajpai—Nehruvians, neoliberals and hyper-realists) projecting Sino-Indian relations, but our analysis would suggest that Prime Minister Modi's policy tends to straddle between the thoughts of the neoliberals and hyper-realists. Bajpai points to the differences between the three schools regarding India's policy towards China (what it ought to be):

   Nehruvians, neoliberals, and hyperrealists have quite different perspectives on China...

   Nehruvians in the end believe that India can create the conditions for peace and cooperation with the giant to the north much as it can with Pakistan. Neoliberals argue that economics can lead the way even with China, that a pragmatic approach to the border can bring about a stable relationship, and that a tacit alliance with the US can contain Chinese influence. Hyperrealists see a rising China as aggressive and expansionist, and therefore argue that only Indian military power and a containment of China by a ring of Asian powers will hold Beijing in check.

Bajpai, 'Pakistan and China in Indian Strategic Thought', 822.

2. Jizhe, 'China's Data Chief Admits Fraud and Deception in Statistics'.
3. Gupta, *War and Diplomacy in Kashmir, 1947–48*, Chapters 4 and 5.
4. Reid, *Envoy to Nehru*, 220, 233–34, Chapter 16.
5. The American Assembly, *Atoms for Power*. This background paper provides details for US efforts to establish international atomic energy control including India's program.
6. Gopal, *Jawaharlal Nehru*, 235, Chapters 3 and 5.
7. Sardar Patel was to caution Nehru. When China invaded Tibet in October 1950, Patel wrote to Nehru that

> [C]ommunism is no shield against imperialism and that the Communists are as good or as bad imperialists as any other. Chinese ambitions in this respect not only cover the Himalayan slopes on our side but also include important parts of Assam.... Chinese irredentism and Communist imperialism are different from the expansionism or imperialism of the Western Powers. The former has a cloak of ideology which makes it 10 times more dangerous. In the guise of ideological expansion lies concealed racial, national or historical claims.

Quoted by Guha, 'An Asian Clash of Civilisations?', 53.

8. *Selected Military Writings of Mao Tse-tung*. The connection between 'initiative' and 'superiority' and 'passivity' and 'inferiority' is on page 236. Page 214 notes that China's strength is not enough and allies are needed and this adds to China's tasks in international propaganda and diplomacy.
   Selected Works of Zhou Enlai, 43. This book explains the task to liberate Taiwan and Tibet, and ensure frontier security for China. Page 99 of the book notes that China should be flexible in its diplomatic work, rely on the progressives, unite with the middle of the road forces and split the diehards: 'It is wrong to think that the world is simply divided into two conflicting camps....'
9. Peissel, *The Secret War in Tibet*. This is a detailed account of Nehru's secret diplomacy and sell-out of the Tibetan cause to placate China.
10. For a chronological account of Sino-Indian relations since the 'liberation' of Tibet by China in 1950, see Chakravarti, *India's China Policy*.

11. In 1954, Nehru sought to discuss all pending questions but Zhou Enlai only wanted to discuss issues which were 'ripe for settlement'. Mullik, *The Chinese Betrayal* 150–51.

12. Maxwell, *India's China War*, 65–170. This book shows in detail the escalating rhetoric, evasive actions and border clashes which wrecked mutual trust on both sides.

13. Kavic, *India's Quest for Security*, Chapters 2–4.

14. Subcommittee on National Security and International Operations, Committee on Government Operations, and US Senate. *Peking's Approach to Negotiations*, 77 and 79.

15. One of the significant events during this period was the building of 800-km Karakoram highway linking Pakistan and China through Pakistan-held Kashmir; India made very low-key protest. On 3 May 1962, five months before the Sino-Indian border war, China began negotiations with Pakistan to transfer land in Pakistan-side Kashmir, contiguous areas to China border. On 2 March 1963, A Sino-Pakistan Agreement was signed, with China gaining 2,500 square miles of Kashmir area in addition to the 1,600 square miles of area which Pakistan was anyway not effectively controlling. Through China's participation in building the Karakoram highway and taking possession of disputed Kashmir territory, China had become a party to the Kashmir dispute. Zhou Enlai, during his visit to Pakistan in February 1965, the joint communique, basically reiterated Pakistan's position on the Kashmir issue—the Kashmir dispute is to be resolved "in accordance with the wishes of the people of Kashmir as pledged to them by India and Pakistan."

16. Jinnah had this conversation with US embassy officers in Karachi in May 1947 and indicated the availability of Pakistani bases in return for US support against Indian expansionism and Soviet imperialism. The USA adopted this course in the early 1950s.

17. Churchill's letter is reproduced in Gopal, op. cit., 237.

18. Sinha and Athale, *History of the Conflict with China, 1962*.

19. A.R. Basu noted in 1991 that India and China's bilateral cooperative relationship had lot to do with India's weak national governments. Thus, India's policy towards China was being governed by the desire to avoid damaging, external disputes because of continuing political instability at home. See Basu, 'India's China Policy in Historical Perspective', 103–15.

20. Gupta, op. cit., Chapters 4 and 5, tells the story.

21. The Agreements of 1993, 1996, 2003 and 2005 provided that both sides "shall maintain peace and tranquility in the border areas pending the final resolution of the border conflict." In addition, both began a cooperative economic relationship to pursue a multilateral rules-based trading regime and promote Asian economic integration. For example, in the WTO, China and India cooperated in resisting Western pressure to incorporate investment liberalization disciplines into WTO instrument.

22. However, the border tensions did take another strategic turn when, in 2010, Pakistan allowed between 7,000 and 11,000 Chinese troops to enter Pakistan-controlled Kashmir (in Gilgit and Baltistan) to help in the construction of a high-speed rail and road link from eastern China to the Chinese-built naval port of Gwadar in Pakistan. Indian protests led to counter-protests by China. During his December 2010 visit to India, Chinese Premier Wen Jiabao was to refer to Sino-Indian disagreements on border issues as a "'historical legacy that would not be easy to resolve and would take a fairly long period of time." See Frankel, 'The Breakout of China–India Strategic Rivalry in Asia and the Indian Ocean', 4.

23. Surjit Mansingh, in her commentary on the changing nature of relationship between India and China during the Rajiv Gandhi and Narasimha Rao governments, noted that the normalization of relationship between the two countries at this time could not be interpreted as a guarantee to a cooperative approach. Instead,

> Normalization does not imply that divergences in strategic perspective between India and China have suddenly converged, or that conflicts of interest and differences of opinion on a range of issues have disappeared, or that trade and other economic transactions between China and India are blossoming at even a respectable fraction of the rate sustained between China and other nations of the Asia-Pacific region. Such fancies belong to the "Hindi–China bhai" (Indians and Chinese are brothers) sentiment of the mid-1950s.

See Mansingh, 'India–China Relations in the Post–Cold War Era', 285–86.

24. Baru, *1991: How P. V. Narasimha Rao Made History*, Chapters 5–8.

25. During Manmohan Singh's visit to China in January 2008, economic ties were the centre piece and a conscious attempt was made by both India and China to stay away from contentious issues. As Alka Acharya noted at that time, by contrast to earlier five-year efforts (either through the visits or the penning down of Strategic Partnership Agreements),

> [This visit] seems almost like a contemplative pause or an introspective interlude—taking cognisance of the miles yet to cover between them, but responding to similar strategic concerns that are increasingly confronting the two countries. It was marked by a resolve to get this crucial equation right because, as Manmohan Singh said, the rise of India and China must be seen as a "global public good" which will benefit the world—a statement which acquires significance in the light of impending reports of a global economic slowdown and the importance of developing economies such as India and China in cushioning it.

See Acharya, 'India–China Relations', 10–13. Manmohan Singh also maintained that India is not interested in joining any formal containment alliance aimed at China and that it will maintain its strategic autonomy. Similarly, Swaran Singh points out that both countries began to look at multilateral forums to provide each with a relatively neutral playground in which the two countries began to gradually assert their common interests in addressing their regional and global challenges. Singh was to observe very accurately in 2011,

> No doubt, their difficult bilateral engagement also impacts their interactions at the multilateral level and their mutual trust deficit circumscribes their joint strategies in multilateral forums. Yet, on balance, contemporary Sino-Indian relations seem to mark a clear shift in the center of gravity from a bilateral to a multilateral matrix. This shift is now discernible enough to stand scrutiny and also to guide the future direction of Sino-Indian equations.

See Singh, 'Paradigm Shift in India–China Relations', 155. There are several authors who suggest that around this time, competition gave way to cooperation and dialogue. Authors cite joint institutional arrangements for economic exchange, joint energy bids in Iran and other countries and joint naval exercises. For example, see Athwal, *China–India Relations: Contemporary Dynamics*; Rusko and Sasikumar, 'India and China', 99–123.

26. Smith, 'Trump Should Read India's Playbook on Taunting China'.
27. Tibet has remained a thorny issue between the two countries. While Indian anxieties relate to China's military build-up and infrastructure development in Tibet, including the building of dam rivers that rise in Tibet and flow into India, China remains insecure about the Tibetan question which has been kept alive by the Dalai Lama in India and the large Tibetan refugee population of about 120,000 to create trouble for China in Tibet. See Sikri, 'The Tibet Factor in India China Relations', 55–71. Also see, Dingl, 'Building China–India Reconciliation', 139–63.
28. Beijing's desire to mitigate ethnic separatist problems along with its concerns about Islamic militancy in its Uighur Muslim minority, while ensuring that it sustains friendly relations with Pakistan, also generates coincidence of interests with India. Eradication of terrorism and energy security would remain two dominant areas of cooperation between China, India and other neighbouring countries in South Asia.
29. Jacques, *When China Rules the World*.
30. One of the recurring issues between the two countries, not easily resolvable, is about water disputes. While the recent concerns pertain to China's proactive dam building in Tibet and its ability to stop water flow of Brahmaputra, India's water concerns go back to the 1950s. In 1950, Sardar Patel was to write in a letter to Prime Minister Nehru, 'In our calculations we shall now have to reckon with communist China in the north and in the northeast, a communist China which has definite

ambitions and aims and which does not, in any way, seem friendly disposed towards us'. Quoted by Holslag, 'Assessing the Sino-Indian Water Dispute', 20.

31. The Joint Statement read:

> The leaders agreed that simultaneous re-emergence of India and China as two major powers in the region and the world offers a momentous opportunity for realisation of the Asian Century. They noted that India–China bilateral relations are poised to play a defining role in the 21st century in Asia and indeed, globally. The leaders agreed that the process of the two countries pursuing their respective national developmental goals and security interests must unfold in a mutually supportive manner with both sides showing mutual respect and sensitivity to each other's concerns, interests and aspirations. This constructive model of relationship between the two largest developing countries, the biggest emerging economies and two major poles in the global architecture provides a new basis for pursuing state-to-state relations to strengthen the international system.

> See Press Information Bureau, 'Joint Statement Between the India and China during Prime Minister's Visit to China'.

5

Pakistan Policy—Déjà Vu or Something New?

India–Pakistan relations have remained troubled since the partition of India in 1947. Despite the success of the South Asian refugee regime (a bilateral arrangement between India and Pakistan to resettle the displaced population living in refugee camps after partition) and despite the successful conclusion of the Indus Water Treaty in 1960, the India–Pakistan conflict has endured, fuelled by the unsettled issue of Kashmir and by Pakistan's desire to achieve power parity in the region.[1] Pakistan has steadfastly insisted that Kashmir is a disputed territory and a piece of unfinished business left over from a religion-grounded partition. While Pakistan was able largely to neutralize the power differential between it and India by aligning with the United States, it has also resorted to proxy wars, what T.V. Paul has termed 'asymmetric strategies', in order to respond to India's increasing economic prowess and superior conventional military capability. Unrest in India's Kashmir and the inability of successive Indian governments to respond effectively and in a way that might satisfy the Valley's Muslim population have facilitated Pakistan's pursuit of an asymmetric strategy of conducting a proxy war against India.

The late 1990s witnessed some important developments in India's foreign policy. Vajpayee is credited with shifting India's foreign policy with regard to the United States, China and Pakistan in a direction which Manmohan Singh pursued with diligence. However, the two prime ministers' new approach of engagement towards Pakistan has not stood the test of time: while Pakistan appeared to behave in a consistently predictable manner, India by contrast has emerged as weak through the loss of its credibility internally and externally and the loss of its authority vis-à-vis Pakistan. A pattern of engagement followed by confrontation between the two countries has been enduring and consistent. The 1999 Lahore Declaration, signed by Vajpayee and Nawaz Sharif (the first major agreement between the two countries since the 1972 Simla Accord) was almost immediately followed by the Kargil War when Pakistani forces occupied strategic positions on the Indian side of the LoC. In July 2001, Pervez Musharraf and Vajpayee met for a two-day summit in Agra. This was followed six months later by an attack on the Indian Parliament by LeT and JeM. In 2006, Musharraf and Manmohan Singh agreed to put in place an Indo-Pak institutional terrorism mechanism. This was then followed by the 18 February 2007 bombing of the Samjhauta Express (the India–Pakistan train service) near Delhi, killing 68 people and injuring a dozen others. In September 2008, Manmohan Singh and Asif Ali Zardari announced the opening of several trade routes between the two countries and this was followed two months later by the 26 November Mumbai attack that killed 166 people. Pakistan's subsequent unwavering denial of complicity in the attack and its refusal to bring the perpetrators to justice effectively scotched the dialogue between the two countries.

It would be six years before the resumption of dialogue appeared to become once more a possibility: in May 2014, Narendra Modi began to re-engage Pakistan by inviting Pakistan's Prime Minister Nawaz Sharif to New Delhi on the occasion of his swearing-in ceremony and began in earnest to engage the Muslims of Kashmir, invoking Vajpayee's agenda of *Insaniyat* (humanity), *Jamhooriyat* (democracy) and *Kashmiriyat* (Kashmiri ethnic identity of pluralistic culture). However, two sets of high-level talks had to be cancelled due to both India's and Pakistan's irreconcilable positions: the Modi government was to insist upon discussing only 'terrorism-related issues', without the involvement of any third party (meaning the

Kashmiri separatists). This was a no-starter for Pakistan where the Kashmir issue remains a matter of domestic legitimacy. The LoC violations continued to occur despite Modi's personal efforts (the sidebar talks at the Ufa meetings, Modi's surprise Lahore visit in 2015) to bring the dialogue between the two countries back on the table. Since the 2003 ceasefire agreement along the 720-km-long LoC and the 198-km-long international border between India and Pakistan, as many as 2,058 ceasefire violations have been recorded. And the situation after Modi's conciliatory gesture remained basically unchanged; in all, some 583 violations were recorded in 2014, 405 in 2015 and 377 through 15 November 2016. Then the Pathankot attack on the Indian Air Force base took place on 2 January 2016, barely a few days after Modi's surprise Lahore visit. In July 2016, the Valley erupted in a mass protest against the killing of the home-grown Mujahideen young leader Burhan Wani, putting the credibility of the coalition government of the Peoples Democratic Party (PDP)–BJP in the state of Jammu and Kashmir in jeopardy. Indian attempts at a reconciliation and restraint approach towards Pakistan were to continue until the September 2016 Uri attack when India responded with a surgical strike against the launch pads of the militant groups by crossing over the LoC. This was followed once again, in December 2016, by Pakistan based terrorists' two-pronged attack in Nagrota and Ramgarh area of Samba (Jammu region) near the international border.

In this chapter, contrary to the general observation that the Modi government's policy towards Pakistan's has remained at best ad hoc and that Modi's approach follows the same path as that of the previous leaders (on-and-off dialogue and a self-imposed restraint vis-à-vis Pakistan and Pakistan-based terrorist-based adventurism on the Indian territory), we will show that that there has been in fact a slow and steady evolution towards a firm and coherent Pakistan policy in the present government. Indeed, Pakistan remains a challenging issue for the Modi government as has been the case for all previous Indian governments and during its first two years in office, the Modi government did give the impression that its policy towards Pakistan lacked coherence. Instead, we will assert that this impression is misplaced. Consistent with our argument of a paradigmatic shift in Modi's foreign policy, we suggest in this chapter that (a) although it has taken the Modi government some time to align its strategic policy choices with its policy instruments, this should not be interpreted as a lack of a Pakistan policy and (b) his government can be credited with freeing India from its earlier Pakistan policy trajectory of a 'punctuated incrementalism'.

Modi and Pakistan

During its first 18 months, the Modi government certainly presented a picture of pursuing what Brahma Chellaney has termed a 'zig-zag' policy. The Modi government's on-and-off engagement with Pakistan did go through different versions, resulting in inconsistencies and producing a sense of déjà vu—following, as some have suggested, the footsteps of earlier governments along the well-trodden path of a failed foreign policy towards Pakistan.[2] Doubtless India's Pakistan policy under Modi looked to any outside observer to be full of U-turns and flip-flops, with both serious external and domestic implications for the functioning of the PDP–BJP coalition government in the state of Jammu and Kashmir and, in turn, for Pakistan's response to India, the one feeding upon the other. The responses and counter-responses of both India and Pakistan to their engagement or disengagement with each other did read more like a soap opera than anything else. Pakistan continued to behave predictably—ensuring that the Kashmir issue remained alive on the global platform while denying its own participation in cross-border terrorism. The Modi government also gave the impression that it was not able to make up its mind whether to engage or play hard ball with Pakistan or to do both. The Modi government, like its predecessors, was criticized for lacking a comprehensive national policy to deal with domestic militancy and cross-border terrorism as well as for not being able to cope with the complex internal reality of Kashmir's unrest, a state of affairs of which Pakistan has been more than happy to take advantage. This impression was further confirmed by India's more conciliatory policy turn following the 2 January 2016 airbase attack in Pathankot near the LoC by heavily armed Pakistan-based terrorists that killed seven military personnel. The attack came just a week after Modi's 'surprise' stop-over visit to Nawaz Sharif in Lahore in late December 2015 as the Indian prime minister was en route from Afghanistan to India and an India–Pakistan agreement to hold CBD, covering all issues of contention between the two countries. After the Pathankot attacks and in the face of criticism by the opposition parties, the Modi government chose a path of dialogue and reconciliation with Pakistan and allowed a team of Pakistani investigators to tour the base and collect evidence. But that policy was to take yet another U-turn in early July when, in Kashmir, Indian soldiers killed Burhan Wani, a 22-year-old home-grown Hizbul Mujahideen, igniting a wildfire of violent protests throughout the Valley. Pakistan, taking full advantage of the situation, sought once again to internationalize the Kashmir issue and, in an effort to win support from the Valley's Muslim population, declared Wani a martyr for the Kashmiri *azadi* (freedom) cause. Two months later, in September 2016, at the 71st session of UN General Assembly, Nawaz Sharif raised the Kashmir issue, accusing India of being in 'illegal occupation' of Jammu and Kashmir, and demanded a plebiscite and an independent enquiry into the deaths that had taken place in the wake of the unrest in the Valley. Sharif privately approached high-level representatives from the United States and other countries but failed to obtain their support. India, for its part, repeated its charge that Pakistan was a terrorist state.

Then came India's unexpected, pattern-breaking response to a heavily armed militant attack on Indian Army brigade headquarters in Uri near the LoC on 18 September 2016 that killed 19 military personnel (17 outright, 2 later in hospital).

Within a week of the attack, Modi had put the Indo-Pakistani water-sharing agreement, the Indus Water Treaty, back on the table for re-assessment and within 11 days the Indian Army launched 'surgical strikes', crossing over the LoC into Pakistani territory and attacking militant camps and which Modi announced publicly. This was something quite new in recent memory and the response has been judged by most observers to have been a game changer in India's Pakistan policy and a true shift away from how India has traditionally handled Pakistan.

This shift was evident during the 4 December 2016 Sixth Ministerial Conference of the Heart of Asia—Istanbul Process (HoA—IP) at Amritsar (the goal of these conferences is to galvanize regional cooperation amongst 14 partner countries for peace, security and development in Afghanistan). Pakistan was unable to prevent the passage of an India-led anti-terrorism resolution which clearly suggested that Pakistan-based terrorist groups were jeopardizing the security situation in Afghanistan. The Amritsar Declaration read,

> We strongly call for concerted regional and international cooperation to ensure elimination of terrorism, in all its forms and manifestations, including dismantling of terrorist sanctuaries and safe havens in the Heart of Asia region, as well as disrupting all financial, tactical and logistical support for terrorism. In this regard, we call upon all states to take action against these terrorist entities in accordance with their respective national counter terrorism policies, their international obligations and the UN Global Counter Terrorism Strategy 2006.[3]

Pakistan media reported that this meeting had been a disaster, nor did the Indian prime minister and the Afghan president let the opportunity slip by to get their digs in at Pakistan.

Our discussion of Modi's Pakistan policy revolves around three major assertions. First, we maintain that India definitely has a coherent Pakistan strategy consistent with the new foreign policy paradigm even if the Modi government chose a winding road to sort out its Pakistan strategy. The problem has been how to reconcile its Pakistan policy goals which might appear contradictory in nature, given on the one hand India's inability to resist the exigencies of its hard-line domestic constituency and on the other hand mounting external pressure, particularly from the United States, to engage Pakistan. When some suggest that the Modi government has no Pakistan policy, their emphasis is on the implementation, on the governmental actions, successful or unsuccessful, in achieving its policy objectives and goals. The Modi government has been consistent, even emphatic, in the articulation of its policy objectives towards Pakistan. Where it can be faulted is in not selecting relevant solutions and at times choosing not-so-relevant policy options.

Second, we point out that Modi's policy, just like that of his predecessors, is hampered by the shifting dominant actors in Pakistan within the context of the ongoing hybridity of its regime (army versus the civilian government). With the alternating relevance of the two institutions and their respective leaders, the Modi government's responses sometimes can be seen as out of sync, more reactive rather than proactive. This has resulted in great dissatisfaction among Modi's major political constituencies and several policy communities who have clearly expressed the unacceptablity of the status quo policy instruments of choosing between engagement with or retaliation against Pakistan, as pursued by the previous governments of Vajpayee and Manmohan Singh.

Third, our narrative of the Modi government's engagement or disengagement with Pakistan suggests that if there is a failure of the Modi government, it has been the failure of policy instruments rather than of policy goals and this has serious implications for the new foreign policy paradigm. Major policy changes do require a serious disturbance to the status quo. Any expected changes upon the groups targeted by the policy also require an understanding of the complexity of the problem addressed—in this case, the constraints imposed by Pakistan's Army upon Pakistan's civilian government. The Modi government's insistence on a 'terror first' agenda and the widely publicized 'no third party involvement' in any India–Pakistan dialogue on Kashmir has had serious consequences for its moving forward on its Pakistan policy goals. Not only did it push Nawaz Sharif into a corner vis-à-vis his popular Army Chief Raheel Sharif, but it also breathed new life into the Kashmiri nationalist and separatist groups. At the same time, however, consistent with its agenda of 'terror first', after the Uri attack on an army base, the Modi government has been able to punish Pakistan through strategical strikes, galvanizing domestic support in India. On the other hand, the Modi government and its coalition partner, the PDP, did not handle effectively the four-month ongoing protests in the Kashmir Valley. By blaming Pakistan for the actions of stone-pelting youths, it ignored that there is a genuine discontent amongst the Valley's population, the genesis of which can be traced in part to distrust of the PDP–BJP coalition government in view of its ineffectiveness and in part as well to a growing religious fundamentalist agenda being pushed forward aggressively by Hindu nationalist groups emboldened by the electoral success of the BJP in Hindu-majority Jammu. It has taken a while for the Modi government to recognize these challenges—the constraints of a hybrid regime in Pakistan and its interconnectivity with India's domestic politics in Kashmir Valley. But it has begun to align its policy instruments, such as the comprehensive bilateral dialogue and a proactive response to terrorists-based activities in accordance with its policy objectives but the adjustment has been slow. At any rate, shortfalls in policy implementation (the Modi government's back-and-forth tough talk, punctuated with sudden episodes of engagement with Pakistan) should not be viewed as an absence of a coherent policy.

The following discussion is divided into three parts. The first section elaborates on India's ongoing challenges and the constraints which all Indian governments, Modi's included, have had to face vis-à-vis Pakistan. The second section describes Modi's Pakistan policy objectives, the origins of which can be traced to the pre-Modi era—preventing the export of terrorism and ensuring a crisis-free, geo-politically stable and economically inter-linked neighbourhood. The third section describes the emergence of the Modi government's coherent Pakistan strategy, tracing its evolution from the 2014 election campaign, through Modi's initial articulation of India's neighbourhood policy, along the bumpy road up to the September 2016 attacks and, finally, to the post-Uri policy world.

India's Ongoing Challenges with Pakistan

In order to formulate a Pakistan policy, the Modi government, like its predecessors, has had to come to grips with the three major impediments to achieving any peaceful relations with Pakistan. India's three major challenges are (a) the hybrid regime in Pakistan and its reliance on 'asymmetric strategies' of supporting militant groups and conducting a proxy war in Indian Kashmir,[4] (b) the Kashmir issue as played out domestically—its irredentist and secessionist aspects and (c) the China factor. One should add to these the Modi government's ongoing difficulties in governance with a coalition partner with a soft nationalist agenda in the state of Jammu and Kashmir, a domestic challenge which has serious implications for India's ability to handle a Pakistan always ready to exploit any opportunity to raise the Kashmir issue for its own domestic consumption.

Pakistan's Hybrid Regime and Proxy War in Kashmir: Although in 2013, Pakistan witnessed a remarkably smooth and peaceful transfer of power from one elected democratic government to another with Nawaz Sharif, the leader of the Pakistan Muslim League-N, receiving an overwhelming majority, Pakistan's regime type has not abandoned its hybrid characteristics. A hybrid regime is one where democratic governments function under the threat of military intervention. These regimes tend to seek popular legitimacy through disputes with the result that rivalry issues become symbolic rallying points for the regime.[5] Under these conditions of hybridity, Pakistan's military continues to use militant groups as proxies to control Afghanistan and destabilize India. In his 2014 book *The Warrior State: Pakistan in the Contemporary World*, T.V. Paul makes four significant assertions which explain the working of the hybrid regime in Pakistan: first, Pakistan's dominant elites share the ideological worldview of creating a strong national security environment based on military might and in which Islam plays a crucial role in defining the Pakistani identity; second, the Pakistani elite's 'warrior state' ideal and military security-first approach—strike first and use military force to recover territory—is a product of the elites' 'Hobbesian worldview with a religious coloration'; third, the geostrategic location of the country has facilitated the pursuance of this 'hyper-national security' agenda by the elites, continuously seeking power symmetry with India, with the resulting consequences of an enduring rivalry between the two countries, a shifting of resources to war-making and an unholy alliance with Islamic militant groups; fourth, the geostrategic location has put a 'geostrategic curse' on Pakistan, allowing it to benefit from vast amounts of foreign assistance, but taking away any impetus to pay attention to its own internal needs, including the requirement of seeking legitimacy from its own population.[6]

The lack of democratic identity combined with an anxious worldview and a fear of India provide Pakistani elites with a rationale for conducting proxy warfare In Kashmir, that India has never accepted partition produces a legitimizing basis for Islamic and fundamentalist identities while the BJP rhetoric of Akhand Bharat only serves to buttress such worldviews. With a weak civilian government operating in a hybrid regime, the Pakistan Army's continuing involvement in Kashmir carries with it potent validating symbolism domestically. Christine Fair and Sumit Ganguly, in their respective works, have suggested that Pakistan's foreign policy and security establishment have propagated several myths to pursue their so-called vital interests—amongst which, the 'most durable and persistent legend that Pakistan has promoted is that it faces an existential threat from India'.[7] Fair also argues in her book *Fighting to the End: The Pakistan Army's Way of War* that the Pakistani military has been central in shaping Pakistan. Its revisionist agenda is driven by an ideological agenda as defined by Islam rather than by security considerations. Not only would Pakistan like to take possession of the territory of Jammu and Kashmir from India but it also seeks to prevent India's 'inevitable if uneven ascendance' in South Asia and beyond.[8]

The Kashmir issue allows the army to disseminate legitimizing propaganda to cement its hold on power, particularly given a weak civilian government. Consequently, four wars have taken place between India and Pakistan, with Pakistan initiating each of these. Cross-border terrorism has resulted in attacks in several Indian cities, the most deadly being the 2008 November Mumbai attack. LoC violations by the Pakistani Army have remained the norm. The November 2003 ceasefire agreement between the two countries brought to a near halt a proliferation of border violations—in 1982, some 8,376 incidents on the border in which 76 civilians and 58 troopers were killed and in 2003, another 2,045 incidents in which 59 civilians perished. For the first two years after the agreement, things remained calm but thereafter, ceasefire violations began to occur with increasing frequency: 3 in 2006, 21 in 2007, 77 in 2008, 28 in 2009, 44 in 2010 and 62 in 2011, becoming still more frequent and at an explosive rate: 114 in 2012, 347 in 2013, 583 in 2014 and 405 violations in 2015. India–Pakistan relations have since reached another low after the September 2016 Uri attack and subsequent LoC strikes and violations.

Beginning with the 27 October 1947 tribal invasion, there is a long history of Pakistani covert operations in Kashmir and proxy war with India. The Kashmiri people suffered at the hands of the tribals that year (looting and the killing of many civilians) and consequently welcomed the Indian intervention which resulted from the princely state of Jammu and Kashmir's accession to India. However, Kashmir remains an Achilles heel for New Delhi, as two policy decisions at the time of the tribal invasion have come back to haunt Indian foreign policy. The first of these policy decisions had to do with the conditional acceptance of the state's accession to India and the Indian government's assertion that once law and order had been restored in Kashmir and the invaders had been pushed out, the question of accession should be settled by a reference to the people. The second policy failure had to do with taking the tribal invasion complaint to the UN Security Council in 1948. This gave legitimacy to the Pakistani claim that Kashmir was a disputed territory. It effectively put India and Pakistan on an equal footing and gave Pakistan a stake in the resolution of the issue. The Government of India's complaint explained the circumstances leading to the accession of the state of Jammu and Kashmir to India and provided evidence of Pakistan's involvement in aiding the tribal invaders who were still occupying a substantial portion of the state's territory. It requested the Security Council to 'prevent Pakistani government personnel, military and civil, from participating and assisting in the invasion of Jammu and Kashmir state and to deny the invaders (a) access to any use of its territory for operations against Kashmir, (b) military and other supplies and (c) all other kinds of aid that might tend to prolong the present struggle'. As per the ensuing 13 August 1948 UNCIP Resolution, both India and Pakistan consented to a ceasefire and a truce agreement. But most significantly, Part 3 of the resolution bound India and Pakistan to hold a plebiscite in the state. It recommended 'to the Government of India and Pakistan … to create proper conditions for a free and impartial plebiscite to decide whether the State of Jammu and Kashmir is to accede to India or Pakistan'.[9] The resolution effectively put Pakistan at par with India even though India's initial complaint had been earlier verified as legitimate by the UNCIP delegates who had visited the state in July 1948 and were shocked by what they saw. Pakistan's admission that it had sent troops to the state of Jammu and Kashmir did not enter into the deliberations of the Security Council. Moreover, because the resolution asked both the countries to withdraw their troops, it almost amounted to denying the accession treaty's legality and to making Kashmir a disputed territory until a plebiscite should be conducted under peaceful and fair conditions. The Security Resolution's implications were clear and continue to present challenges for India until this day: it has allowed both Pakistan and the secessionist groups in the Kashmir Valley to keep the Kashmir issue alive by providing a legitimate basis to their demands for a plebiscite.

Nehru's decision to take India's complaint to the Security Council had clearly backfired. He had failed to appreciate the Anglo-American geo-political interests in the region. The pre-eminent US concern with regard to South Asia was to prevent a major disruption in the existing balance of power in the region. The United States believed that, so long as serious tensions and hostilities between India and Pakistan remained, both the countries would continue to be economically and politically unstable. Therefore, it would seek to prevent the escalation of the Kashmir crisis into a general war between India and Pakistan. For their part, the British, recognizing the strategic importance of Pakistan, took a pro-Pakistani stance in the Security Council by relying exclusively upon the information provided by the Governor of North-West Frontier Province Sir George Cunningham to the effect that the tribesmen were acting on their own and that the Pakistan government had been unable to prevent the tribal invasion. Gower Rizwi has suggested that the British belief that the atrocities committed by the Maharaja of Kashmir were the root cause of the Kashmir conflict pushed them to a pro-Pakistani stance.[10] The United States also played a significant and extensive role in moving away from the initial Indian complaint of Pakistani aggression on Indian Territory to an enlarged one to include all problems connected with India–Pakistan relations. Most significantly, it aligned itself with Pakistan's claim that Kashmir was a disputed territory and India could not make a legal, political or moral claim to this territory. Brands, in his extensive study on the Indo-US relations, points to the US role as that of a 'reluctant neo-imperialist' and to the Kashmir dispute as 'a ploy, a case of diplomatic posturing' on the part of the Truman administration.[11]

Some have suggested that, even prior to India taking the complaint of Pakistani aggression to the Security Council, the United States was aware of some activity by the Soviets in the Ladakh region and felt that India's policy of non-alignment did not provide it with an opportunity to control either the Chinese or the Soviet expansion in the region.[12] India's adherence to its policy of non-alignment was to emerge as a serious obstacle to arriving at any understanding of the commonality of the Indian and the US strategic interests in the South Asian region. The United States became increasingly tied to Pakistan, providing it military and economic support. Following the 1948 Security Council Resolution, it acquired military bases in Pakistan-occupied Kashmir with adjoining boundaries with China and the Soviet Union and during 1954 and 1955, the Eisenhower administration signed three different military assistance agreements with Pakistan—the US–Pakistan Mutual Defense Assistance Agreement (1954), the Defense Support Assistance Agreement (1955) and the Mutual Cooperation Agreement (1955). Eisenhower did try to assure Nehru that the US agreements with Pakistan should not be viewed as anti-India, that the United States would continue to provide economic and other assistance to India and that in case India required military assistance, such a request 'would receive most sympathetic consideration'. Nehru, by now distrustful of American intentions, rejected the offer. Pakistan was to emerge from it all with a legitimate political agenda: to satisfy its internal needs and, at every opportunity, to take advantage of its geostrategic location. Given its strategic geo-political location, the great powers such as the United States and later on China have helped Pakistan's quest for power parity with the result that the Pakistani military elite have come to overestimate its power potential. As Tatyana L. Shaumian has noted,

> [T]he involvement of Pakistan in U.S. military and strategic designs and further development and expansion of U.S.–Pakistan military

cooperation did not help to resolve the contradictions between India and Pakistan retained from the colonial epoch. On the contrary, the concentration of modern U.S. arms, obtained by Pakistan (under the pretext of a threat of invasion posed by Afghanistan and the Soviet Union), in the regions bordering on Indian territory has considerably aggravated relations between the two countries.[13]

Domestic Aspects of the Kashmir Issue: Domestically, India was to face major challenges in the state of Jammu and Kashmir. A number of factors were to sow the seeds of public disenchantment amongst the Muslim population of the Valley against the Indian State: the involvement of Hindu fundamentalist groups in the post-1947 ongoing communal violence against Muslims; the urging by the Jammu-based Hindu nationalist party, Praja Parishad; the arrest in 1953 of Sheikh Abdullah who had begun to entertain thoughts of an independent Jammu and Kashmir, competing identity-based demands in three regions of the state; and a slow and steady integration of the state within Indian federal structure, thus making much of the special status accorded to the state under Article 370 of the Indian Constitution redundant (other than the citizenship and property-based rights component of the special status). To this list should be added the corrupt governance of several centrally sponsored regional governments and the denial of public and electoral space to the dissident groups. All this was eventually to result in a mass-supported political insurgency in 1989. As was to be expected, Pakistan would take advantage of every opportunity both to internationalize the Kashmir issue and to provide military support to the militant groups in the Valley.

Since the mid-1960s, Pakistan has supported peripheral, small-scale, organized, covert organizations in the Kashmir Valley. Among these were the Students and Youth League (formed in 1964), the Master Cell and its five subsidiaries and the Revolutionary Council (the latter two formed in 1965), all of which sought the liberation of the state. These groups carried out intermittent operations against the Indian State with Pakistan's support by initiating small-scale grenade attacks, arson and stone-pelting incidents. In 1971, a new group, Al-Fateh, was involved in a bank robbery in Srinagar and the hijacking of an Indian Fokker Friendship Plane to Pakistan. Some 250 students were arrested in connection with Al-Fateh's anti-state activities. However, these covert operations remained marginal in the state until 1989. All this was to change in 1989, when the Kashmiri masses supported openly a political insurgency demanding azadi from India. What had begun in the 1960s as a small-scale 'informal war', interrupted in 1965 by Pakistan's failed 'Operation Gibraltar', was now transformed into a mass-supported azadi movement. In Azad Kashmir, Pakistan supplied training and weapons to both the nationalist groups (led by the Jammu and Kashmir Liberation Front, demanding freedom from the Indian State) and the irredentist Islamic groups (led by Hizbul Mujahideen seeking unification with Pakistan). The mass-based political insurgency, accompanied with the slogan of azadi, was to resonate in the Valley. In response to arbitrary killings of anyone suspected of supporting India and to targeted arson, the Valley's small Hindu minority, almost in its entirety, fled the Valley. The civilian government collapsed and was unable to handle the year-long spate of daily massive popular protests. Praveen Swami, who has carefully traced the covert war in his 2007 book *India, Pakistan and the Secret Jihad* correctly points out that pre-1989, 'covert warfare was not in itself adequate to capitalize on conditions as they existed on ground, and transform them into a mass uprising'.[14] Nevertheless, Pakistan's role and the global tide towards Islamic fundamentalism cannot be denied.

India's threefold strategy of aggressively eliminating the militants, controlling the border so as to make it difficult for Pakistan to provide covert military assistance and trying all the while to engage moderate separatist groups in dialogue proved successful in initiating an electoral process in 1996. The events of 9/11 and the subsequent war on terror were to strengthen India's hand to a limited extent in isolating Pakistan in its cross-border adventurism. Pakistan's own internal logic, dictated by the legitimacy requirements embedded in its hybrid regime, remain the root cause for the perpetuation of Pakistan's modus operandi of covert and proxy war.

The China Factor: China has emerged as an important player in this proxy war. China and Pakistan have remained steadfast strategic partners since 1966 when Chinese military assistance began. With a formal strategic alliance in 1972 and economic cooperation agreements in 1979, China has emerged as Pakistan's largest supplier of arms. The 1,300-km-long Karakoram Highway, started in 1960s with China's aid and finished in 1979, connects western China's Uighur Autonomous Region to Gilgit-Baltistan which was part of the princely state of Jammu and Kashmir and is now under Pakistan's administration. The highway was among the first of China's massive construction projects and one of the important components of Beijing's strategy for the Silk Road connectivity; it will become the main artery for the CPEC. In early 2013, Pakistan approved the transfer of operational control of Gwadar port, strategically located on the Arabian Sea and at the mouth of the Persian Gulf, from Singapore's Port of Singapore Authority (PSA) International to Chinese Overseas Port Holdings Ltd. The port is only about 400 km away from the Strait of Hormuz, a key global oil supply route. It was commissioned by General Musharraf, with China underwriting 75 per cent of the $248 million construction costs, while the PSA won a 40-year contract to manage the facility, starting in early 2007. On 5 July 2013, during Prime Minister Nawaz Sharif's visit to China, the two countries signed the CPEC Memorandum of Understanding. With construction to be completed by 2030, the CPEC is about integrated links to the Chinese One Road, One Belt and to the 21st Century Maritime Silk Route, intended to link Kashgar in China's Xinjiang province to the Gwadar deep-sea port close to Pakistan's border with Iran. After an active consultation of Chinese authorities, Pakistan has prepared a plan to construct three corridors: the western alignment, the central alignment and the eastern alignment, the last mentioned constituting the first phase of connectivity. While Pakistan is to benefit in terms of infrastructural development (roads, railways and ports), creating employment and securing energy security, China obtains direct access to Gwadar Port. The CPEC will give China land access to the Indian Ocean, cutting the present nearly 13,000 km distance by sea (from Tianjin to the Persian Gulf through the Strait of Malacca and around India), to a mere 2,000 km road journey from Kashgar to Gwadar. Priyanka Singh notes,

> [T]he idea of connecting China to the strategically important waters of the Arabian Sea though has evolved over a period of time, way back to when the Karakoram Highway was constructed during the 1960's and 1970's. The strategic highway built through the only land link between China and Pakistan (read Gilgit Baltistan) in many ways blueprinted the idea of an intensive connectivity network of what is today envisaged as the grand CPEC project.[15]

While the CPEC project has given a great boost and confidence to Pakistan, it has created serious geo-political concerns for India. Gilgit-Baltistan (known until 2009 as the Northern Areas) and through which the CPEC connectivity corridor is to pass is considered by India to be part of Pakistan-occupied Kashmir and therefore disputed territory.

A part of the princely state of Jammu and Kashmir, the Gilgit Agency was leased to the British by the Maharaja due to its strategic location in relation to Afghanistan and China. Although remaining a part of the princely state, it was administered by a British officer and a police force, manned by the British, called the Gilgit Scouts. With the departure of the British, the agency went back to the direct rule of the Maharaja who appointed a new governor, Brigadier Ghansar Singh. However, with the help of the Gilgit Scouts, in October 1947, Pakistan was able to establish its control over these northern territories. In 1963, Pakistan ceded part of the region to China—5,180 square km in Shaksgam Valley—in order to facilitate the construction of the Karakorum Highway which would provide China with an unfettered road access to the Gulf. Despite ongoing human rights violations against the region's majority Shia population and its ambiguous constitutional status (until 2009 when it was given limited autonomy, the area was neither included in the Pakistani Constitution nor given an autonomous status), the region has received minimal attention, both within Indian and the international circles. China's intentions to build the economic corridor has brought Giglit and Baltistan into the strategic geo-political game. In addition to raising concerns with the Chinese about the disputed border, Prime Minister Modi has effectively introduced the narrative of Gilgit and Balistan into India's Pakistan policy. These concerns have been repeatedly expressed by India to China, including during Prime Minister Modi's visit to China in 2015 and at the 2016 G20 Summit hosted by China in Hangzhou.

Regional Governance: In addition to these three ongoing challenges, the Modi government's inexperience in the regional governance in the state of Jammu and Kashmir (where in 2015 it was able for the first time to form a coalition government) and its consequent mishandling of the killing of a 22-year-old home-grown Hizbul Mujahideen leader gave an excellent opportunity to Pakistan once more to internationalize the Kashmir issue. July 2016 will be etched for a long time in the memory of Kashmiri Muslims as a *mensis horribilis* (horrible month). The killing of Wani and two of his associates by the security forces (including the Jammu and Kashmir Police, Rashtriya Rifles and the CRPF), while the Valley was in the midst of Eid festivities, was to unleash a state of pandemonium. Burhan, who had been one of the most recognizable faces of the militancy, has acquired posthumously the status of *shaheed* (martyr) along with Maqbool Butt and Afzal Guru (the former hanged on 11 February 1984 and the latter on 9 February 2013) for openly challenging the dominant State power and keeping alive Kashmiri resistance against the Indian State. During the period from July to November 2016, the Kashmir Valley remained engulfed in continuing protests and violence. Stone-pelting crowds (including women and children) were responded to harshly by the security forces' so-called 'non-lethal' pellet guns, fired at close range; the result was the death of 70, the blinding of some 500 and injury to more than 15,000 civilians, the majority of whom were under the age of 25. The Valley remained under curfew for more than three months as the streets became open sites of contestation between the Kashmiri masses defying curfew (mostly young men but including children and women as well) and the State. The Central government rushed additional troops to the Valley to curb the ongoing cycle of violence. All communication channels were kept closed—no Internet or mobile service was available.

No doubt the immediate catalyst to the 2016 unrest has been the unpopular partnership government that had been formed in March 2015 by the PDP (soft nationalist) and BJP (staunch Hindu–India nationalists) on the basis of an Agenda of Alliance (AoA); both parties having agreed to disagree on their ideological contradictions and to concentrate on a good governance agenda. All the while, the people in the Valley have been suspicious of the BJP's motives (namely, ultimately to revoke the special status of the state under the Indian Constitution). During the first 10 months of the coalition government, the AoA remained largely undelivered. From the start of the coalition government, two gestures by Jammu and Kashmir's chief minister, PDP leader Mufti Sayeed, prompted particularly strong negative reactions from the BJP and other groups adhering to the hard-core Hindutva agenda. Mufti Sayeed had publicly expressed his gratitude to the separatists and to Pakistan for ensuring a successful electoral process and had released from prison Masarat Alam who had played a significant role in the 2010 stone-pelting rallies in the Valley. Both were calculated moves on part of Mufti Sayeed to reassure the people of the Valley that the PDP remained committed to its soft nationalist agenda and to engagement with the separatist groups in the Valley. An indefensible 10-month delay by the Central government in committing financial support to the state towards the rehabilitation of thousands of victims of the 2014 flood created a deep disillusionment in the Valley with both India and the state government. One could add to the list of irritants the continuance of the Armed Forces Special Powers Act (AFSPA), the 'beef politics' (some BJP activists' attempt to enforce an outdated law banning the consumption of beef) and the cancellation of the NSA's talks with Pakistan due to the latter's invitation to meet with the separatist Hurriyat leaders. The result has been a huge credibility gap for the Modi government and the ironic unintended consequence of giving a new lease on life to the Hurriyat leadership which, in the past few years, had lost much of its relevance in the Valley. Hurriyat leaders, under the banner of the Joint Resistance Group, have once again become major actors in the mobilization of the Valley by giving calls for continuous protests and marches, whether to the mosques, to martyrs' graveyards or to Srinagar's famous Lal Chowk, and by promulgating a weekly shut-down calendar.

It took the Modi government a while to realize that the July 2016 protests in the Valley had more to do with indigenous political and identity-based issues rather than any open role Pakistan might have played. The government's response for several weeks was to insist that it had all been Pakistan's doing and that only a very small minority of the population was actually involved in the unrest. Although the Kashmiri youth spearheaded the violent protest and although Pakistan was upping the rhetoric of 'disputed Kashmir' within international circles, the more than three-month old agitation against the states—Indian and regional—emerged as evidently much broader based, inclusive and diverse (workers, trades people, businessmen, men, women, civil society associations, employed and unemployed alike). Different demands, whether for good governance and/or autonomy within or outside the Indian State, irredentist for association with the Pakistani Islamic State, all came to coalesce under the single banner of azadi. State actions to control the mass protest through the usage of force, the denial of public space for protest and tough restrictions on mobility and information for the Valley's already-angry and grieving population met with a near hysterical, often provocative, response in rest of India, only aggravating the Valley's alienation from and resistance to the Indian State. The day Burhan was killed, the Indian news channels, some with great bravado, talked in detail about the army operation to capture Burhan and his two colleagues and displayed the faces of the militants' corpses on television—apparently without realizing the consequences of such coverage. The Kashmiri masses, for all that the great majority abhor violence, nevertheless did admire the courage and commitment of these local young men to openly challenge the Indian State.

Both the regional government and the Indian government remained ineffective in reassuring the masses. It was almost a week after the killing of Burhan that Prime Minister Modi made his first statement which was basically to advise the security forces to exercise restraint and see to it that civilians were not harassed. Demonstrating an unfortunate lack of insight into the Kashmiri political reality, Home Minister Rajnath blamed Pakistan for the bloodshed and pointed out that the current crisis was basically between the separatists and the country. Largely due to Singh's and the BJP's insistence on blaming Pakistan for inciting violence in the Valley and to their treating the mass protests about the killing of Wani as an exclusively law-and-order problem, the home minister's four visits to the Valley proved largely fruitless in bringing about even a semblance of normalcy to the Valley. Although the government made a commitment to replace the pellet guns with 'less lethal' chilli-based pelargonic acid vanillyl amide, also called nonivamide, shells, this gesture came rather late in the game. Prime Minister Modi's vocabulary aimed at invoking calm emphasizing keywords such as *mamta* and *ekta* (motherly affection and unity) and *vikas* and *vishwas* (development and trust) rang hollow and fell on deaf ears. Instead, the prime minister was seen not to have followed up on his promises, made during the 2014 election campaign in the Valley, to deliver and carry forward his commitment to Vajpayee's Kashmir agenda of Insaniyat, Jamhooriyat and Kashmiriyat. While speaking the language of compassion and trust-building, Modi did not refrain from invoking Pakistan's role with regard to Kashmir violence and taking Pakistan to task for human rights violations in Baluchistan, Gilgit and Baltistan. All this did not sit well with Kashmiris and the unrest might well have continued unabated had it not been for a brazen attack by Pakistan-supported JeM militants on Indian Army brigade headquarters near Uri. The Modi government had been handed an unhoped gift by Pakistan—India was suddenly in a position to concentrate the international community's attention on cross-border terrorism and on Pakistan's open support of the jihadi groups and, moreover, it could now work on the Kashmir issue internally, focusing on its intended governance agenda as per the AoA, thereby taking Pakistan out of the Kashmir equation.

Modi's Policy Goals

Harsh Pant is correct when he points out that the Modi government, since coming to power, 'has been gradually reshaping underpinnings of India's Pakistan policy'.[16] This policy, moving beyond the historical straddling between *Jhappi* (big embrace or a hug) and *Katti* (no talking, temporary coldness),[17] is a part of the larger framework of Modi's foreign policy goals: of active engagement with its immediate and extended neighbourhoods; of multilevel alignments, pursuing a diversity of interests in diverse settings with diverse powers; and of developing the 'India brand' globally. Within this broader framework, the Pakistan policy is a narrower subset of policy objectives. And, in their articulation, there has certainly been no inconsistency. First and foremost, dealing with the exporting of terrorism and with cross-border terrorism remains on top of India's agenda. The government has been working hard to translate India's deep concern about the export of terrorism, particularly coming from Pakistan, into a significant global agenda item. Modi has engaged several global powers such as the United States, the United Kingdom, China, Malaysia and Singapore to agree to combating terrorism as one of the major areas of cooperation between India and other countries. Therefore, the primary goal of India's Pakistan policy is to dismantle safe havens for terrorist and criminal networks as well as to thoroughly disrupt all financial and tactical support for networks such as Al-Qaeda, LeT, JeM, the D-Company and the Haqqanis. Also, the Indian government continues to reiterate its call for Pakistan to bring to justice the perpetrators of the November 2008 terrorist attack in Mumbai. Added to this list are now the recent Pathankot airbase and Uri army camp attacks. A natural corollary or extension of this objective is the protection of India's territorial integrity. The LoC is to be considered sacred and its violations are not to be tolerated.

The second major goal, a crisis-free, geo-politically stable and economically inter-linked neighbourhood is directly tied to one of India's primary foci—pursuing its dream of becoming a superpower. And that is possible only if India emerges as a leader of South Asia. To achieve this goal, Modi knows well that becoming a credible regional power translates first from the solid conviction by the global powers, particularly China and the United States that India can indeed become such a regional force. Dialogue and negotiation with Pakistan fall within the purview of this broad goal. However, the Modi government wants to dictate the terms for negotiations which are fourfold: (a) development of trade and economic connectivity; (b) discussion of terror list, then other issues; (c) the Kashmir issue can be on the negotiation table but no third party is to be involved—there are only two parties involved in the dispute and the separatist leaders of Kashmir have no locus standi in the matter and (d) cooperation with China to tame its immediate and challenging neighbour, Pakistan, with regard to both cross-border terrorism and bringing peace to Afghanistan.

Modi personally controls the narrative in order to present India as capable of pursuing a balanced position with regard to a difficult neighbour. India's credibility in this regard vis-à-vis the great powers is essential in order not to jeopardize its own great power prospects. How it presents its actions to the great powers vested in the region is an essential element in developing the India brand globally. As a policy entrepreneur, Modi has managed to sound a balanced tone with, on the one hand, India's usage of 'surgical strikes' against Pakistan in response to the latter's role in exporting terror and, on the other hand, by maintaining something like 'surgical restraint' vis-à-vis Pakistan. The restraint was evident in India's cautious way of referring to these very limited military actions. The strikes were aimed towards the militants' launch pads based across the LoC, on the Pakistani side. In short, India was not to tolerate any terrorist action. But by not overtly declaring war, it allowed Pakistan the opportunity to save face by denying that any such action had taken place while maintaining a rhetoric of retaliation should Pakistan ever come under attack. (This was reminiscent of India crossing over the Myanmar border in 2015—although allegedly in consultation with the Myanmar government—and conducting military operations causing sufficient casualties on the militant groups who had killed 18 army men in Manipur.)

Modi made sure to balance his vow to his fellow countrymen and women that the sacrifice of 'our' 18 soldiers would not be in vain (accompanied by the tough rhetoric of the BJP leaders, e.g., Ram Madhav's call to the army to claim 'for a tooth a jaw'), by calling as well on the people of Pakistan to go to war against poverty, unemployment, illiteracy and infant mortality. Turning down the volume on the earlier domestic rhetoric of threats of retaliation and declaration of open war on Pakistan, at the BJP National Council meeting at Kozhikode Beach in Kerala in his first speech after the Uri attacks, Modi directly addressed the people of Pakistan rather than their government.

> I want to say that India is ready for a war.... India is ready for a war on poverty. Let both countries fight to see who would eradicate poverty first.... I want to tell the youth of Pakistan, let's have a war on ending unemployment.... I want to call out to the children in Pakistan, let's declare war on illiteracy. Let's see who wins. Let's declare war on infant mortality and maternal deaths.[18]

By emphasizing the importance of Pakistani public opinion, Modi and his ministers are playing on the Pakistani fear and memory of the 1965 war which, although ended in a military stalemate, had a major psychological effect on Pakistan; after all, the Indian forces had reached very near to Lahore and Sialkot, two major centres in the heartland of Pakistan.

Modi has sent clear messages to his domestic constituency, to the Pakistani Army and public and to the great powers that India is ready to mount an all-out public relations offensive to isolate Pakistan diplomatically and expose its activities in exporting terror and in the killing of innocent people, and that Pakistan is responsible for exporting terrorism across the world, 'While India exports software, Pakistan exports terrorism across the world'; '*Hindustan na kabhi aatankwaad ke saamne jhuka hai, aur na kabhi jhukega*' (India has never tolerated terrorism and will never do so in the future); 'And a day will come when the people of Pakistan will go against its own government to fight terrorism'. Rather more shrilly, Pakistan's Army Chief General Sharif was quick to respond verbally to India's surgical strikes,

> Any aggression, born out of deliberate intent or even a strategic miscalculation, will not be allowed to go unpunished and will be met with the most befitting response. We will be highly relentless in defending our motherland against entire spectrum of threat.[19]

The upshot is that Modi had succeeded in turning the world's attention to Pakistan as the exporter of terrorism, to India's zero tolerance of terrorism and to his mission of promoting inclusive development, both in India and in the region. Modi, it would appear, has been able to reassure the world that India can use force against Pakistan without thereby risking an escalation into full-scale war.

These two overarching goals—to deal with the exporting of terrorism and with cross-border terrorism and to ensure a crisis-free, geo-politically stable and economically inter-linked neighbourhood—have their origin in the pre-Modi era, but these have been pursued historically by India in the absence of a coherent Pakistan policy. First, the LoC emerged as sacrosanct when, in 1999, both the United States under President Bill Clinton and China opposed the Pakistan adventure in Kargil which had entailed Pakistan crossing the LoC. The Indian Armed Forces reacted with a vigorous military action but by staying within the confines of the Indian side of LoC. The line is now deemed to be fixed de facto in international thinking even though Kashmir remains an issue on the UN Security Council agenda. It has achieved a moribund status because no major power wants to revive it in the Security Council and the demand instead is that the two sides, India and Pakistan, maintain a bilateral dialogue to resolve their issues, particularly including Kashmir. Pakistan's repeated plea for UN action (whether for third party or UN mediation, plebiscite, surrender of Kashmir valley to Pakistan, joint administration of Jammu and Kashmir by the governments of Pakistan and India, etc.) has been fundamentally ignored by major global actors.

Second, since the 2001 attack on the Indian Parliament, terrorism has remained the fundamental issue in the bilateral relations of the two countries. Consistently, each successive Indian government has been adamant in proposing that an amicable resolution to their outstanding issues can only be reached if Pakistan both commits to and implements a policy to get rid of the usage of Pakistani territory for supporting terrorist groups. In 2003, addressing the UN General Assembly, in a forceful statement, Vajpayee asserted that

> New Delhi would not dialogue with Islamabad as long as Pakistan continues to sponsor terrorism in Kashmir.... A dialogue would take place between India and Pakistan, only when cross border terrorism was stopped or eradicated and then we can dialogue on the other issues between us.[20]

However, Vajpayee did shift his position, asserting that 'history can be changed but not geography'. He will always be credited with boldly introducing some of the most comprehensive confidence-building measures (CBMs) between India and Pakistan: the 2003 ceasefire on the LoC, the creation of the

Delhi–Lahore bus service, the signing of the Lahore Declaration and a promise to deal with the demands of Kashmiris from humanitarian and democratic perspectives. Vajpayee and Musharraf, after their meeting at the 12th SAARC summit in 2004, initiated a 'Composite Dialogue Process' of bilateral meetings at all levels. Later in 2004, continuing with the Vajpayee initiatives, newly elected Prime Minister Manmohan Singh announced a reduction in troop deployments to Kashmir. For the next couple of years, matters continued on a promising trajectory and despite the 2007 Samjhauta Express train terrorist attack near New Delhi (killing 68 people and injuring dozens more), the fifth round of talks on the review of nuclear and ballistic missile-related CBMs were held as planned. In 2008, Asif Ali Zardari and Manmohan Singh announced the opening of several trade routes, including across the LoC. All this progress, however, came to an unexpected sudden halt with the November 2008 Mumbai attack that resulted in the death of more than 160 people.

Third, a global perception of the key role of Pakistan-based and -supported terror groups as the centre of international jihad has gained currency in the international public discourse in recent years. Now US ambassadors in India freely make statements with increasing frequency pointing to Pakistan's need to control its jihadis. This is a major shift from a past when Indian policy-makers often complained about Pakistan's support of terror groups (which Pakistan ritually denied) and were wary of international opinion which held terrorism to be a strictly bilateral issue. With the rise of ISIS, and growing jihadi violence in the Middle East and the Gulf region, and China's concern about the influence of jihadis coming from Pakistan into Xinjiang, the world community is now looking at Pakistan's role for the first time with serious and sustained attention.

The Modi government was to get an opportunity to turn international opinion in its favour and to bring about the diplomatic isolation of Pakistan when, on 18 September 2016, four heavily armed Pakistan-based militants attacked an Indian

Army camp, the brigade headquarters in Uri (just 10 km away from the LoC on the Indian side), killing 17 soldiers and injuring another 30. This was one of the deadliest attacks on security forces in two decades. It had been preceded nine months earlier by an attack on the Pathankot Air Force base in January 2016 (for which a Kashmir-based militant coalition, the United Jihadi Council, operating from Pakistan took responsibility while India pointed to JeM) to which India had responded with restraint and engaged Pakistan diplomatically. A five-member team from Pakistan arrived in India, the first time that Pakistani intelligence and police officials had done so, but nothing came out of their investigation and the Modi government had to face criticism domestically for its willingness of engaging with Pakistan despite the continuation of attacks. It therefore came as no surprise when, in the immediate wake of the Uri attack, the Indian prime minister strongly condemned the incursion and had very harsh words for Pakistan: 'We will leave no stone unturned to isolate Pakistan in the world'. For the first time ever, Indian troops crossed over the LoC and attacked terrorist camps. This, according to many, has ushered in a new era in India's relationship with Pakistan—from strategic restraint to strategic strike (Shivshankar Menon, the former foreign secretary in Congress-led governments, was however to disagree, stating in an interview with Karan Thapar, that India has in the past engaged in pre-emptive strikes as well). India was careful to declare that these strikes were targeted against the terrorist camps and thus by implication were not intended against Pakistan. In addition, the government suggested a review of the water-sharing agreement and Pakistan's most-favoured nation status. Narendra Modi's response has been viewed as restrained but firm.

It would appear that just before launching its counter-strike, India had already begun to court international opinion in its favour. *The New York Times* reported that Ajit Doval spoke by telephone with the US NSA, Susan E. Rice, hours before the strike got underway. She was to later release a statement saying the United States expects Islamabad to 'take effective action' to combat terrorist groups.[21] In an interview with Suhasini Haidar of *The Hindu*, the US Ambassador to India Richard Verma, in his first interview since the Uri attack, stated that the United States condemned cross-border attacks, that India and the United States remained closely connected post- Uri and that the US intelligence agencies offered support in the wake of the Uri terror attack. Referring to the US policy towards Pakistan, he asserted,

> [We] have also been quite tough on Pakistan, right from the President, the Secretary of State, the Secretary of Defence and the NSA, about the need for Pakistan to crack down on its safe havens, to crack down on the use of proxies to carry out terrorist attacks. We have to stand united and we stand in solidarity with India on that front.[22]

There was general global condemnation of the Uri attack. Indian Ministry of External Affairs spokesperson was quick to release a collection of statements by a number of countries. Russia strongly condemned the attack:

> In view of the attack on the Indian air base at Pathankot in January this year, we note with concern the resurgence of terrorist attacks near the Line of Control. It is alarming, and according to New Delhi, the attack on military unit near the town of Uri was committed from the territory of Pakistan.[23]

Similarly, France, calling India its strategic partner, stated, 'More than ever, we stand alongside India.... We call for decisive actions to be taken within the respect of international law against terrorist groups targeting India and in particular, Lashkar-e-Tayibba, Jaish-e-Mohammad and Hizb-ul-Mujahideen'.[24] Germany was to issue a statement declaring that it 'stands firmly on the side of India in the fight against terrorism. Every country has the responsibility to take decisive action against terrorism, which emanates from its own territory'.[25] The Modi government had fully achieved its objective of creating a global awareness of the central role of Pakistan-based and supported terrorist-groups and bringing about Pakistan's diplomatic isolation in this area.

These subtle atmospheric changes are significant because change in language and awareness is often a prelude to change in policy at the bilateral and international levels. Indian diplomacy in the Modi era has sharpened the international awareness of the problem of Pakistan as a significant element of international terrorism which creates problems for regional security. Modi's personal diplomacy in his foreign visits has emphasized this message. Even if Pakistan's Army ritually rejected claims that Pakistan was the source of terrorism against India, its refusal to bring the alleged jihadis to justice has raised doubts about the credibility of its denials and, furthermore, points to the existence of an apparent fault line between the elected Prime Minister Nawaz Sharif and the powerful Army chief.

Modi's Strategy: A Gradual Reshaping of India's Pakistan Policy

Modi's Election Campaign: During his election rallies, despite no mention being made of the nature of the foreign policy his government might adopt, Modi did drop certain hints not only about seeking peace in the neighbourhood but also about getting tough with Pakistan. Indeed, he gave what amounted to confusing signals about his likely approach towards India's neighbour. His first speech after his being announced as the BJP's prime ministerial candidate was to a rally of ex-servicemen at Rewari, Haryana, in which he urged Pakistan to embrace the path of peace and leave the path of bombs because it has not done any good to the people, especially the youth and the poor. 'From the land of Mahatma Gandhi, let us give a message of peace to the world'. At the same time, criticizing the UPA government, he emphatically declared,

> [W]hen we were praising the work of our soldiers in Uttarakhand, Pakistan was killing our soldiers. And see the misfortune, the defence minister said people dressed in Pakistan army uniform came. Imagine

how our soldiers would feel. Delhi remained unbothered. For them, such events keep happening. Then a Minister said people join the army so die ... what can be worse? If one cannot cry for the soldiers and is stone-hearted let it be but do not insult our soldiers please.[26]

This was consistent with the BJP approach: as an opposition party, it had consistently blamed the Congress party for allowing Pakistan-based terrorist groups to create havoc on the LoC as well as for creating a fragile environment in Kashmir.

Confusing signals from Modi, though few and sporadic, continued during the final weeks of the election campaign. In an interview with *The Economic Times*, Modi suggested that he would follow Vajpayee's footsteps in matters of foreign policy.[27] On 26 March 2014, addressing a public meeting in Jammu, Modi assured Kashmiris that he would follow the path shown by Vajpayee on Kashmir—Insaniyat, Jamhooriyat and Kashmiriyat. 'It is my wish to complete the work started by Vajpayee.... It is my wish and I will come repeatedly here for that'.[28] Some have suggested, although it is denied by the BJP, that he had sent emissaries to meet the Kashmir hard-line separatist leader Syed Ali Shah Geelani to seek his assistance in resolving the protracted issue of Kashmir. In his pre-election interview with Asian News Network, Modi responded to Smita Prakash's query about the anticipated muscular foreign policy towards the neighbours (the '56 inch chest policy'), Modi's answer (which he was to repeat after taking office) was emphatic: the days of bullying or of a muscular response were over. In Hindi, he stated: *aankh dekhany ke zamane bheet gaye; aankh melany ka yug hai* (the days are gone when one could approach others with anger. It is the era of working together). However, this soft and cautious approach was followed by posters at the Wagah border in Attari showing Modi 'issuing a symbolic warning apparently to those who spread cross-border terrorism'. *The Economic Times* reported that this had been the first time a leader aspiring to the position of prime minister had issued such a warning to a neighbouring country during the Parliamentary elections.

Unsurprisingly, Modi's ambiguous signals on Pakistan during the campaign gave rise to two different sets of expectations. One segment of the Indian electorate expected that, as a right-wing politician, Modi would have a better chance to strike a peace deal with Pakistan following Vajpayee's path, building upon his groundwork and that, in light of his development and growth agenda, he would give precedence to the pursuance of greater economic/trade linkages rather than resort to retaliation with Pakistan. It seemed to them that, if elected, Modi would be well-placed to find opportune conditions in Pakistan where Nawaz Sharif's centre-right party had also placed development and the economy above nationalism. In contrast, the other segment of the electorate, consisting of hard-core Hindutva and BJP followers, hoped for an aggressive 'eye-for-an-eye' treatment of Pakistan. This constituency has consistently maintained the view on Pakistan, expressed unequivocally by the Bharatiya Jana Sangh, the earlier version of the BJP—it questions the very circumstances in which Pakistan was born.

> Pakistan came into existence through the planned working up of Muslim hostility towards Hindus in India and it is keeping that hostility alive to sustain itself against the natural, historical, economic and cultural factors that point to the reunification of the two States. To that end its rulers have from the very first day been looking upon India as their enemy number one and behaving accordingly.[29]

Jana Sangh's solution is the annulment of partition and the reunification of integrated India. Despite the BJP's nuanced official position and its underscoring of good and friendly relations with the neighbouring countries including Pakistan, the earlier Jana Sangh position seems to retain a significantly greater emotional purchase with most of the BJP constituencies, largely reflecting their Hindu nationalist proclivities. They view with disdain India's failure with regard to the Kashmir issue (the failure unequivocally to declare India's sovereignty over the whole of Jammu and Kashmir including those areas under Pakistan and China's occupation) and India's inability, militarily, to control Pakistan's irredentist interventions and punish Pakistan for cross-border terrorism. They also regard the United States' pro-Pakistan tilt and its military assistance to Pakistan as a prominent source of threat to India in particular and to the South Asia region in general.

Irrespective of these conflicting expectations, Modi, by his own admission, was not prepared to speak out on foreign affairs before getting elected as he apparently felt he needed to learn more about the subject. However, C. Raja Mohan quite perceptively summarized Modi's intentions in invoking Vajpayee arguing that it would allow Modi greater latitude, if elected, in pushing forward India's policy goals as well as in establishing a distance between himself and the traditional BJP agenda.

> Modi's emphasis on Vajpayee's foreign policy legacy is politically significant for a number of reasons. It has offered much-needed reassurance all around that India will not abandon its traditional nuclear restraint, continue to seek peace with neighbours and promote regional prosperity through the economic integration of the subcontinent. In reclaiming the Vajpayee legacy, Modi is also distancing himself from the breathtaking political opportunism of the BJP when it sat on the opposition benches since 2004. Under the leadership of L.K. Advani, the BJP simply discarded Vajpayee's foreign policy legacy.[30]

This confusion lingered after the elections and the formation of a solid majority UPA government.

Post Elections: Modi began his tenure amid great hopes and excitement regarding regional diplomacy. Both within and outside of India, Modi's gestures to invite SAARC leaders, including Pakistan's Nawaz Sharif, were seen as a fresh beginning to India–Pakistan relations. Even within Pakistan, Modi's emphasis on the neighbourhood, on regional stability and peace, and on the development of interpersonal relationships between the leaders of the neighbouring countries outside formal diplomatic channels met with a relatively positive reception outside the jihadi and religious hardliner community. Upon his departure for New Delhi, Nawaz Sharif told reporters in Lahore, 'I am carrying a message of peace. Dialogue is the only solution.... This is a chance to reach out to each other. Both governments have a strong mandate. This could help in turning a new page in our relations'.[31] The Kashmir Valley's mainstream political parties as well as separatist groups welcomed Modi's initiative of inviting Sharif. They expressed the hope that this would mark a new beginning in Indo-Pak relations. Modi continued with the Vajpayee theme of Insaniyat, Jamhooriyat and Kashmiriyat. On 4 July 2014, on the occasion of the opening of the Katra rail link, connecting the Valley with the rest of the country, he once more assured the Jammu and Kashmir populations that his message to the people of Jammu and Kashmir is that 'the government wants to carry forward the former Prime Minister Atal Bihari Vajpayee's plan in the state. [His] aim is to win the hearts of the people of the state'. A similar message was repeated on 22 November 2014 in Kishtwar in Jammu and Kashmir, 'democracy, humanity and Kashmiriyat, these words of Atalji have made special place in the hearts of Kashmiris and have ignited a hope in every Kashmiri youth about better future'.[32]

However, the initial euphoria of kick-starting a newer and fresher approach to India–Pakistan relations quickly gave way to a chilly climate between the two nations. The first official meetings since Modi had taken over the reins of power, the foreign secretary-level talks between Sujatha Singh and her Pakistani counterpart Aizaz Ahmad Chaudhry, scheduled for August 2014, were called off at the last minute because of a proposed meeting between Hurriyat leaders and Pakistan's high commissioner in Delhi. To the Indian government's assertion that Pakistan had to decide whom it wanted to engage with—the government of India or the separatists— Pakistan reacted strongly and negatively. While the Modi government laid down the law that India and Pakistan's official talks were to take place in a strictly bilateral mode, as set out in in the Simla Agreement of 1972, and that there was no place for a third party, Pakistan opined that such meetings had happened in the past. Questioning the sincerity of Pakistan, the Indian Ministry of External Affairs spokesperson, Syed Akbaruddin, said,

Indian foreign secretary conveyed to the Pakistani high commissioner today, in clear and unambiguous terms, that Pakistan's continued efforts to interfere in India's internal affairs were unacceptable. It was underlined that the Pakistani high commissioner's meetings with these so-called leaders of the Hurriyat undermines the constructive diplomatic engagement initiated by Prime Minister Modi in May on his very first day in office.[33]

An unintended consequence of the Modi government's hard-line stance was to bring the Kashmir issue back into prominence and give the Kashmiri separatists an active platform to which they had been slowly losing access during the last decade. In addition, it weakened Nawaz Sharif's domestic ability vis-à-vis the army to push for an improvement of relations with India. Pakistan was left with no choice but to go back to the only issue, Kashmir, which it believes gives it an upper hand and legitimacy with its own domestic constituency. Its response was swift and unambiguous: Kashmir was not a part of India. Tasneem Aslam, Pakistan's Foreign Office spokesperson, asserted, 'The High Commissioner of Pakistan did not interfere in India's internal affairs. Pakistan is not subservient to India. It is a sovereign country, a legitimate stakeholder in the Jammu and Kashmir dispute'. In his speech to the UN General Assembly, in September 2014, Nawaz Sharif did not let slip the chance to blame India for missing an opportunity to engage Pakistan in a peace dialogue, for not adopting the course of high statesmanship and for reminding the world that the Kashmir dispute remains 'the core issue' between the two countries. Moreover, he reiterated Pakistan's historic commitment and duty to support and advocate the right to self-determination of the people of Jammu and Kashmir.

This whole episode of the cancellation of foreign secretary-level talks also coincided with an escalation of ceasefire violations by Pakistan. In early October 2014, 5 Indian civilians were killed and 34 injured in cross-border firing in the Arnia sub-sector of Jammu. The Modi government's response was tough. India retaliated strongly, resulting in the death of 15 Pakistani civilians. India's Defence Minister Arun Jaitley was categorical in asserting, 'If Pakistan persists with this adventurism, our forces will make the cost of this adventurism unaffordable'. Mr Jaitley further added that India as a responsible state can never be an aggressor but

> at the same time it has a paramount duty to defend its people and its territory. Our Armed Forces, particularly the Army and the BSF in this case, have only one option—that is to respond adequately and defend our territory and our people.[34]

Another minister, Venkaiah Naidu, added, 'Pakistan will be made to understand what the response of India is'. Meanwhile, Modi, asking for an end to any political debate on Pakistan's so-called aggression, made it clear that 'The enemy has realized that times have changed and their old habits will not be tolerated'.[35] Pakistan's response was as aggressive as that of India. Its Defence Minister Khawaja Asif, while blaming India for starting the LoC violations, vowed that Pakistan would 'respond befittingly to Indian aggressions'. Raising the tension bar, he invoked the 'nuclear' word, 'We do not want the situation on the borders of two nuclear neighbours to escalate into confrontation. India must demonstrate caution and behave with responsibility'.[36]

Tension between the two countries was evident during the 18th SAARC summit, held in Kathmandu in November 2014. Despite the fanfare and pre-discussion about the SAARC agenda where India did take the lead in defining it, the summit did not accomplish much due to the chilly relations between India and Pakistan over the Kashmir issue. A handshake at the end of the summit by the two prime ministers, Pakistan's Nawaz Sharif and India's Modi, was considered to be the saving grace of the fruitless discussions by eight countries.

Meanwhile, as a spate of firing along the LoC continued intermittently during November and December 2014, claiming lives on both sides, a battle of words was in full swing between the two countries.[37] Amit Shah, the BJP president, during a visit to the Hindu-dominated R.S. Pura town in Jammu and Kashmir repeated Indian Home Minister Rajnath Singh's threat to Pakistan, 'If Pakistan resorts to firing, we will definitely give a befitting reply to them'. In Pakistan, Nawaz Sharif was having his own domestic troubles. Anti-government protests by two opposition groups, led by the Sufi cleric Tahir-ul-Qadri and the charismatic cricket star turned politician Imran Khan, crediting Nawaz Sharif's victory to electoral fraud, threatened the survival of the civilian government. Some have suggested that the Pakistani military was behind Qadri and Khan's campaign. In early November, a suicide bomber killed 60 people on the Pakistani side of the Wagah India–Pakistan border. Although three different Pakistani-based militant groups claimed responsibility for the attack, Pakistan's military was quick to blame India. In a televised interview, Hamid Gul, the former chief of the ISI, accused India, 'We offered our hand in friendship, and this is how they repay us'.[38]

In December 2014, two days after the shocking massacre by the Pakistani Taliban of about 150 students in Peshawar's army-run school, a Pakistani court granted bail to Zaki-ur-Rehman Lakhvi, the commander of LeT and the man behind the Mumbai attack which had killed 166 people in 2008. India, which had been already concerned with the slow pace of Lakhvi trial, was incensed by the bail and asserted that such a gesture by the Pakistani court system served 'as a reassurance to terrorists who perpetrate heinous crimes'.[39]

India's hawkish policy towards Pakistan was in full swing in the early part of 2015. In January, Defence Minister Manohar Parrikar directed the security forces not to hold back but to retaliate with 'double the force'. One month later, he also cautioned Pakistan that India had no choice but to 'neutralize terrorists through terrorists only': *kaante se kaanta nikalta hai* (only with the help of a thorn can you remove a thorn). The NSA Ajit Doval coined the term 'defensive aggressive' for this hawkish strategy which he suggested could prove to be very disastrous for Pakistan. In his speech at SASTRA University in February 2014, he asserted that this strategy was to be based upon taking advantage of Pakistan's vulnerabilities to India's advantage. The telling line in the speech was, 'You can do one Mumbai, you may lose Baluchistan'. Pakistan has consistently accused India of assisting through funding and arming the insurgents in Baluchistan, a province that has been waging a struggle for independence since it was incorporated into Pakistan in 1947. Doval also proposed something similar to Parrikar's solution of using a thorn to remove a thorn, 'Pakistanis are not our well-wishers, we will tackle Taliban in the way we want'. And one of the strategies he recommended was to counter funds with funds, an obvious allusion to the insurgents in Baluchistan.

The Indian Army's successful cross-border attack against rebels in Myanmar in late June 2015 in retaliation for the deaths of Indian soldiers in Manipur on 18 June was accompanied by an open message by Rajyavardhan Singh Rathore, minister for information and broadcasting. Asserting that Prime Minister Modi had given the go-ahead to annihilate the two insurgent camps, the minister said, based on effective intelligence, 'We will carry out surgical strikes at the place and time of our own choosing. Friendship and zero tolerance will go hand in hand. This is a beginning. India is strong. This message should go to everyone.'[40] Although Home Minister Rajnath Singh took Rathore to task in a 20-minute closed-door meeting (where it appears he asked the latter to take precautions while making statements out in the media), the harm had been done. In February, after Obama's Republic Day visit, Modi once again took the initiative to re-engage Pakistan and deployed Foreign Secretary Jaishankar for a SAARC Yatra. While Pakistan expressed hope that the foreign secretary's visit would lead to the resumption of an Indo-Pak dialogue, India's expectation was to find ways to take forward the process of normalization of relations between the two countries. Pakistan's reaction to Rathore's tough talking and hawkish statements was characteristically swift. Pakistani Interior Minister Nisar Ali Khan pointed out, 'Pakistan is not like Myanmar. Those having ill designs against Pakistan should listen carefully that our security forces are capable of matching response to any adventurism'.[41] He also warned India that his country could not be cowed by the threats from across the border. While Nawaz Sharif's reaction was controlled—calling Indian statements 'irresponsible and imprudent'—the former military ruler Pervez Musharraf forcibly expressed both Pakistan's willingness and capacity to retaliate by invoking the 'N' word:

> We do not want to use nuclear capability but if our existence comes under threat, who do we have these nuclear weapons for? Don't attack us, don't challenge our territorial integrity because we are not a small power, we're a major and nuclear power. Don't push us. We should have self-confidence that their (Indian) dream to denuclearise Pakistan is not possible. We won't let their end game materialize.[42]

No wonder that, despite the good intentions expressed and the owning up to a collective responsibility to ensure peace and promote development during the BRICS and Shanghai Cooperation Organisation summits, July 2015 Ufa agreement to hold the NSAs talks in New Delhi was bound to be a failure.[43] Pakistan remained adamant in its demand to discuss the issue of Kashmir during the NSA talks while the Indian government did not budge from its insistence that dialogue must be held only on terrorism and that the Ufa agreement did not include Kashmir on the agenda.

War of words was to continue until November when Modi initiated informally a conversation with Nawaz Sharif at the Paris Climate Summit. In September 2015, in response to Indian Army Chief Dalbir Singh Suhaag's remarks on India's preparedness for the 'swift, short nature of future wars' in light of recurring LoC violations by Pakistan, the Pakistani Army chief warned India of the 'unbearable cost' of war, 'Let me reiterate that our armed forces stand fully capable to defeat all sorts of external aggression. If the enemy ever resorts to any misadventure, regardless of its size and scale—short or long—it will have to pay an unbearable cost'. He also unequivocally made the Kashmir issue, an 'unfinished agenda of partition', the foremost agenda item in bringing about enduring peace between India and Pakistan.[44] Indian Army Chief Suhaag's remarks were made at the Tri-Service Seminar organized as part of the 1965 war's golden jubilee celebrations, which were also attended by Vice President Hamid Ansari, Defence Minister Manohar Parrikar and the three Service chiefs. This newly developed mobilize-fast and hit-hard doctrine (informally called 'Cold Start', initially invoked in response to the terrorist attack on Parliament) was viewed with concern by Pakistan.

Towards a Cohesive Strategy—Pre-Uri Attack of September 2016: At the end of November 2015, during the Conference of Parties (CoP) Climate Summit in Paris, as a result of a brief face-to-face meeting, Modi and Nawaz Sharif directed their respective foreign secretaries to initiate the process of renewal of talks, including meetings between the NSAs of the two countries. Although described as a courtesy meeting by the Ministry of External Affairs, it set in motion, at least from the Indian side, the beginning of an articulation of a coherent Pakistan strategy. While India was not keen on publicizing this brief encounter for the obvious reason of not giving an opportunity to the opposition parties to question the government on this issue in the ongoing Parliamentary session, Nawaz Sharif, however, spoke enthusiastically about their encounter which he described as warm and friendly and where both the leaders had been willing to put all issues on the table for discussion. As a matter of fact, before the Modi–Sharif meeting in Paris, the two NSAs Retired Lt General Naseer Janjua (rumoured to be close to the then Army Chief Raheel Sharif) and Ajit Doval had spent weeks exchanging proposals through Pakistan High Commissioner Abdul Basit. *The Indian Express* reported that Basit spoke with Doval on several occasions during mid-November. In these exchanges, Foreign Secretary Jaishankar was also involved.[45] This resulted in Nawaz Sharif indicating just a few days before arriving in Paris that Pakistan was ready for dialogue with India without preconditions, making it easier for Modi to convince Pakistan to come to the dialogue table. At the summit, in an interview with a Pakistani reporter, he stated that both India and Pakistan desired to move forward and that the Indian prime minister was open to look at Pakistani issues: *Achchhi guftagu hui hai, achchhe andaaz mein hui hai, achchhe mahaul mein hui hai … unke taraf se bhi izhaar kiya gaya hai ki hamaare mamlaat badhane chahiye (*they had a good talk, done in a good style, in a good environment. From their side, a desire has been expressed to take forward our issues).[46]

The venue was, incidentally, quite appropriate for Modi who for the first time was sending a message to the world that India could take a leading role in driving climate change and provide both symbolic and concrete international leadership in this area. The world leaders had been pushing both countries to restart their dialogue. The Obama and Cameron administrations expressed their keenness to see a resumption of dialogue between India and Pakistan. UN Secretary-General Ban Ki-moon had also asserted at the Paris Summit that he was convinced that dialogue was the only way forward for improving relations between Pakistan and India and that he had urged the leaders of both countries to resolve their differences through talks.

On 6 December, the two NSAs Retired Lt General Janjua and Doval met in Bangkok. The meeting was also attended by Jaishankar, the PM's special envoy on counter-terrorism Asif Ibrahim, Joint Secretary (PMO) Vinay Kwatra, Jawed Ashraf, joint secretary in the PMO and Pakistan's Foreign Secretary Aizaz Ahmad Chaudhry. This was a win-win situation for both the countries. India was able to stick to its condition of bilateral talks on Kashmir without any third-party involvement and to receive commitments from Pakistan for the early completion of the Mumbai attacks trial. A third-country venue made Hurriyat a non-issue, whereas Pakistan was able to get all issues of concern, including Kashmir, on the table. The two NSAs in their joint statement referred to the broad scope of the talks as well as the inclusion of issues for discussion pertaining to 'peace and security, terrorism, Jammu and Kashmir, and other issues, including tranquillity along the LoC'. This was followed on 9 December by Foreign Minister Sushma

Swaraj's visit to Islamabad for the Heart of Asia Conference on Afghanistan. Swaraj and her Pakistani counterpart Sartaj Aziz announced the launching of a comprehensive bilateral dialogue (CBD) between the two countries whose twofold aim was to address the issues of concern through dialogue, and to establish cooperative relations between the two countries. Ten agenda items were placed under the dialogue rubric: peace and security, CBMs; Jammu and Kashmir; Siachen; Sir Creek; the Wular Barrage/Tulbul project; economic and commercial cooperation; counter-terrorism, narcotics control; humanitarian issues; people to people exchanges; and religious tourism. Mrs Swaraj explained the modus operandi of the CBD, 'How this dialogue process should be taken forward will be decided in a meeting between our Foreign Secretaries, who will work on scheduling and modalities of the process. Scheduling means which all pillars, when, what modalities and who all Secretaries will hold it'.[47] Mrs Swaraj also explained the adaptability of the dialogue when she added, 'It will have additional components apart from those in the composite dialogue'.

Although the announcement linked the new dialogue to the earlier structured Composite and Resumed Dialogues, the new process had specificity to it and was coupled with an accompanying mechanism—for behind-the-scenes and closed-door discussion on thorny and touchy topics under the purview of NSAs. For the first time, operational matters were to be discussed away from the media and by the operational people (significantly the security experts who would take forward talks on terrorism), the CBD was the political venue where the political masters—ministers and the bureaucracy—were to take charge.

What were the chances of the success of the CBD in normalizing the relations between India and Pakistan when the 'comprehensive dialogue' (Gujral and Sharif's agreement arising out the 1997 SAARC summit, followed by another attempt by Vajpayee and Musharraf in 2004), the 'resumed dialogue' (kick-starting of stalled discussions by the Manmohan Singh government), and Track 1 and Track 2 diplomacy (state attempts coupled with those by both non-state and extra-state actors) have all met with failure? The chances had certainly appeared good until the 18 September Uri terrorist attack which created once again an interruption in the pursuance of this strategy. They appeared good then and may yet show promise for three reasons: First, the CBD contains a comprehensive list of concerns underlying India–Pakistan relationships and has the flexibility to mould the dialogue according to the evolving discussions. What is also significant is India's assurance that it is prepared to move its cooperation along at a pace with which Pakistan is comfortable. After six terrorists from JeM held security forces at Pathankot Air Force Station at bay for three days and killed one soldier, one would have expected India to have backed off the dialogue process and, indeed, the Kargil War and the Mumbai attack had seen the stalling of talks between India and Pakistan under the composite and renewed dialogue process. But in the Pathankot case, however, India's response was restrained and entailed using the neutral term 'non-state actors' to describe the attackers. Nawaz Sharif promptly discussed the terrorist strike at a high-level meeting in Islamabad which was attended by his NSA Naseer Khan Janjua, Foreign Secretary Aizaz Ahmad Chaudhry and Foreign Policy Chief Sartaj Aziz; Janjua reported on his discussions with his Indian counterpart, Ajit Doval. Following the meeting, Sharif spoke with Prime Minister Modi, condemning the attack and assuring him of a prompt response. Consequently Pakistan set up a six-member team, headed by Additional Inspector General of Punjab's Counter-Terrorism Department Rai Tahir, to investigate the attack on the basis of evidence provided by India. In addition, there were reports that Pakistan had detained 31 JeM suspects in custody but JeM Chief Masood Azhar was not among them and his whereabouts were unknown. Although there was not much progress on the investigation and the scheduled foreign secretary talks were postponed to a later date (Doval announced that there would be no talks without action on the ground), both sides had, nevertheless, created a new framework suited for a hybrid regime, with each recognizing the others' limitations and within the new framework of Indian foreign policy.

Second, it is the NSAs who came to be charged to work behind the scenes on thorny issues outside the media glare. It is the first time that the NSAs have been entrusted with issues related to terrorism. The Bangkok meeting was a test case for India and its successful outcome, setting forth the agenda for Swaraj, and Aziz's announcement of a CBD did allow India and Pakistan to create this dual process of engagement with Pakistan. *The Economic Times* reported that Aziz and Swaraj had mentioned that 'the Bangkok meeting was a good meeting and the issues were complex but were not dealt in an accusatory manner but in a constructive way'.[48] At Bangkok, the range of security issues covered by the NSAs was wide and it included a discussion of 'peace and security, terrorism, Jammu and Kashmir and other issues, including tranquility along the Line of Control'.[49] After this meeting, it was expected that the NSAs would continue to cover the discussion of these and other related security concerns and then set the agenda for the CBD, once India and Pakistan get back to a new normal.

Third, India has come to realize the structural constraints associated with Pakistan's peculiar hybrid regime—neither purely civilian nor purely military. Hybrid regimes are based on logrolling the interests of the several components of the coalition where the lesser interests are sacrificed for the core interests aimed at maintaining regime solidarity.[50] And for Pakistan's Army, the existential threat posed by India to Pakistan and the Kashmir issue are the two main drivers of its domestic legitimacy. In other words, in a hybrid regime, as previously mentioned, both military and civilian partners have to be engaged. India's acknowledgement that Pakistan's Army needs to be fully involved if there is to be any progress made on India–Pakistan's enduring problems will likely bear fruit for the peace process. During the initial discussions—pre-Pathankot attack—Pakistan's NSA did come from the army ranks and was considered to be the appointee of the then Army Chief Sharif. Through Janjua, India established direct links with the Pakistan

Army, in the expectation that any agreement, if achieved, would have the army's blessing. While it remains to be seen how the new Army Chief General Javed Bajwa handles India–Pakistan relations, one suspects that it will not be much different from the approach of General Raheel Sharif who enjoyed huge popularity among the Pakistani citizenry. He was admired, among other things, for his swift actions in punishing several officers and soldiers who had failed to prevent the massacre of 160 children in Peshawar, in launching the offensive against the Islamic militants in North Waziristan and in restoring law and order in Karachi—cleaning up the city by dismantling the armed groups and organized crime. Raheel was also well received by the Washington establishment. In 2014, during his official visit to the United States, he was conferred the US Legion of Merit for his leadership. During his official five-day visit to the United States in November 2015, he reiterated Pakistan's commitment to eradicating terrorism and extremism from Pakistani soil. While he stressed the need for resolution of the Kashmir issue, the US administration impressed upon him the need to resume the India–Pakistan dialogue. With the Uri attack, India and Pakistan lost a window of opportunity, which, we think, Modi will reopen once the right opportunity arises.

Were it to be successful in activating the dual process of dialogue—the CBD and the NSAs' operational meetings—and were it to move beyond the recent Pathankot and Uri fiasco, the Modi government would almost certainly see a positive impact on the situation in Jammu and Kashmir, which unfortunately remains to this day unsettling. The PDP–BJP partnership in Jammu and Kashmir, instead of improving India's relationship with the Kashmir Valley, has produced the opposite effect. The separatist leaders who, up to the December 2014 elections, had been marginalized in the state have once again come to occupy a prominent public space. Through a consistent mishandling by the BJP government and the hard-core Hindu nationalists in Jammu of the Kashmiri political identity issues (ranging from the release of the separatist leader Masrat Alam by the Mufti government, the raising of the Pakistani flag, the pitting of

Kashmiri flag vs Indian flag, to the infamous 'Beef Ban' and the killing of Burhan Wani accompanied by pellet gun attacks on the protesters), the nationalists/secessionists groups have once again taken control of the Kashmir agenda. By India making a vocal and public issue of not allowing Hurriyat to meet with the Pakistani high commissioner before the foreign secretaries' talks in August 2014, the Modi government inadvertently gave great legitimacy to the separatists in the Kashmiri public arena. While the Modi government, like its predecessors, has a tough task ahead in reconciling Kashmiri and Indian nationalisms, the fact of getting Pakistan on its side will have the added advantage of isolating the nationalists and the separatists in the Valley.

It is important to note here that the new strategy of the new version of Track 2—dual process of dialogue—had the result of changing the Pakistani rhetoric on Kashmir, if only for a short period. Within this context, it is interesting to note that Nawaz Sharif's speech made in Muzaffarabad in 2016 on 3 February, a day which is observed both in the Kashmir Valley and in Pakistan as Kashmir's Solidarity Day, was different from that of the preceding year. Compared to his 2015 comments about Kashmir as the 'jugular vein of Pakistan' and accusing India of insincerity in resolving the Kashmir issue, Sharif's February 2016 remarks struck a clear note of reconciliation and expressed hopes for the CBD, 'Kashmir issue is a test for current leadership of Pakistan and India and people of both countries cannot prosper until the lingering issue is resolved'. It is worth comparing these remarks as well to his 2015 speech made in Mirpur city in Azad Kashmir, 'If war in Kashmir further prolonged India would have to pay a heavy price for it. On the occasion of Kashmir Day I want more intensity in the freedom struggle'.[51] However, all this was to change six months later with the killing of Burhan Wani in Kashmir in July. Nawaz Sharif was to call him a martyr and attempted once again to open the Kashmir issue at the global level.

Post-Uri Attacks: The question which we need to ask ourselves is whether Modi's new diplomatic structure and dual process strategy for an Indo-Pakistani dialogue with its acknowledgement that in Pakistan the real power in military and foreign affairs lies with the Army still remains a viable option after the Uri attacks. In line with its primary foreign policy goals, the Modi government's response to the Uri attacks remains consistent with the twofold Pakistan policy agenda: to urge Pakistan to end cross-border terrorism and to work towards creating a crisis-free, geo-politically stable and economically inter-linked neighbourhood. With its surgical strikes against the militant launch pads across the LoC, the Indian government has urged Pakistan to end the terrorism, and at the same time, it has sent a message that it is willing to exercise soft power and restraint because it chooses to do so and not because it is required to do so. Moreover, it has given the Indian Army and the Ministry of Defence authority to engage in retaliatory action as a signal to Pakistani officials and the public that there are costs involved in terrorist activities against India. It has also managed to isolate diplomatically Pakistan, both globally and within the neighbourhood. Bangladesh, Afghanistan, and Bhutan joined India in cancelling their participation in the 2016 SAARC meeting originally scheduled to be held in Islamabad in November. The three blamed Pakistan for creating an environment which was not conducive to the successful holding of the regional meeting. Later, Sri Lanka and Nepal were also to join the boycott. In addition to the terrorism issue, another message was being sent to Pakistan, namely that Islamabad was impeding progress on other fronts such as trade, energy, and road connectivity in the region and the neighbouring countries would go on without Pakistan in pursuing their own agenda of regional connectivity.

In response to the Uri attack, a precedent setting 'surgical strike' was carried out across the LoC on terrorist camps in Pakistani-controlled Kashmir which Pakistan denied. Surgical strikes have set a new norm in terms of how the Modi government intends to respond to any future cross-border attacks. Shivshankar Menon, the former foreign secretary in Manmohan Singh's government, maintains that previous governments have been involved in similar pre-emptive strikes but that the difference this time is that the Modi government has publically acknowledged that a cross-border assault by Indian troops had taken place. Just how significant is this development?

First, the 'strategical strike' is being presented by the government and viewed by the population at large as something like a tectonic shift in Modi's policy towards Pakistan (a shift to zero tolerance towards terrorist groups supported by Pakistan and operating within India) and 'debunking the traditional myth of zero operational space between unabated terror by Pakistan and a nuclear war'.[52] Prime Minister Narendra Modi followed through on his warning that those responsible for the Uri attack 'would not go unpunished'. As we have shown earlier, consistent with his global agenda of combating terrorism, India promptly moved to mobilize international support for its surgical strike against terrorists. Foreign Secretary Jaishankar briefed envoys of 25 countries in New Delhi, thus ensuring the diplomatic isolation of Pakistan. But mostly, the biggest change in Modi's policy has been for the Ministry of Home Affairs to give the military, and particularly the Border Security Forces, an increased latitude to deal with any similar instances of LoC violation. The military is delighted with the political will of the Modi government to support the army and to do so publicly.

Second, surgical strikes have achieved the aim of conciliating the domestic constituency—looking for retaliation against Pakistan and retribution for its state-sponsored terrorism. But most significantly, the BJP has used 'surgical strikes' and the public popularity of the army. The Modi government has taken full advantage of the perceived success of surgical strikes during its electoral campaigns in Uttar Pradesh (UP), Uttarakhand, Punjab, Goa and Manipur. The BJP's posters, used in the UP election campaign, showed Modi, with his clenched fist upraised, threatening Pakistan; in the background is the military imagery of an armed soldier and a reference to the 'surgical strikes'. Another portrayed Modi as Lord Ram and Pakistan's Prime Minister Nawaz Sharif as his foe Ravana. Another poster, which drew open criticism from former chief minister of Jammu and Kashmir, Omar Abdulla, stated: *Hum tumhe maarenge aur zaroor maarenge. Lekin vo bandook bhi humaari hogi, goli bhi humaari hogi, waqt bhi hamaara hoga, bas jagah tumhaari hogi* (We will kill you, definitely kill you. But the gun, bullet and time will be decided by us. Only the place will be yours). Defence Minister Manohar Parrikar compared Indian troops to Hanuman 'who did not quite know their prowess before the surgical strike'. With the BJP's religious discourse at full tilt to portray the muscular nature of the Indian state, Modi chose during the rallies to pay homage to the soldiers who had fulfilled their duty towards the *Veer Bhumi* (land of the brave), 'Our army's valour is being discussed across the country these days. We used to hear earlier that Israel has done this. The nation has seen that Indian army is no less than anybody'.[53] The army was more than willing to assist Modi's party and raised no objections to the politicization of the military. This is in sharp contrast to the army's earlier insistence upon keeping army actions outside the political arena. General Malik, after the Kargil War (1999), had openly voiced his objections to NDA election posters featuring the three military chiefs. Writing about an episode when, on the occasion of Raksha Bandhan (the annual rite of sisters tying rakhis around their brothers' wrists), representatives of Vishwa Hindu Parishad (VHP) visited army headquarter on 23 August 1999, bringing rakhis for the troops in Kargil, Malik refused to meet them and restricted their entry on to the army premises:

> The armed forces were anguished because they were getting sucked into electoral politics as a result of the blatant effort to politicise the war for immediate electoral advantage. At one stage, in desperation, I had to send across a strong message through the media, 'Leave us alone; we are apolitical'.[54]

After the Uri attack in September, the government's assertion that it may indefinitely suspend the meeting of the Indus water commissioners of India and Pakistan and review the Indus Water Treaty was directly aimed towards the domestic constituency. In November 2016, while campaigning on behalf of his party for the 2017 Punjab Assembly elections, Modi assured the farmers that 'blood and water cannot flow together' and the waters in Sutlej, Beas and Ravi rivers 'belong to India and our farmers', and 'now every drop of this water will be stopped and [he] will give that to farmers of Punjab and Jammu and Kashmir and Indian farmers. [He is] committed to this'. Modi added that his government had formed a task force to make sure that farmers in Punjab and the rest of the country 'get each drop of water due to them'.[55] However, in the foreign policy circles, there continues a discussion whether the treaty should be abrogated outright or whether a policy of restraint might be preferable. The latter consideration has in mind China's response to any Indian action. China does not have a treaty on waters with India but has the capacity to control the flow of waters of two rivers covered under the Indus Water Treaty—the Indus and the Sutlej—which originate in Tibet.

Third, the Modi government has successfully pursued a strategy aimed at the diplomatic isolation of Pakistan. This strategy is motivated not only by Pakistan's failure to curb terrorism but also by Islamabad's impeding progress on other fronts such as trade, energy and road connectivity in the region. This isolation is evident in parallel regional agreements being pursued by India with its neighbours but excluding Pakistan. The most significant of these is the Chabahar agreement between India, Afghanistan and Iran. For the first time in its history, the South Asia Subregional Economic Cooperation (SASEC), established in 2001 and comprising Bangladesh, Bhutan, India, the Maldives, Nepal and Sri Lanka, launched a 10-year action plan in September 2016 with the goal of promoting greater economic cooperation among the member countries. The plan over the next 10 years is to extend physical linkages not only within SASEC but also with East and Southeast Asia. In a similar move, when Pakistan withheld its support for a road project connecting the South Asian countries, India signed the Motor Vehicles Agreement with Bangladesh, Bhutan and Nepal, leaving Pakistan out of it. Beyond these regional groupings, Modi also took the case of terrorism to the BRICS

Summit held in Goa in October 2016. Before the start of the summit, Russian President Vladimir Putin asserted that the five-nation bloc of emerging economies (Brazil, Russia, India, China and South Africa) was 'determined' to cooperate in the fight against terrorism. The Goa declaration, in a tougher stance and with stronger language than in any previous BRICS Summit document, sought to push the international community to adopt a comprehensive approach in combating terrorism, including the recruitment and movement of terrorists including foreign terrorist fighters. Following upon Modi's foreign policy agenda on terrorism, the declaration called upon the global community 'to work together to expedite the adoption of the Comprehensive Convention on International Terrorism (CCIT) in the UN General Assembly without any further delay'. Held immediately after the Goa BRICS Summit, the BIMSTEC Outreach Summit discussions (comprising Bangladesh, India, Myanmar, Sri Lanka, Thailand, Nepal and Bhutan) spoke to the issue of terrorism in strong and unequivocal language.

> Terrorism continues to remain the single most significant threat to peace and stability in our region.... We condemn in the strongest terms the recent barbaric terror attacks in the region.... We strongly believe that our fight against terrorism should not only seek to disrupt and eliminate terrorists, terror organisations and networks, but should also identify, hold accountable and take strong measures against States who encourage, support and finance terrorism, provide sanctuary to terrorists and terror groups, and falsely extol their virtues.[56]

Despite various speculations to the contrary, Pakistan participated in the Herat of Asia Conference, held in December 2016 at Amritsar in India. Although there was no bilateral engagement on the sidelines of the Conference, Pakistan's High Commissioner to India Abdul Basit's statement described a shifting attitude in Pakistan. On the eve of the conference, he expressed Pakistan's keenness to get dialogue under way and affirmed Pakistan's desire to do so along the lines of the CBD which the two countries had announced on the occasion of Swaraj's visit to Islamabad in December 2015. This comprised dialogue on all outstanding issues, including terrorism and Jammu and Kashmir. No doubt this Pakistani gesture followed upon the strong global condemnation of the terrorist attacks in India compounded by India's strategy calculated to diplomatically isolate Pakistan. But it has also responded to the negative public opinion it was facing domestically. Pakistan's *The Nation* newspaper, considered to be close to the Pakistani government, and the military establishment, has warned the government about the consequences of its isolation. It asked Pakistan to clearly define its policies to its allies and act accordingly to those policies. It asked Pakistan to move away from its differentiation of good Taliban (so-called 'freedom fighters' both in Kashmir and Afghanistan) from the bad Taliban.

> Modi's statement (Pakistan the mothership of terrorism) shows just how committed New Delhi is when it comes to isolating Pakistan globally. From cancelling the SAARC summit to boycotting Pakistani artistes, the Modi regime is hell-bent on weakening Pakistan at every international forum.... When and if isolated, the impact would be drastic, and Pakistan would never want that.[57]

Journalist Cyril Almeida reported in Pakistan's English daily newspaper *Dawn* that the relationships between the army and the civil government appear strained as a result of Indian post-Uri action. In a high-level meeting between the heads of the civil government and the military where the army leadership was taken to task and the ISI head Lt General Rizwan Akhtar was ordered 'to take a trip to all of his provincial directorates and instruct them regarding not obstructing police action against the Jaish or Lashkar-e-Taiba'.[58] Moreover, Almeida also alerted about China's concerns about Pakistan. 'Specifically', Almeida wrote, 'while Chinese authorities have conveyed their willingness to keep putting on technical hold a UN ban on Jaish-i-Mohammad leader Masood Azhar, they have questioned the logic of doing so repeatedly'.[59] Not only was the story made to disappear from newspaper but Cyril Almeida was also placed on the Exit Control List which prevents certain people from leaving the country. By isolating Pakistan diplomatically,

India has rattled Pakistan while holding the upper hand in determining the timing for a restart of the dialogue process.

In sum, the Modi government has ushered a new era in India–Pakistan relations—with a clarity of goals and a set of policy instruments tailored to implement those goals. As policy instruments must take into account the behaviour and actions of both state (army and the civil government) and non-state actors in Pakistan, these might on the surface appear ad hoc and reactive. What we have attempted to show in this chapter is that Modi's Pakistan policy has moved beyond the punctuated incrementalism—straddling between 'Jhappi' and 'Katti' and has categorically enunciated the broad principle of Terrorism First. Once the commitment, followed by action to control the exporting of terrorism and cross-border terrorism, is made by Pakistan, all discussions are to take place through a CBD, the new Track 2 process. Recognizing the political realities of a hybrid regime in Pakistan, the Modi government has introduced a new and hopefully stable diplomatic structure for a fruitful Indo-Pakistani dialogue. This process takes into account that the real power in Pakistan in military and foreign affairs lies with the Pakistani Army, but that there is a fault line between the civil and military authority within Pakistan. India has shown in its post-Uri response that India can effectively use international public opinion to put pressure on Pakistan to act responsibly on the LoC, to contain the export of terrorism into India and to show that its judiciary and political authority are sufficiently independent-minded to curb the wrong-doing of the past by various terror groups which have enjoyed state support. Because the damage has already been done by earlier attacks on Indian targets, punishing the wrongdoers would not, of course, alter the past but would be intended rather to appease Indian public opinion and to indicate a change in direction within Pakistan. With concrete action on the terrorism file, there is hope that other issues can be discussed in an unhurried, incremental fashion, to be pursued through CBD that would allow the various constituents within India and Pakistan feel comfortable and respected. However, we would also caution the Modi government to take seriously Kashmir discontent. There are unquestionably deep and genuine discontent and alienation amongst the population of Jammu and Kashmir. India needs to pay attention to the identity-based and governance demands. If it does so, then Pakistan will find itself isolated and without a leg to stand, either domestically or internationally, to push for the Kashmiri cause.

Notes

1. See Robinson, 'Too Much Nationality', 344–65.
2. See Shivshankar Menon's interview with Karan Thapar on 'To the Point'—'It wasn't a surgical strike but pre-emptive strike against terror launching pads: Shivshankar Menon', 19 November 2016. Available at: http://indiatoday.intoday.in/programme/shivshankar-menon-former-nsa-india-pakistan-relations-karan-thapar/1/814949.html (accessed on 18 May 2017).
3. Nanda, 'Heart of Asia Conference'.
4. Paul, *Causes of the India–Pakistan Enduring Rivalry*, 12.
5. Tremblay and Scofield, 'Institutional Causes of India–Pakistan Rivalry', 225–50.
6. See Paul, *The Warrior State*.
7. Fair and Ganguly, 'Five Dangerous Myths about Pakistan', 73.
8. See Fair, *Fighting to the End*.
9. United Nations, 'United Nations Official Documents: Resolutions and Decisions of the Security Council 1948, Security Council Official Records, Third Year'.
10. Rizwi, 'Nehru and the Indo-Pakistan Rivalry over Kashmir, 1947–64', 22.
11. Brands, *India and the United States*.
12. Robert Turnbull, a reporter with *The New York Times* who, in October 1947, reported that Nicol Smith, a trained intelligence agent, had recently visited the region and had brought the news of some pro-Russian activity in Leh, the capital of Ladakh.
13. Shaumian, 'India's Foreign Policy', 1164.
14. Swami, *India, Pakistan and the Secret Jihad*, 27.
15. Singh, 'CPEC: Corridor of Discontent'.
16. Pant, 'A Seismic Shift in India's Pakistan Policy'.
17. Sood, 'Uri as Inflection Point'.
18. Mathew, 'PM Modi Speaks to People of Pakistan: Let Us Go to War Against Poverty, Unemployment … Let's See Who Wins'.
19. *The Hindu*, 'Pakistan Army Chief Lashes out at India'.

20. Quoted by H.M., 'Foreign Policy Position of Bharatiya Janata Party Towards Issues of India Pakistan Relations', 284.
21. Barry and Masood, 'India Claims "Surgical Strikes" across Line of Control in Kashmir'.
22. *The Hindu*, 'We Stayed Closely Connected with India after Uri Attack.
23. Balasubramanian, 'Condemning Uri Terror Attack, France, Russia Score Direct Hits against Pakistan'.
24. Ibid.
25 Ibid.
26. http://www.narendramodi.in/nation-is-very-proud-of-our-servicemen-who-make-sacrifices-for-the-nation-narendra-modi-at-rewari/ (accessed on 18 May 2017).
27. C. Raja Mohan in his musing over the new government's foreign policy suggests that

> Modi's emphasis on Vajpayee's foreign policy legacy is politically significant for a number of reasons. It has offered much-needed reassurance all around that India will not abandon its traditional nuclear restraint, continue to seek peace with neighbours and promote regional prosperity through the economic integration of the subcontinent. In reclaiming the Vajpayee legacy, Modi is also distancing himself from the breathtaking political opportunism of the BJP when it sat on the opposition benches since 2004. Under the leadership of L.K. Advani, the BJP simply discarded Vajpayee's foreign policy legacy.

Mohan, 'The Legacy of Vajpayee and Singh'.
28. Bukhari, 'Kashmir in Modi's First Year'.
29. Kishore, *Jana Sangh and India's Foreign Policy*, 149.
30. Mohan, 'The Legacy of Vajpayee and Singh'.
31. *Dawn*, 'Modi Inauguration a "Great Opportunity" for a New Chapter: Jhanil'.
32. Bukhari, 'Kashmir in Modi's First Year'.
33. Bagchi, 'Modi Govt Shows Pakistan Its Tough Side'.
34. *The Indian Express*, 'India Warns Pakistan as Tension Escalates at LoC'.
35. *The Indian Express*, 'We Have Responded with Courage to Ceasefire Violation by Pakistan'.
36. *Dawn*, 'Pakistan Capable of Responding to Indian Actions: Defence Minister'.
37. According to one report, over 550 incidents of ceasefire violations took place in 2014. See Jamwal and Hans, 'Pakistan–India: Ceasefire Violations and Effects on Civilians in Border Areas of Jammu and Kashmir'.
38. Saeed, 'India and Pakistan: A Debilitating Relationship'.
39. Massod and Welsh, 'Key Suspect in 2008 Mumbai Attacks Granted Bail'.

40. *News World India, in,* 'Myanmar Operation Has Changed Mindset, Those Who Fear India Are Reacting: Parrikar'.
41. *Dawn,* 'India Will Carry Out Military Strikes at Any "Place and Time," Says Minister'.
42. *The Times of India,* 'We didn't Build Nukes to Fire on Shab-e-Baraat', Musharraf Says'.
43. The joint statement at Ufa was issued by two foreign secretaries. It had five specific steps to be taken by the two sides: (a) a meeting in New Delhi between the two NSAs to discuss all issues connected to terrorism, (b) early meetings of DG BSF and DG Pakistan Rangers followed by that of DGMOs, (c) decision for release of fishermen in each other's custody, along with their boats, within a period of 15 days, (d) mechanism for facilitating religious tourism and (e) both sides agreed to discuss ways and means to expedite the Mumbai case trial, including additional information like providing voice samples.
44. *The Times of India,* 'Pakistan Army Chief Raheel Sharif Warns India of "Unbearable Cost" in Case of War'.
45. See more at http://indianexpress.com/article/india/india-news-india/indo-pak-nsas-meet-in-bangkok-discuss-terrorism-jk/#sthash.rsiP7IhK.dpu (accessed on 18 May 2017).
46. http://indianexpress.com/article/india/india-news-india/pm-modi-meets-nawaz-sharif-at-un-climate-summit-in-paris/#sthash.n9BGBv6T.dpuf (accessed on 18 May 2017).
47. *The Tribune,* 'India, Pak Say Yes to Dialogue, No to Cricket'.
48. http://articles.economictimes.indiatimes.com/2015-12-09/news/68899718_1_foreign-secretaries-composite-dialogue-india-and-pakistan (accessed on 18 May 2017).
49. Patil, 'India–Pakistan Relations'.
50. The concept of hybrid regime is discussed by Tremblay and Schofield in explaining the institutional causes of India–Pakistan rivalry. See Tremblay and Schofield, 'Institutional Causes of India–Pakistani Rivalry', 225–50.
51. Bukhari, 'Kashmir and Pakistan's Predicament'.
52. Lamba, 'Restraint to Retribution'.
53 Jyoti, 'Modi Praises Indian Army for Surgical Strikes'.
54. Quoted by Shukla, 'Army Silent as Soldier, Surgical Strikes Feature in BJP Election Posters'.
55. Jamwal, 'In the Din over the Indus Waters Treaty, the Climate Change Factor Has Been Overlooked'. Jamwal raises a very significant point, quoting the University of Kashmir Earth Science scientist, Shakil A. Romshoo, that

> However, the real crisis will strike when there will not be enough water in these rivers to share with Pakistan ... since the mid-1990s,

there is a significant decline in streamflow [the flow of water in a river or stream] in the three western rivers, the Jhelum, Chenab and Indus…. Reduced streamflow is not an immediate concern for India because, for at least the next five decades, there will be no acute water scarcity on its part of the Indus basin as glaciers will continue to melt and supply water.

56. Sajjanhar, 'BRICS, BIMSTEC, and Anti-Terrorism'.
57 Neelakantan, 'We Are on Verge of Global Isolation'.
58. Siddiqa, 'Cyril Almeida's Story Points to Old Fault Lines and New Strains in Pakistan Army–Govt Relationship'.
59. Sajjanhar, 'BRICS, BIMSTEC, and Anti-Terrorism'.

Concluding Reflections

Our preceding discussion has clearly laid out the reasons why Prime Minister Narendra Modi government can rightfully claim to have ushered in a new interpretative framework for foreign policy ideas. In fact, the new framework is different enough from the old one that it truly constitutes a 'paradigm shift'; with it come substantial changes in the policy discourse, goals and instruments. Not only has Modi succeeded in breaking with the past but certain essentially irreversible policy actions, particularly in the security arena, also have the potential to form an enduring new legacy—Modi's legacy. The new normative framework and the cognitive script of Indian foreign policy are those of multilevel alignments rather than of non-alignment or its later version, strategic autonomy. In our discussion, we have focused on the cognitive and discursive structure of non-alignment which, despite pragmatic and incremental changes during its history, did produce a continuity in Indian foreign policy that was maintained until Modi's arrival on the Indian national scene. Modi as policy entrepreneur has introduced a new foreign policy language, with a distinctive content, abandoning the prevailing status quo and its strategy of 'punctuated incrementalism'. In short, Modi's foreign policy team has brought about a radical shift. It has moved Indian foreign policy-making away from a historical consensus and time-honoured framework, the origins of which lay in the idealism of the Nehru era, the self-affirmation of post-Independent India and the politics of the Cold War.

In creating a symbiotic relationship between the domestic and foreign policy agendas, the Modi government's foreign policy has been transformative. Through foreign policy instruments, particularly multilevel alignments with both the global and the emerging powers, it has been pursuing diligently and systematically a domestic neoliberal agenda of growth, on the one hand, and the goal of inclusive development *Sabka Saath, Sabka Vikas,* on the other. Modi has intertwined major programmes such as Make in India, Smart Cities, Energy Security and Start-ups to bring the Indian diaspora and the global powers to actively engage with the Indian economy through their financial, technological and know-how contributions. Modi's multilevel alignment strategy, that is, pursuing a diversity of interests in diverse settings with diverse powers, appears to be bearing fruit. The major global powers have not disappointed Modi and have entered into consequential agreements with India. The successful pursuance of multilevel alignments has allowed Modi not to get boxed into a corner. Thus, partners which might have been pursuing conflictual policies vis-à-vis each other have willingly concluded agreements with India: Japan–China; the UAE–Iran–Israel; the US–Great Britain–France–Australia–Russia. The kind of agreements which Modi has signed with these countries range from civil nuclear agreements to cyber security protocols and infrastructure investment. In the areas of security and countering terrorism, Modi has been successful in pinning down bilateral agreements for cooperation in counter-terrorism, maritime security and defence. Even though he has been in office for a relatively short time, it is no exaggeration to say that Modi has established his credibility as a world leader. His critical leadership role at the Paris Climate Summit was acknowledged by other world leaders. The WIN/Gallup survey for ORB Internationals 'International World Leaders Index', conducted at the end of the year 2015, places Modi as the seventh most popular leader in the world. This has all to do with Modi's personal style, substance and the proactive, determined leadership which has made the world forget that he is the same Gujarat chief minister who, in 2002, was denied visas by various countries for his alleged association with one of the world's most heinous pogroms against Muslims. Trust and confidence are the words which have typically been used in conjunction at the conclusion of various agreements with other countries. At the signing of a new security pact between India and Australia in November 2014, which also included a commitment to sign a free trade agreement within a one-year time frame, Prime Minister Tony Abbott described himself and Modi as 'can-do PMs'. During Modi's visit to the United Kingdom in November 2015, Prime Minister David Cameron played down concerns about Modi's role in the Gujarat massacres: ignoring the protests against Modi over religious intolerance in India, speaking at a joint press conference, Cameron expressed his wish to transform the relationship between the two countries and make it 'one of the leading global partnerships'. Similarly, French President Hollande, during a three-day visit on the occasion of India's Republic Day, confirmed 'the historic relationship' between the two countries and praised Modi for his leadership role during the Paris Climate Summit. He acknowledged that the climate agreement signed in Paris 'owes much to Prime Minister Modi'.

We now turn to the future. In this concluding section, we briefly explore some of the challenges and some of the opportunities that lie ahead for Modi's transformative foreign policy agenda. We maintain that external challenges, however significant and uncertain, are manageable. But we caution that two domestic challenges—the Hindutva agenda of the Sangh Parivar and the Kashmir issue—have the capacity to distract from and even sidetrack that agenda.

External Challenges

Although China is to remain one of India's major focal concerns, we assert that the relationship between the two countries will most probably continue on the status quo path, riddled with minor provocations and disagreements relating to the long-standing border dispute. China will have to work out its opposition to India, as a non-signatory of the Non-Proliferation Treaty, becoming a member of Nuclear Suppliers Group. As we have described earlier, both countries are continuously seeking opportunities to create win-win situations in diplomatic and security arenas. They are engaged in what they perceive as a positive-sum game, exploring potential gains in their relationship which are greater than the costs. And we expect the transactional nature of this relationship to continue. On the Indian side, Modi needs Chinese investment to develop India's economy—the Modi government's domestic economic agenda requires China to satisfy India's huge needs for investment in infrastructure and for that purpose, it seeks to make Beijing an active partner in India's economic development in the long run. India should continue to be cautious in its handling of China with regard to the Indian Ocean and the South China Sea. As mentioned earlier in our discussion, despite various domestic calls to get tough on China and play hard ball, particularly in regard to the border dispute, the Modi government has used careful language pointing to its commitment to working through international laws and protocols. As Walter Anderson and Dániel Balázs[1] have suggested, this has resulted in Beijing maintaining its composure so far as the Indian foreign policy of multilevel alignment and India's strategic partnership with the United States and Japan are concerned, while 'India has been cautious in its handling of China's differences with the United States, most prominently the South China Sea'. This cautious attitude was evident in Moscow, for example, when in April 2016, the foreign ministers of India, China and Russia issued a joint communique:

> Russia, India and China are committed to maintaining a legal order for the seas and oceans based on the principles of international law, as reflected notably in the UN Convention on the Law of Sea (UNCLOS). All related disputes should be addressed through negotiations and agreements between the parties concerned. In this regard the Ministers called for full respect of all provisions of UNCLOS.[2]

Despite Modi's proactive neighbourhood engagement, China has continued to make inroads, although with varying degrees of success, in most of the South Asian countries, namely Pakistan, Nepal, Sri Lanka and Bangladesh. Certainly, Pakistan and Nepal stand out as successes. Nepal, with over 94 per cent of its exports going through India (two-thirds consumed in India itself, the remaining third shipped from the port of Kolkata), eager to expand its trade with China, has been successful in getting both India and China to construct rail lines to increase their respective trade ties. But it is Pakistan which will continue to occupy a large space in Indian foreign policy. One of the areas of major concern for India has been China's all-out support for Pakistan and its huge investment in building the CPEC. Some have suggested that through the CPEC construction, China is acknowledging Pakistan's sovereignty over the disputed territory of Gilgit-Baltistan. Moreover, there are concerns about China continuing not to back Indian demands that Pakistan stop supporting the jihadi militant groups that are carrying out terrorist attacks across the border in India. China, for example, stood by its ally in April 2016 by using a technicality (insufficient evidence) at the UN Security Council in the matter of designating Masood Azhar, the JeM Chief, as an international terrorist, despite the fact that the JEM has been declared an international terrorist organization by the UN since 2001. But, on the other hand, China shares a common interest with India in halting the export of terrorism from Pakistan's territory, as this could adversely impact China's own security in the not too distant a future. Indeed, China has consistently stuck to its public stand that it is against all forms of terrorism and that it remains involved in international cooperation against terrorism—therefore its reliance on a technicality in Azhar's case to support Pakistan makes sense. There is also no doubt that in investing in CPEC, given Pakistan's security conditions, failing state institutions and corruption, China is undertaking a huge risk. With Washington getting tough on Pakistan in recent times largely due to the latter's continuing support of the terrorist groups causing havoc in Afghanistan, India is also cognizant of the fact that China has come to occupy a larger strategic space for Pakistan and if Pakistan needs to be tamed, then India's best bet is China. The successful completion of CPEC would require China to push Pakistan to deal with, among other security concerns, the questions of terrorism, its human rights abuses in Gilgit-Baltistan and the autonomy demands of Baluchistan.

Fareed Zakaria points out in his 15 December 2016 *Washington Post* opinion piece (comparing China's ambitions vs those of Russia), that China, despite its status as the world's super economic power with exponentially expanding military power and geo-political strategic print in Asia and Africa, 'has become a status quo power' and 'whether on climate change or peacekeeping, China has been willing to play a more constructive role in recent years than ever before'. Instead, what Zakaria suggests is that we should be wearier of Putin and Russia whose goal 'appears to be to overturn the US-created international order, even if this means chaos'[3] and to prevent US attempts to create a unipolar world. Within such a context, India's challenge would be how to redevelop its ties with Russia with which, in the past, it had extraordinarily close relations. Since the mid-2000s, the relationship between the two countries has changed, largely due to India's growing strategic partnership with the United States. There was a time when India entirely depended on Moscow to equip its armed forces. Now the United States has taken over as India's top arms supplier. Even during the post–Cold War era, defence trade had remained the raison d'être for strategic relations between the two nations.

Moscow's recent repositioning in South Asia will certainly pose challenges for India in the coming years. While Russia works on developing its strategic influence in the region, aligning on critical issues with China and Iran to create a multipolar space, three issues would appear to be of concern to India: Russia's engagement with the Taliban, its support for the CPEC project and a revised armed forces policy involving joint military exercises with Pakistan. India's MEA has expressed concerns over Russia's attitude of distinguishing the Taliban from the ISIS. The belief prevails in the MEA that Russia regards the Taliban as a national military-political movement and ISIS as a global jihadist movement which could destabilize Russia's 'near abroad'—central Asia. Within that context, Russia is prepared to engage the Taliban politically. *The Times of India* reported in mid-December 2016 that India has warned Russia about engaging the Taliban, categorically denouncing their role as terrorists. The MEA spokesperson, while not anticipating any downward trend in the India–Russia bilateral relationship, said,

> In so far as the Taliban is concerned, they have to respect the internationally agreed red lines, give up terrorism and violence, sever all ties with al-Qaida, agree to follow democratic norms and not do anything which will erode the gains of the last 15 years.[4]

During 2015–16, the chiefs of Pakistan's Army, Navy and Air Force travelled to Russia and a flurry of high-level bilateral exchanges resulted in the signing of a deal for the sale of four MI-35 attack helicopters to Islamabad. This was considered a major policy shift on the part of Russia in response to a growing strategic partnership between the United States and India. In September 2016, Russia and Pakistan held their first-ever joint military drills dubbed 'Friendship-2016', reflecting growing military ties between the two former Cold War rivals. This was done despite India's hope that Russia would cancel the joint drills in the aftermath of the Uri attack. Russia and Pakistan have also initiated bilateral energy cooperation between the two countries with a possibility for greater Russian investment in Pakistan's oil and gas sector. In October 2015, Pakistan and Russia signed a major agreement to build a 1,100-km liquefied gas pipeline from Lahore to Karachi at an estimated cost of US$2 billion. No longer is Russia's policy towards Pakistan being defined by the India–Russia nexus. And, moreover, Russia's open engagement of Pakistan goes against the Modi government's policy of globally isolating Pakistan so long as Pakistan continues with its policy of proxy wars and support of the jihadi groups.

Should India be concerned about Russia's overt gestures towards Pakistan? Russia was one of the few countries which named Pakistan in its condemnation of the Uri attack. 'We note with concern the resurgence of terrorist attacks near the

Line of Control. It is alarming and according to New Delhi, the attack on the military unit near the town of Uri was committed from the territory of Pakistan'. While Pakistan newspapers reported that the joint military exercise would be conducted at the Pakistan Army's High Altitude School at Rattu in Gilgit-Baltistan and at a special forces training centre at Cherat in Khyber Pakhtunkhwa, the Russian embassy assured India that the drill was not to be held in any disputed areas, such as Gilgit-Baltistan, or the Pakistan-controlled part of the Kashmir region. Modi's late December 2015 visit to Russia (his first State visit) was an attempt to renew engagement between the two countries, particularly a deepening of the defence partnership. Two major announcements between the two countries were the purchase of five S-400 supersonic air defence systems from Russia and, in pursuance of Modi's 'Make in India policy', an invitation to the Russian private sector to participate in the joint manufacturing of defence products in India in order to develop a strong defence manufacturing base in India. India's challenge will be how to continue to cooperate with Russia on many issues, including its partnership in the areas of energy and weapons development without reverting to the old relationship of *Hindi Rusi bhai-bhai* (Indians and Russians are brothers). Given Russia's ambition and its desire to neutralize the prevailing global unipolarity, India's challenge will remain in the near future how to balance its relationships with Russia and yet continue to stick with its multilevel alignment strategy. India might find that it is in the interest of Russia to cooperate with India as a means of successfully positioning itself vis-à-vis China.

China and Russia have recently developed an uneasy friendship as both countries are competing for influence in Central Asia. Although this relationship began in 1994, to be solidified later through the 2012 Strategic Partnership Agreement, it has been China's President Xi Jinping who, since he came to power in 2013, has become a key driver in the intensification of bilateral relations between the two countries. The 2014 Strategic Agreement signed by Xi and Putin has led to a collaboration in the energy sector (a landmark 40-year gas supply agreement between Gazprom and China National Petroleum Corporation). Since 2015, Russia has been one of the five largest recipients of Chinese foreign direct investment. This investment is fundamentally to coordinate and link the Chinese government's One Belt and One Road project to the Russian-led Eurasian Economic Union (EEU). Furthermore, as a result of Western sanctions over Ukraine and the chilling of relations with the United States and Europe, Russia was to make open gestures to embrace China which the latter has reciprocated. China expressed verbal support for Russia's annexation of Crimea with its rationale of Crimea's historical links with Russia. China has also backed Russia's intervention in Syria. At the APEC forum held in Peru in November 2016, China and Russia agreed to promote the APEC bloc by fostering regional and economic growth strategies as well as upholding security and stability in Central and Northeast Asia and regions neighbouring their countries' borders. Russia for its part has supported China's stance on South China Sea, particularly the Chinese position opposing interference by powers outside the region. In 2016, China and Russia also conducted their first joint naval drills in the South China Sea.

India' challenge as well as its opportunity is how to insert itself into this uneasy friendship between China and Russia. One of the possibilities which India might exploit is the common desire of all three countries to build a multipolar or multiplex global system within which China and India would play a global role than at present role. But all this will have to be integrated in India's newly formulated multilevel alignment strategy. Russia, particularly given its current severe economic downturn, needs India, and India would benefit from enhanced energy and defence cooperation with Russia. Modi's first State visit to Russia resulted in agreements opening venues for Russia's participation in building nuclear power plants in India (Russia plans to build a dozen nuclear reactors in India over the next 20 years) and for India's continued use of Russian small and large weaponry. During the India–Russia Annual

Summit in Goa, following the BRICS meeting in October 2016, India and Russia signed billions of dollars of defence and energy deals, including the Rosneft-Essar deal (a group led by Rosneft, the giant majority state-owned Russian oil company, is to acquire 98 per cent of Mumbai-based Essar Oil, and with it a 400,000 barrel-per-day refinery and port at Vadinar in Gujarat for US$12.9 billion). India also proposed that it would buy surface-to-air missile systems and stealth frigates from Moscow. At this meeting, Modi was to remind Russia that 'Ours is a truly unique and privileged relationship' and bring Russia within its multilevel alignment strategy. Moreover, the Modi government's continuation of using forums such as the BRICS, the G20 and the G77, organizations not dominated by the West, would assist India in balancing its relationship with Russia. In short, one of India's challenges in the future will clearly pertain to the dynamic emerging between China and Russia where India will need to figure out how to insert itself in this relationship.

Internal Challenges

The external challenges confronting Modi's foreign policy agenda are daunting but manageable. But the toughest challenges are internal. There are two outstanding domestic issues the Hindu Sangh Parivar's Hindutva agenda and the off-again, on-again unrest in the Kashmir Valley—which could jeopardize the government's foreign policy agenda. Both issues threaten to weaken the Modi government's political legitimacy. If not handled well, unrest in the Valley can cause the central government's loss of its ability to resolve the Kashmir issue on its own terms and result in making Pakistan a party to Indian decision-making.

A real challenge to Modi's transformative policy agenda has been raised by the Hindu Sangh Parivar's mounting violence against India's religious minorities, Dalits and Adivasis and its growing intolerance of free speech and expression. Since the overwhelming Parliamentary success of the BJP, combined with the initial state electoral victories in Maharashtra and Haryana, the Hindu right wing has been emboldened and now seeks radically to change the secular normative framework of the Indian State. These fringe but powerful forces threaten the global ideological consensus which has developed in support of India as a nation that would transcend the divisive parochial forces of caste, language and religion. After all, unofficial civil wars regarding religion and caste would not be a novelty in India, the 1992 destruction of the Babri Mosque and accompanying violence being a case in point.

Starting with campaigns for 'home coming' through *ghar wapsi* (the reconversion of those Hindus converted to Christianity and Islam and the bringing them back to their *ghar* [home], under the Hindu umbrella), and for 'cultural cleansing', the Hindu extremist fringe's activities during the past two years have taken violent overtones. In perhaps the biggest *ghar wapsi* exercise in Khoramdanga village of West Bengal, some 150 tribals, 98 per cent of whom were Christian, were reconverted to Hinduism. In May 2015, five separate attacks were carried out against Christians in their places of worship in the BJP-controlled state of Madhya Pradesh. And still more worrisomely, during a September 2015 meeting with leaders of the Rashtriya Swayamsevak Sangh (RSS), Minister of State for Tourism Mahesh Sharma is reported to have said, 'We will cleanse every area of public discourse that has been westernised and where Indian culture and civilisation need to be restored—be it the history we read or our cultural heritage or our institutes that have been polluted over years'.[5]

However, it was the murder of M.M. Kalburgi in August 2015 which drove communal disharmony to a fever pitch. Kalburgi had been an outspoken Indian scholar who drew the ire of religious groups for denouncing superstition and idol worship. As a result of his murder, more than three dozen writers, historians, filmmakers and scientists resolutely handed back their national awards as a mark of protest against intolerance.

The BJP reaction was that those writers and others were left-wing liberals and ideologically opposed to the BJP agenda. The BJP national secretary Siddharth Nath Singh denied that the party was being soft on the issue of 'intolerance' but chillingly added that '[they] feel that the ideological inclinations of the writers who have either resigned or have returned their awards should be looked into. You will get the answer'.[6]

In September 2015, a 50-year-old man in northern India was killed in a mob lynching, allegedly over rumours that his family had been storing and consuming beef at home. Again, Mahesh Sharma, Minister of State for Tourism and the BJP representative of the implicated constituency, underplayed the severity of the actions of the mob and qualified it as 'an accident' occurring 'due to some misunderstanding' and should not be perceived as a communal incident. Several other BJP party leaders, such as Sangeet Som, Sakshi Maharaj and Sanjay Baliyan made provocative and controversial statements. Modi and Shah, the party president, tried to do damage control. It is reported that Modi expressed his anger with these party leaders for making incendiary remarks. Amit Shah, Home Minister Rajnath and Finance Minister Arun Jaitley tried to reassure the outraged public of the BJP's stance on the Dadri lynching. Shah said that the lynching of a Muslim man over beef-eating rumours in Dadri of Uttar Pradesh was 'wrong' and the perpetrators should be punished. Arun Jaitley also added,

I feel it is extremely important that people indulging in this [behaviour] are strongly criticised ... those who are using these methods must introspect whether they are adding to the quality of Indian democracy, or reducing the credibility of India as a country before the eyes of the world.[7]

However, the country was waiting for Modi to speak. On 8 October, Modi broke his silence at a Bihar election rally, 10 days after the incident, but instead of referring specifically to the Dadri incident, he confined his comments to the general observation that Hindus and Muslims should fight poverty and not each other.

The intolerance debate was further fuelled by the suicide of a Dalit student Rohith Vemula at Hyderabad Central University echoing the frustrations of those from scheduled castes and tribes (SCs and STs), resulting from various forms of discrimination on campus. Loud protests against actions of the NDA government took place at several different campuses across the country. These included IIT Madras (over the banning of a students' forum), Hyderabad University (the suspension of Rohith Vemula and four other Dalit students from the university hostel at the insistence of the BJP government), the Film and Television Institute of India (FTII), Pune, the Aligarh Muslim University (over the minority status of the institution), University of Delhi (over a seminar on the Ayodhya temple) and JNU (over the protest and arrest of the student leader for raising slogans in favour of Kashmir's secessionist movement and in protest against the hanging of Afzal Guru and Maqbool Bhat).

As the July 2016 unrest in the Kashmir Valley intensified, a vocal public outrage was expressed by the so-called nationalists against anyone who openly expressed the opinion that Kashmiri protest had indigenous roots and that alienation of the population was real, and not Pakistan sponsored. In 2016, there were regular reports of the ill treatment of Kashmiris outside the Valley. In April 2016, the rhetoric of national vs anti-national was in full swing during a clash over a cricket match between Muslim and out-of-state non-Muslim students at the National Institute of Technology in Srinagar. The state's BJP spokesperson, Sunil Sethi, asked the state government to take action against all elements who were indulging in anti-national slogans and hoisting Pakistani flags. He maintained that not only were such activities anti-national but also amounted to supporting and propagating terrorism and separatism in the state and rest of the country. He urged the state government to facilitate activities which promoted Indian nationalism.

Despite the fact that Modi had campaigned exclusively on the development, anti-corruption and anti-dynastic rule agendas and without in any way invoking religion, his electoral success brought with it a great burden of anxiety among liberals and Muslims. Indeed, there was not a single Muslim elected to the Parliament under the BJP banner. Some of these anxieties were apparently relieved when the BJP formed a partnership government with the soft nationalist PDP party of the Kashmir Valley. A majority of the Indian electorate had elected Modi based on his promise of a changed politics. Modi's silence on religion both during and post elections is no doubt indicative of his complete understanding of the ideological underpinnings of his party. The BJP, the VHP and the RSS have consistently opposed the secular normative basis for the nation. Instead, they have pushed the principle of Hindu *rashtra* (one Hindu culture—'there can be many flowers but one garland; many rivers, but one ocean') and the notion of *pitrabhumi* (fatherland, land of one's birth, one's ancestors) and *punyabhumi* (sacred land of the Hindus). The Hindutva concept, in a symbiotic relationship with the notions of pitrabhumi and punyabhumi, maintains that all other cultures and religions within India are to be subordinated to Hindu traditions, religion and culture. There would appear to be an emerging trend of intolerance of differences, of that which is not Hindu in both the religious and cultural senses that is accompanied by a denial of the free speech and expression given to Indian citizens under a democratic constitution. Increasingly, a word against Bharat or Mother India is perceived in official quarters as an act of being anti-Indian or anti-national.

Ashutosh Varshney, writing after the first 100 days of the BJP electoral victory, suggested that the prospect of India witnessing a period of communal unrest and violence 'is not a foregone conclusion'. The electoral constraints and the desire for power, which require the ruling party to construct a winning coalition across different partners, require both 'alliance-building and ideological-moderation'. In underlining Modi's challenges in reconciling the development agenda and maintaining communal peace in India, he points to what he believes to be Modi's real challenge: 'The ideological proclivities of his party are in direct conflict with the political and constitutional realities of India. Given this clash, Modi's leadership will play a decisive role in how India evolves in the new future. The likelihood is that moderation will prevail'.[8]

Unfortunately, Modi's long silences on the ongoing communal violence and intolerance have fostered the impression that either he does not care or he does not have the capacity to control the extremist elements of the Hindu nationalist right. His reliance on disciplining his party members behind closed doors with regard to their irresponsible statements does not seem to have had much of an effect on the extremist Hindu elements. Modi's credibility in handing the Hindu chauvinist groups is suffering both within and outside India and could very well have a serious negative impact on the pursuance of those enlightened transformative and proactive endeavours with foreign partners that are aimed at providing strong, even essential, support to the domestic economic agenda. Shashi Tharoor was to succinctly summarize India's growing loss of reputation globally when he pointed out that 'For a government that is unduly proud of its international standing, the BJP administration in the national capital seems curiously oblivious to the great damage being done to India by global perceptions of the changed climate in a famously argumentative democracy'[9] President Obama himself, in the final speech of his 2015 Republic Day visit, categorically cautioned the Modi government that India would only succeed if it didn't 'splinter along religious lines'. He was to repeat his concerns during a speech at a National Prayer Breakfast, delivered in Washington, D.C. on 5 February 2015.

> Michelle and I returned from India—an incredible, beautiful country, full of magnificent diversity—but a place where, in past years, religious faiths of all types have, on occasion, been targeted by other peoples of faith, simply due to their heritage and their beliefs—acts of intolerance that would have shocked Gandhiji, the person who helped to liberate that nation.[10]

The other internal challenge is the Kashmir issue. In its mishandling of the July 2016 unrest, the BJP government gave

Pakistan an upper hand. Pakistan did not waste a single moment of time and not only internationalized the issue but also gave moral support to the Kashmir cause. Had the Uri episode not happened, the Kashmir unrest would have continued with the same intensity as it had from July to early September 2016. India needs to resolve the issue of Kashmir on its own terms and with the support of the population of Jammu and Kashmir. By acknowledging that there is a real political, identity-based problem, it can make Pakistan redundant with no stake in the resolution of the Kashmir issue.

The BJP government was to mishandle the spiralling Kashmir Valley unrest which began as a result of the killing of the home-grown Hizbul commander Burhan Wani on 8 July by the security forces, resulting in the death of 70 people and injury to 15,000, including 5,000 security personnel. Never before had the Valley seen such unrelenting violence, literally on a daily basis. And never before had the Valley witnessed Kashmiri people from all walks of life and from every corner (in all its 10 districts) united against the actions of the security forces and united in expressing demands for 'azadi' (freedom). Public expression of grief at the death and injury of their loved ones was met with anger and frustration by both the Indian and the state governments, including the state police. City streets became the sites for contestation between the security forces and the resisting Kashmiris on almost a daily basis. Day-to-day living was interrupted for more than five months by the unrelenting imposition of curfews and corresponding calls of shutdown by the separatist leaders, by restrictions on mobility and communication including the usage of mobile phones, Internet services and by the control over information through the censorship of press (the latter, however, short-lived due to widespread national and international condemnation). The BJP's insistence on blaming Pakistan for inciting violence in the Valley and their treating the mass protest for the killing of Wani as an exclusively law-and-order problem added fuel to the fire. PM Modi's calming words of *mamta* and *ekta* (motherly affection and unity) and *vikas* and *vishwas* (development and trust) fell on deaf ears precisely for the reason that the prime minister had not been able to follow up on his promises made during the 2014 election campaign in the Valley to tangibly deliver and carry forward his commitment to Vajpayee's Kashmir agenda of Insaaniyat, Jamhooriyat and Kashmiriyat. While speaking the language of compassion and trust- building, Modi also had not refrained from invoking Pakistan with regard to Kashmir violence and taking Pakistan to task for human rights violations in Baluchistan, Gilgit and Baltistan. All this was not to sit well with Kashmiris.

There is no doubt that since 1948, Pakistan has emerged as the most essential emblem of Kashmiri resistance and is revered by Kashmiri Muslims for consistently challenging the Indian State. It is also apparent that Pakistan's motives in morally and militarily supporting Kashmir are largely self-interested. However, for a Kashmiri Muslim, Pakistan is a symbol of local resistance against India. The raising of Pakistani and Islamic flags is nothing new. This has been going on since the accession of the state to India and during any protest movement when Kashmiris have felt their religious identity or political identity is being threatened. However, the Indian government needs to acknowledge two realities with regard to Kashmir: (a) the Valley's resistance is complex, fluid, flexible and multi-sited with interlayered realities and (b) its key characteristic is scattered and regular everyday resistance to the Indian State by the ordinary Kashmiri Muslim. If the Indian State wishes to better understand the protracted character of the Kashmir conflict, it must pay specific attention to at times habitual (e.g., celebrating Eid only when the Pakistan Mullah declares the holiday), and at times 'conscious' actions/resistance of the Kashmiri masses and their dynamic interaction with the organized resistance by groups such as the Hurriyat. What strategy the Valley's Muslims adopt depends upon how the State reacts to Kashmiri agitation, and this in turn impacts upon the ordinary Kashmiri resisters' response: whether they will demand good governance or azadi or both, or whether they will join in with the secessionists and nationalists in their collective public protests.

Only by understanding this everyday reality of Kashmiri resistance will the Modi government be able to isolate Pakistan and deprive it of its symbolic status so far as Kashmiris are concerned. The Uri incident and accompanying Indian strategy of isolating Pakistan gave the Modi government an excellent opportunity to push its agenda of development in the state. One of the most significant actions it has undertaken to undermine Pakistani influence is to review officially the 1987 decision to suspend construction on the Tulbul navigation project. There has been an ongoing dispute between India and Pakistan over the Tulbul project since 1987. India proposed to build the barrage in 1984 on the Jhelum River, at the mouth of Wular Lake, India's largest fresh water lake, at Sopore in the Kashmir Valley. According to the original Indian plan, the barrage was expected to be 439-feet long and 40-feet wide, and would have a maximum storage capacity of 0.30 million acres feet of water. India claims that the barrage would make the river navigable in summer, while Pakistan objects that it violates the 1960 Indus Waters Treaty. The Jhelum River through the Kashmir Valley below Wular Lake provides an important means of transport for goods and people. To sustain navigation throughout the year, a minimum depth of water is needed. The Modi government, if successful in going ahead with this project, may start to get Pakistan out the radar of Kashmiris. This might be a wishful thinking as the road ahead remains challenging.

If the troublesome and potentially volatile Hindutva and Kashmir issues can be managed competently—and there is no guarantee that the Modi government will be able to do so—then there are several important positive factors, institutional as well as personal of the prime minister himself, that argue for his government's successful design and pursuit of foreign policy. We have pointed out the innovative and successful elements of foreign policy design but can perhaps dwell more in concluding on the exceptional personal strengths of

Narendra Modi on which rest the best hopes for a solution to the two large domestic threats we have identified. Modi has so far been able to sustain unblemished a public image of transparency, probity, generosity, vision and great ambition for the nation. He has so far succeeded in retaining much of his political capital at home and abroad although the honeymoon period is over. He still enjoys a broad measure of domestic support and goodwill. His foreign policy actions have led to tangible agreements which promise substantial benefits for India as in infrastructure development. Modi has shown himself to be an agent of real change functioning with the support of a disciplined and performance-oriented diplomatic and military machinery and has earned the confidence of the public at large, especially after the surgical strikes against Pakistan. Finally, he has shed the baggage of non-alignment because of which multilevel alignment has now become the backbone of India's foreign policy. The paradigm shift has indeed taken place and Modi government's foreign policy is well-placed to handle the external challenges, as mentioned above, but the two domestic challenges—the Hindutva agenda of the Sangh Parivar and the Kashmir issue—have the capacity to sidetrack Modi's agenda, creating major domestic distractions in pushing forward the new foreign policy paradigm.

Notes

1. Anderson and Balázs, 'Why China Isn't Too Worried by Expanding US–India Ties'.
2. Sajjanhar, 'India and China'.
3. Zakaria, 'Vladimir Putin Wants a New World Order'.
4. *The Times of India*, 'India Cautions Russia and Iran against Engaging with Taliban'.
5. Available at: http://www.dnaindia.com/india/report-modi-government-rss-plan-to-cleanse-india-of-western-culture-roadmap-to-be-prepared-2123479 (accessed on 26 May 2017).

6. *The Indian Express*, 'As Writers Continue to Return Award, BJP Says Check Their Ideological Inclinations'.
7. Tharoor, 'Why India's Intolerance Problem Is Hurting Its Global Reputation'.
8. Varshney, 'India's Watershed Vote', 44.
9. See note 7.
10. Remarks by the President at National Prayer Breakfast, 5 February 2015. Available at: https://www.whitehouse.gov/the-press-office/2015/02/05/remarks-president-national-prayer-breakfast (accessed on 26 May 2017).

Bibliography

Abraham, Itty. 'The Future of Indian Foreign Policy'. *Economic and Political Weekly* 42, no. 42 (2007, 20–26 October): 4209–12.

———. 'From Bandung to NAM: Non-Alignment and Indian Foreign Policy, 1947–65'. *Commonwealth and Comparative Politics* 46, no. 2 (2008): 195–219.

Acharya, Alka. 'India–China Relations: Towards a "Shared Vision"'. *Economic and Political Weekly* 43, no. 4 (2008, 26 January–1 February): 10–13.

Aijazuddin, F. S. ed. *The White House and Pakistan*. Oxford: Oxford University Press, 2002.

Anderson, Walter K. 'The Domestic Roots of Indian Foreign Policy'. *Asian Affairs* 10, no. 3 (Fall, 1983): 45–53.

Anderson, Walter, and Dániel Balázs. 'Why China Isn't Too Worried by Expanding US–India Ties'. *The Diplomat*, 17 June 2016. Available at: http://thediplomat.com/2016/06/why-china-isnt-too-worried-by-expanding-us-india-ties/ (accessed on 15 May 2017).

Appadorai, A. *Select Documents on India's Foreign Policy and Relations, 1947–1972*, vol. 1. New Delhi: Oxford University Press, 1982.

Athwal, Amardeep. *China–India Relations: Contemporary Dynamics*. London and New York, NY: Routledge, 2008.

Ayres, Alyssa. 'Three Takeaways on U.S.–India Defense Ties'. Forbes, 29 August 2016. Available at: http://www.forbes.com/sites/alyssaayres/2016/08/29/three-takeaways-on-u-s-india-defense-ties/#7091af937c61 (accessed on 15 May 2017).

Bagchi, Indrani. 'Modi Govt Shows Pakistan Its Tough Side, Calls off Foreign Secretary-level Talks'. *The Times of India*, 19 August 2014. Available at: http://timesofindia.indiatimes.com/india/Modi-govt-shows-Pakistan-its-tough-side-calls-off-foreign-secretary-level-talks/articleshow/40382419.cms (accessed on 15 May 2017).

Bajpai, Kanti. 'Pakistan and China in Indian Strategic Thought'. *International Journal* 62, no. 4, India Emerging: Strength and Challenge (Autumn, 2007): 805–22.

———. 'Modi's Foreign Policy—How's It Going?' *Global Brief: World Affairs in the 21st Century*, 2 September 2016. Available at: http://globalbrief.ca/blog/2016/09/02/modi%E2%80%99s-foreign-policy-%E2%80%93-how%E2%80%99s-it-going/ (accessed on 15 May 2017).

Balasubramanian, Shyam. 'Condemning Uri Terror Attack, France, Russia Score Direct Hits against Pakistan'. *The Times of India*, 21 September 2016. Available at: http://timesofindia.indiatimes.com/ india/Condemning-Uri-terror-attack-France-Russia-score-direct-hits- against-Pakistan/articleshow/54429098.cms (accessed on 15 May 2017).

Bandyopadhyaya, J. *The Making of India's Foreign Policy: Determinants, Institutions, Processes and Personalities*. Bombay: Allied Publishers, 1970.

Barry, Ellen, and Salman Masood. 'India Claims "Surgical Strikes" Across Line of Control in Kashmir'. *The New York Times*, 29 September 2016. Available at: http://www.nytimes.com/2016/09/30/world/asia/kashmir- india-pakistan.html?_r=0 (accessed on 15 May 2017).

Baru, Sanjaya. *1991: How P. V. Narasimha Rao Made History*. New Delhi: Aleph Book, 2016.

Basu, A.R. 'India's China Policy in Historical Perspective'. *Contemporary Southeast Asia* 13, no. 1 (1991, June): 103–15.

Benner, Jeffrey. *The Indian Foreign Policy Bureaucracy*. Boulder, CO: Westview Press, 1985.

Bharatiya Janata Party. *Manifesto 2014: Ek Bharat—Shreshtha Bharat*. Available at: http://www.bjp.org/images/pdf_2014/full_manifesto_ english_07.04.2014.pdf (accessed on 12 May 2017).

Brands, H.W. *India and the United States—The Cold Peace*. Boston: Twayne Publishers, 1990.

Brecher, Michael. *India and World Politics: Krishna Menon's View of the World*. London: Oxford University Press, 1968.

Bukhari, Shujaat. 'Kashmir and Pakistan's Predicament'. *Rising Kashmir*, 12 February 2016.

———. 'Kashmir in Modi's First Year'. *The Friday Times*, 29 May 2015. Available at: http://www.thefridaytimes.com/tft/kashmir-in-modis-first- year/ (accessed on 29 May 2017).

Cairney, Paul. *Understanding Public Policy: Theories and Issues*. Basingstoke: Palgrave Macmillan, 2012.

Chakravarti, P.C. *India's China Policy*. Bloomington: Indiana University Press, 1962.

Chaulia, Sreeram. 'BJP, India's Foreign Policy and the "Realist Alternative" to the Nehruvian Tradition'. *International Politics* 39, no. 2 (2002): 215–34.

Chenoy, Kamal Mitra, and Anuradha M. Chenoy. 'India's Foreign Policy Shifts and the Calculus of Power'. *Economic and Political Weekly* 42, no. 35 (2007, 1–7 September): 3547–54.

Chiriyankandath, James. 'Realigning India: Indian Foreign Policy after the Cold War'. *The Round Table* 93, no. 374 (2004, March): 199–211.

Cohen, Stephen. *India: Emerging Power*. Washington, DC: Brookings Institution Press, 2002.

Cohen, Tova, and Ari Rabinovitch. 'Under Modi, Israel and India Forge Deeper Business Ties'. *Reuters*, 23 November 2014. Available at: http://www.reuters.com/article/us-india-israel-ties-idUSKCN0J70L520141123 (accessed on 15 May 2017).

Dalmia, Taru, and David M. Malone. 'Historical Influences on India's Foreign Policy'. *International Journal* 67, no. 4, Canada after 9/11 (Autumn, 2012): 1046.

Davenport, Coral, and Gardiner Harrison. 'Citing Urgency, World Leaders Converge on France for Climate Talks'. *The New York Times*, 30 November 2015. Available at: http://www.nytimes.com/2015/12/01/world/europe/obama-climate-conference-cop21.html?_r=0 (accessed on 15 May 2017).

Dawn. 'Modi Inauguration a "Great Opportunity" for a New Chapter: Sharif'. *Dawn*, 26 May 2014. Available at: http://www.dawn.com/news/1108677 (accessed on 15 May 2017).

———. 'Pakistan Capable of Responding to Indian Actions: Defence Minister'. *Dawn*, 9 October 2014. Available at: http://www.dawn.com/news/1136855 (accessed on 15 May 2017).

———. 'India Will Carry out Military Strikes at Any "Place and Time," Says Minister'. *Dawn*, 10 June 2015. Available at: http://www.dawn.com/news/1187334/ (accessed on 15 May 2017).

DNA. 'Full Speech: PM Modi's Address at the Third India–Africa Forum Summit'. 29 October 2015. Available at: http://www.dnaindia.com/india/report-full-speech-pm-modi-s-addressal-at-the-third-india-africa-forum-summit-2139769 (accessed on 15 May 2017).

Dingl, Shen. 'Building China–India Reconciliation'. *Asian Perspective* 34, no. 4, Special Issue on Seeking Political Reconciliation: Case Studies in Asia (2010): 139–63.

Doval, Ajit. 'Internal Security–Need for Course Correction'. 9 January 2012. Available at: http://ariseawakeyuvabharat.blogspot.ca/2012/01/internal-security-need-for-course.html (accessed on 15 May 2017).

Enlai, Zhou. *'Selected Works of Zhou-en-Lai*, vol. 2. Beijing: Foreign Languages Press, 1989.

Fair, C. Christine. *Fighting to the End: The Pakistan Army's Way of War*. New York, NY: Oxford University Press, 2014.

Fair, C. Christine, and Sumit Ganguly. 'Five Dangerous Myths about Pakistan'. *The Washington Quarterly* 38, no. 4 (2016): 73–97.

Frankel, Francine R. 'The Breakout of China–India Strategic Rivalry in Asia and the Indian Ocean'. *Journal of International Affairs* 64, no. 2, Sino-Indian Relations (Spring/Summer, 2011): 4.

Ganguly, Sumit. *India's Foreign Policy: Retrospect and Prospect*. New York: Oxford University Press, 2012.

———. 'Hindu Nationalism and the Foreign Policy of India's Bharatiya Janata Party'. 2014–15 Paper Series, No. 2, Transatlantic Academy, Washington DC, 2015.

Ganguly, Sumit, and Eswaran Sridharan. 'The End of India's Sovereignty Hawks?' *Foreign Policy* (2013, 7 November). Available at: http://foreignpolicy. com/2013/11/07/the-end-of-indias-sovereignty-hawks/ (accessed on 15 May 2017).

Ganguly Sumit, and Manjeet S. Pardesi. 'Explaining Sixty Years of India's Foreign Policy'. *India Review* 8, no. 9 (2009): 4–19.

Ghosh, Partha S. 'Foreign Policy and Electoral Politics in India: Inconsequential Connection'. *Asian Survey* 34, no. 9 1994, September): 807–17.

Gopal, S. *Jawaharlal Nehru*, vol. 2. Cambridge: Harvard University Press, 1979.

Guha, Ramachandra. 'An Asian Clash of Civilisations? Revisiting the Sino-Indian Conflict of 1962'. *Economic and Political Weekly* 46, no. 44/45 (2011, 5 November): 51–61.

Guldbrandsson, Karin, and Bjoorn Fossum. 'An Exploration of the Theoretical Concepts of Policy Windows and Policy Entrepreneurs at the Swedish Health Area'. *Health Promotion International* 24, no. 4 (2009): 434–44.

Gupta, C. Das. *War and Diplomacy in Kashmir, 1947–48*. New Delhi: SAGE Publications, 2002.

H.M., Sanjeev Kr. 'Foreign Policy Position of Bharatiya Janata Party Towards Issues of India Pakistan Relations'. *The Indian Journal of Political Science* 68, no. 2 (2007, April–June): 275–91.

Hagerty, Devine T. 'India's Regional Security Doctrine', *Asian Survey* 31, no. 4 (1991): 351–63.

Hall, Ian. 'Multialignment and Indian Foreign Policy under Narendra Modi'. *The Round Table* 105, no. 3 (2016): 271–86.

Hall, Peter A. 'Policy Paradigms, Social Learning, and the State: The Case of Economic Policymaking in Britain' *Comparative Politics* 25, no.3 (1993, April): 275–96.

Harshe, Rajen. 'India's Non-Alignment: An Attempt at Conceptual Reconstruction'. *Economic and Political Weekly* 25, no. 7/8 (1990, 17–24 February): 399–405.

Holslag, Jonathan. 'Assessing the Sino-Indian Water Dispute'. *Journal of International Affairs* 64, no. 2, Sino-Indian Relations (Spring/Summer, 2011): 19–35.

Honeyman, Chris. 'Integrative bargaining'. Available at: http://www. beyondintractibility.org (accessed on 12 June 2017).

India Today. 'Narendra Modi's First Independence Day speech: Full text'. *India Today*, 15 August 2014. Available at: http://indiatoday.intoday. in/story/narendra-modi-independence-day-speech-full-text-red-fort/1/377299.html (accessed on 15 May 2017).

———. 'India, Seychelles Sign 4 Pacts to Boost Security Cooperation. *India Today*, 11 March 2015. Available at: http://indiatoday.intoday.in/story/ modi-in-seychelles-sign-4-pacts-security-cooperation/1/423250.html (accessed on 29 May 2017).

Iyengar, Rishi. 'India is Using Its Military Incursions into Burma to Send a Message to Other Countries'. *Time*, 11 June 2015. Available at:

http://time.com/3917362/india-burma-army-operation-militant-attack-pakistan-manipur/ (accessed on 12 May 2017).

Jacques, Martin. *When China Rules the World: The Rise of the Middle Kingdom and the End of the Western World*. London: Allen Lane, 2009.

Jaishankar, S. 'Keynote Address by Foreign Secretary Dr S. Jaishankar at the IFS-IDSA Seminar—India and the Great Powers: Continuity and Change'. 21 November 2016. Available at: http://www.idsa.in/keyspeeches/s-jaishankar-foreign-secretary-india-and-great-powers-continuity-and-change (accessed on 15 May 2017).

Jamwal, Anuradha Bhasin, and Asha Hans. 'Pakistan–India: Ceasefire Violations and Effects on Civilians in Border Areas of Jammu and Kashmir—A Preliminary Report by PIPFPD'. Citizens Action and Concerns for Peace in South Asia, 21 January 2015. Available at: http://www.sacw.net/article10425.html (accessed on 15 May 2017).

Jamwal, Nidhi. 'In the Din over the Indus Waters Treaty, the Climate Change Factor Has Been Overlooked'. Scrollin, 26 November 2016. Available at: http://scroll.in/article/817910/in-the-din-over-the-indus-waters-treaty-the-climate-change-factor-has-been-overlooked (accessed on 15 May 2017).

Jizhe, Ning. 'China's Data Chief Admits Fraud and Deception in Statistics'. *Financial Times*, 9 December 2016. US digital edition (Kindle).

Jones, Bryan D., and Frank R. Baumgartner. 'From There to Here: Punctuated Equilibrium to the General Punctuation Thesis to a Theory of Government Information Processing'. *Policy Studies Journal* 40, no. 1 (2012): 1–20.

Jyoti, Dhrubo. 'Modi Praises Indian Army for Surgical Strikes, Compares It to Israel'. *Hindustan Times*, New Delhi, 18 October 2016. Available at: http://www.hindustantimes.com/india-news/modi-praises-indian-army-for-surgical-strikes-compares-it-to-israel/story-eTqN4s5a3Y70KVv4DRMfWM.html (accessed on 15 May 2017).

Kamath, P.M. 'Need to Correct Some Debilitating Features of Foreign Policy Making in India'. *Indian Journal of Asian Affairs* 10, no. 2 (1997, December): 17–30.

Kavic, L.J. *India's Quest for Security, Defence Policies, 1947–65*. Berkeley, CA: University of California Press, 1967.

Keenleyside, A.A. 'Prelude to Power: The Meaning of Non-Alignment Before Indian Independence'. *Pacific Affairs* 53, no. 3 (Autumn, 1980): 461–83.

Khilnani, Sunil, Rajiv Kumar, Pratap Bhanu Mehta, Prakash Menon, Nandan Nilekani, Srinath Raghavan, Shyam Saran, and Siddharth Varadarajan. *Nonalignment 2.0: A Foreign and Strategic Policy for India in the Twenty First Century*. 2012. Available at: http://cprindia.org/research/reports/nonalignment-20-foreign-and-strategic-policy-india-twenty-first-century (accessed on 15 May 2017).

Kingdon, J.W. *Agendas, Alternatives, and Public Policy*. Boston: Little, Brown and Company, 1984.

Kishore, Mohammed Ali. *Jana Sangh and India's Foreign Policy*. New Delhi: Associated Publishing House, 1969.

Kondapalli, Srikanth. 'Five Big Takeaways from Xi Jinping's Visit to India'. *Economic Times*, 19 September 2014. Available at: http://economictimes.indiatimes.com/opinion/et-commentary/five-big-takeaways-from-xi-jinpings-visit-to-india/articleshow/42845713.cms (accessed on 12 May 2017).

Lamba, Arvinder Singh. 'Restraint to Retribution: Modi's New Normal and Nawaz Sharif's Challenge—Analysis'. *Eurasia Review*, 27 November 2016. Available at: http://www.eurasiareview.com/27112016-restraint-to-retribution-modis-new-normal-and-nawaz-sharifs-challenge-analysis/ (accessed on 15 May 2017).

Lyon, Peter. 'Review: Indian Foreign Policy: The Nehru Years. By B.R. Nanda'. *International Affairs (Royal Institute of International Affairs 1944-)* 53, no. 4 (1977, October): 718.

Mansingh, Surjit. *India's Search for Power: Indira Gandhi's Foreign Policy, 1966–1982*. New Delhi: SAGE Publications, 1984.

———. 'India–China Relations in the Post-Cold War Era'. *Asian Survey* 34, no. 3 (1994, March): 285–86.

Massod, Salman, and Declan Welsh. 'Key Suspect in 2008 Mumbai Attacks Granted Bail'. *The New York Times*, 18 December 2014.

Mathew, Liz. 'PM Modi Speaks to People of Pakistan: Let Us Go to War Against Poverty, Unemployment … Let's See Who Wins'. *The Indian Express*, 25 September 2016. Available at: http://indianexpress.com/article/india/india-news-india/pm-narendra-modi-speaks-to-the-people-of-pakistan-lets-go-to-war against-poverty-unemployment-lets-see-who-wins-3048329/ (accessed on 29 May 2017).

Maxwell, Neville. *India's China War*. Bombay. Jaico Publishing, 1971

———. 'Henderson Brooks Report: An Introduction.' *Economic and Political Weekly* 36, no. 14/15 (2001, 14–20 April): 1189–93.

Mehta, Pratap Bhanu. 'Review: A New Foreign Policy?' *Economic and Political Weekly* 38, no. 30 (2003, 26 July–1 August): 3173–75.

Menon, Shivshankar. *Choices: Inside The Making of India's Foreign Policy*. Washington, D.C.: Brookings Institution Press, 2016.

Miller, Manjari Chatterjee. 'India's Feeble Foreign Policy: A Would-be Great Power Resists Its Own Rise'. *Foreign Affairs* (2013, June): 14–19.

Ministry of External Affairs. '37th Singapore Lecture "India's Singapore Story" by Prime Minister during His Visit to Singapore (November 23, 2015)'. Available at: http://mea.gov.in/SpeechesStatements.htm?dtl/26058/37th+Singapore+Lecture+Indias+Singapore+Story+by+Prime+Minister+during+his+visit+to+Singapore+November+23+2015 (accessed on 12 May 2017).

Ministry of External Affairs. 'India–Saudi Arabia Joint Statement during the visit of Prime Minister to Saudi Arabia (April 03, 2016)'. Available at: http://mea.gov.in/bilateral-documents.htm?dtl/26595/IndiaSaudi_Arabia_Joint_Statement_during_the_visit_of_Prime_Minister_to_Saudi_Arabia_April_03_2016 (accessed on 12 May 2017).

Ministry of Foreign Affairs of the People's Republic of China, 'Joint Communiqué of the 14th Meeting of the Foreign Ministers of the Russian Federation, the Republic of India and the People's Republic of China'. 19 April 2016. Available at: http://www.fmprc.gov.cn/mfa_eng/wjdt_665385/2649_665393/t1356652.shtml (accessed on 29 May 2017).

Misra, K.P., ed. *Studies in Indian Foreign Policy*. New Delhi: Vikas Publishing, 1969.

Mitra, Subrata K. 'The Reluctant Hegemon: India's Self-perception and South Asian Strategic Environment'. *Contemporary South Asia* 12, no. 3 (2009): 399–417.

Mitra, Subrata K., and Jivanta Schöttli. 'The New Dynamics of Indian Foreign Policy and Its Ambiguities'. *Irish Studies in International Affairs* 18 (2007): 19–34.

Modi, Narendra, 'No Partner Has Played Such a Decisive Role in India's Economic Transformation as Japan: PM Narendra Modi'. Joint Press Conference, 12 December 2015. Available at: http://www.narendramodi.in/od/pm-modi-address-at-the-joint-press-statement-with-prime-minister-shinzō-abe-in-new-delhi-386325 (accessed on 29 May 2017).

Mohan, C. Raja. 'The Making of Indian Foreign Policy: The Role of Scholarship and Public Opinion'. ISAS Working Paper 73, Institute of South Asian Studies, National University of Singapore, Singapore, July 2009.

———. 'Panchsheel Myths'. *The Indian Express*, 30 October 2013. Available at: http://archive.indianexpress.com/news/panchsheel-myths/1188853/0 (accessed on 12 May 2017).

———. 'The Legacy of Vajpayee and Singh'. *The Indian Express*, 15 May 2014. Available at: http://indianexpress.com/article/opinion/columns/the-legacy-of-vajpayee-and-singh/#sthash.ql90sD8T.dpuf (accessed on 15 May 2017).

———. 'India's Foreign Policy: Nehru's Enduring Legacy'. 3 October 2015. Available at: http://blog.oup.com/2015/10/india-foreign-policy-nehru-legacy/ (accessed on 15 May 2017).

———. *Modi's World: Expanding India's Sphere of Influence*. Noida, UP: HarperCollins, 2015.

Mullik, B.N. *The Chinese Betrayal*. Bombay: Allied Publishers, 1971.

Nanda, Prakash. 'Heart of Asia Conference: Pakistan "Embarrassed" on Terrorism, but Policy Will Continue'. *Firstpost*, 5 December 2016. Available at: http://www.firstpost.com/india/heart-of-asia-conference-pakistan-embarrassed-on-terrorism-but-policy-will-continue-3139826.html (accessed on 15 May 2017).

NDTV.com. 'Full Text of PM Modi's Statement after Meeting Premier Li Keqiang in Beijing'. 15 May 2015. Available at: http://www.ndtv.com/india-news/full-text-of-pm-modis-statement-after-meeting-premier-li-keqiang-in-beijing-763253 (accessed on 15 May 2017).

Neelakantan, Shailaja. '"We Are on Verge of Global Isolation", Pakistani Media Warns Government and Security Agencies'. *The Times of India*, 17 October 2016. Available at: http://timesofindia.indiatimes.com/world/pakistan/We-are-on-verge-of-global-isolation-Pakistani-media-warns-government-and-security-agencies/articleshow/54891351.cms (accessed on 15 May 2017).

News World India.in. 'Myanmar Operation Has Changed Mindset, Those Who Fear India Are Reacting: Parrikar'. *News World India.in*, 11 June 2015. Available at: http://newsworldindia.in/india/myanmar-operation-has-changed-mindset-those-who-fear-india-are-reacting-defence-minister/52748/ (accessed on 15 May 2017).

Pant, Harsh V. 'Strategic Analysis: Indian Foreign Policy and China'. *Strategic Affairs* 30, no. 4 (2006, October): 760–80.

———. *Contemporary Debates in Indian Foreign and Security Policy: India Negotiates Its Rise in the International System*. New York, NY: Palgrave Macmillan, 2008.

———, ed. 'Introduction'. In *Indian Foreign Policy in a Unipolar World*, 1–19. New Delhi: Routledge, 2009.

———. 'A Seismic Shift in India's Pakistan Policy'. *The Diplomat*, 25 August 2015. Available at: http://thediplomat.com/2015/08/a-seismic-shift-in-indias-pakistan-policy/ (accessed on 15 May 2017).

———. 'India and Russia Struggle to Regain the Past Glow'. *The Diplomat*, 19 October 2016. Available at: http://thediplomat.com/2016/10/india-and-russia-struggle-to-regain-the-past-glow/ (accessed on 12 May 2017).

———. *Indian Foreign Policy: An Overview*. Manchester: Manchester University Press, 2016.

Parameswaran, Prashanth. 'US Official Calls for Permanent Expansion of Malabar Exercises With India'. *The Diplomat*, 17 July 2015. Available at: http://thediplomat.com/2015/07/us-official-calls-for-permanent-expansion-of-malabar-exercises-with-india/ (accessed on 12 May 2017).

———. 'A New "Proactive" Indian Foreign Policy under Modi?' *The Diplomat*, 21 July 2015. Available at: http://thediplomat.com/2015/07/is-india-advancing-a-new-proactive-foreign-policy-under-modi/ (accessed on 15 may 2017).

———. 'India Eyes Stronger Trade Ties with ASEAN States'. *The Diplomat*, 14 January 2016. Available at: http://thediplomat.com/2016/01/india-eyes-stronger-trade-ties-with-asean-states/ (accessed on 12 May 2017).

Parashar, Sachin. 'Modi, Abe Send Message to Beijing on South China Sea'. *The Times of India*, 13 December 2015. Available at: http://timesofindia.indiatimes.com/india/Modi-Abe-send-message-to-Beijing-on-South-China-Sea/articleshow/50156708.cms (accessed on 12 May 2017).

Patil, Sameer. 'India–Pakistan Relations: Bangkok Breakthrough—Analysis'. *Eurasia Review*, 15 December 2015. Available at: http://www. eurasiareview.com/15122015-india-pakistan-relations-bangkok-breakthrough-analysis/ (accessed on 29 May 2017).

Paul, T.V., ed. 'Causes of the India–Pakistan Enduring Rivalry'. In *The India–Pakistan Conflict: An Enduring Rivalry*, 12. New York, NY: Cambridge University Press, 2005.

———. *The Warrior State: Pakistan in the Contemporary World*. New York, NY: Oxford University Press, 2014.

Peissel, M. *The Secret War in Tibet*. Boston: Little Brown, 1972.

PMINDIA. 'Text of PM's 37th Singapore Lecture "India's Singapore Story" During Visit to Singapore'. 23 November 2015. Available at: http://www.pmindia.gov.in/en/news_updates/text-of-37th-singapore-lecture-indias-singapore-story-by-prime-minister-during-his-visit-to-singapore/ (accessed on 29 May 2017).

Prasad, Bimal, ed. *India's Foreign Policy: Studies in Continuity and Change*. New Delhi: Vikas Publishing, 1979.

Press Information Bureau. 'Joint Statement Between the India and China during Prime Minister's Visit to China', 15 May 2015. Press Information Bureau, Prime Minister's Office. Government of India. Available at: http://pib.nic.in/newsite/PrintRelease.aspx?relid=121755 (accessed on 12 May 2017).

———. 'PM Chairs Combined Commanders Conference on board INS Vikramaditya at Sea'. Government of India, Prime Minister's Office, 15 December 2015. Available at: http://pib.nic.in/newsite/PrintRelease. aspx?relid=133265 (accessed on 12 May 2017).

Prindle, David. 'Importing Concepts from Biology into Political Science: The Case of Punctuated Equilibrium'. *Policy Studies Journal* 40, no. 1 (2012, February): 21–44.

Rajendram, Danielle. 'India's New Asia-Pacific Strategy: Modi acts East'. Lowy Institute of International Policy, December 2014. Available at: http://www.lowyinstitute.org/files/indias-new-asia-pacific-strategy-modi-acts-east.pdf (accessed on 12 May 2017).

Ramachandran, *Sudha*. 'The Trouble with India's Projects in Myanmar'. *The Diplomat*, 21 September 2016. Available at: http://thediplomat. com/2016/09/the-trouble-with-indias-projects-in-myanmar/ (accessed on 29 May 2017).

Rana, A.P. 'The Intellectual Dimensions of India's Nonalignment'. *The Journal of Asian Studies* 28, no. 2 (1969, February): 299–312.

———. *The Imperatives of Non-Alignment: A Conceptual Study of India's Foreign Policy Strategy in the Nehru Period*. New Delhi: Macmillan, 1976.

———. 'Nehruvian Tradition in World Affairs: Its Evolution and Relevance to Post-Cold War World Order'. In *Nehru's Foreign Policy: Fifty Years*

On, edited by Surjit Mansingh, 40–68. New Delhi: Mosaic Books, 1998.

Rediff News. 'One Nation Is Spreading Terror in South Asia: PM Modi at G20'. Rediff News, 5 September 2016. Available at: http://www.rediff. com/news/report/one-nation-is-spreading-terror-in-south-asia-pm-modi-at-g20/20160905.htm (accessed on 29 May 2017).

Reid, Escott. *Envoy to Nehru*. Karachi: Oxford University Press, 1981.

Rizwi, Gower. 'Nehru and the Indo-Pakistan Rivalry over Kashmir, 1947–64'. *Contemporary South Asia* 4, no.1 (1995, March): 17–37.

Robinson, Cabeiri Debergh. 'Too Much Nationality: Kashmiri Refugees, the South Asian Refugee Regime, and a Refugee State, 1947–74'. *Journal of Refugee Studies* 25, no. 3 (2012): 344–65.

Roche, Elizabeth. 'President Lays Down Road Map for Foreign Strategy, Security'. *Livemint,* 9 June 2014. Available at: http://www.livemint.com/ Politics/JH8hPuTr5x5zOVe1ZbLlml/President-lays-down-road-map-for-foreign-strategy-security.html (accessed on 29 May 2017).

Roy, Subhajit. 'Derailed Three Years, India–Pakistan Talks Back on Track'. *The Indian Express*, 10 December 2015. Available at: http://indianexpress. com/article/india/india-news-india/time-for-india-pakistan-to-display-maturity-to-do-business-sushma-swaraj/ (accessed on 15 May 2017).

Rusko, Christopher J., and Karthika Sasikumar. 'India and China: From Trade to Peace?' *Asian Perspective* 31, no. 4, Special Issue on 'The BRICs Countries (Brazil, Russia, India, and China) in the Global System' (2007): 99–123.

Saboory, Hamid M. 'President Ghani: Stuck Between India and Pakistan'. *Foreign Policy*, 12 March 2015. Available at: http://foreignpolicy. com/2015/03/12/president-ghani-stuck-between-india-and-pakistan/ (accessed on 12 May 2017).

Saeed, Saim. 'India and Pakistan: A Debilitating Relationship'. *The Diplomat*, 29 November 2014. Available at http://thediplomat. com/2014/11/india-and-pakistan-a-debilitating-relationship/ (accessed on 15 May 2017).

Sajjanhar, Ashok. 'India and China: Asia's Uneasy Neighbors'. *The Diplomat*, 22 August 2016. Available at: http://thediplomat.com/2016/08/india-and-china-asias-uneasy-neighbors/ (accessed on 15 May 2017).

———. 'BRICS, BIMSTEC, and Anti-Terrorism: What Did India Accomplish?' *The Diplomat*, 25 October 2016. Available at: http://thediplomat. com/2016/10/brics-bimstec-and-anti-terrorism-what-did-india-accomplish/ (accessed on 15 May 2017).

Saran, Shyam. 'India and Australia: From a Shared Ocean and Shared Values to Strategic Convergence'. *The Wire*, 27 November 2015. Available at: http://thewire.in/2015/11/27/india-and-australia-from-a-shared-ocean-and-shared-values-to-strategic-convergence- 16249/ (accessed on 12 May 2017).

Schmidt, Vivien A. 'Taking Ideas and Discourse Seriously: Explaining Change through Discursive Institutionalism as the Fourth "New Institutionalism"'. *European Political Science Review* 2, no. 1 (2010): 1–25.

Secretariat of the United Nations. 'Treaties and International Agreements Registered or Filed and Recorded with the Secretariat of the United Nations'. *United Nations Treaty Series* 299 (1958): 57–82. Available at: https://treaties.un.org/doc/publication/unts/volume%20299/v299. pdf (accessed on 18 May 2017).

Sen, Satadru. 'Goodbye to Non-Alignment and All That'. *Economic and Political Weekly* 36, no. 48 (2001, 1–7 December): 4455–57.

Sengupta, Bhabani. 'India in the 21st Century'. *International Affairs* 73, no. 2 (1997): 309.

Sharma, K.P. *Janata's Foreign Policy*. New Delhi: Vikas Publishing, 1979.

Shaumian, Tatyana L. 'India's Foreign Policy: Interaction of Global and Regional Aspects' *Asian Survey* 28, no. 11 (1988, November): 1161–69.

Sinha, P.B. and A. A. Athale. *History of the Conflict with China, 1962*. New Delhi: Ministry of Defence, Government of India, 1992.

Shukla, Ajai. 'Army Silent as Soldier, Surgical Strikes Feature in BJP Election Posters'. *Business Standard*, 8 October 2016. Available at: http://www. business-standard.com/article/current-affairs/army-silent-as-soldier-surgical-strikes-feature-in-bjp-election-posters-116100800315_1.html (accessed on 15 May 2017).

Siddiqa, Ayesha. 'Cyril Almeida's Story Points to Old Fault Lines and New Strains in Pakistan Army–Govt Relationship'. *The Indian Express*, 14 October 2016. Available at: http://indianexpress.com/article/opinion/columns/dawn-journalist-cyril-almeida-banned-pakistan-civilian-govt-military-meet-3081347/ (accessed on 15 May 2017).

Sikri, Rajiv. *Challenge and Strategy: Rethinking India s Foreign Policy*. New Delhi: SAGE Publications, 2009.

———. 'The Tibet Factor in India China Relations'. *Journal of International Affairs* 64, no. 2, Sino-Indian Relations (Spring/Summer, 2011): 55–71.

Singh, Baljit. 'Pundits and Panchsheela: Indian Intellectuals and Their Foreign Policy'. *Background (International Studies Association)* 9, no. 2 (1965, August): 127–36.

Singh, Priyanka. 'CPEC: Corridor of Discontent'. *The Diplomat*, 23 November 2016.

Singh, Swaran. 'Paradigm Shift in India–China Relations: From Bilateralism to Multilateralism'. *Journal of International Affairs* 64, no. 2 (Spring/Summer, 2011): 155–68.

Smith, Jeff M. 'Trump Should Read India's Playbook on Taunting China'. NDTV, 2016, digital edition.

Sood, Rakesh. 'Uri as Inflection Point'. *The Hindu*, 1 October 2016. Available at: http://www.thehindu.com/todays-paper/tp-opinion/Uri-as-inflection-point/article15419823.ece (accesses on 15 May 2017).

Subcommittee on National Security and International Operations, Committee on Government Operations, and US Senate. *Peking's Approach to Negotiations*. Washington, DC: US Government Printing Office, 1969.

Subrahmanyam, K. 'Nehru and the India–China Conflict of 1962'. In *Indian Foreign Policy: The Nehru Years*, edited by B.R. Nanda, 102–30. New Delhi: Vikas Publishing, 1976.

———. 'Forget the Consensus'. *The Times of India*, 29 November 2007.

Swami, Praveen. *India, Pakistan and the Secret Jihad: The Covert War in Kashmir, 1947–2004*. London and New York, NY: Routledge, 2007.

Tellis, Ashley J. 'Back to First Principles: Realizing the Promise of U.S.–India Defense Ties'. Carnegie Endowment for International Peace, 10 December 2015.

Thakur, Ramesh. 'India's Vietnam Policy, 1946–1979'. *Asian Survey* 19, no. 10 (1979, October): 957–76.

Tharoor, Shashi. 'Why India's Intolerance Problem Is Hurting Its Global Reputation'. *Huffington Post*, 2 December 2015. Available at: http://www.huffingtonpost.com/shashi-tharoor/india-intolerance-problem_b_8699164.html#comments (accessed on 15 May 2017).

The American Assembly. *Atoms for Power: United States Policy in Atomic Energy Development*. New York: The American Assembly, Columbia University, 1957.

The Hindu. 'One Nation in South Asia is Spreading Terror in the Region'. *The Hindu*, 5 September 2016. Available at: http://www.thehindu.com/news/national/One-nation-in-South-Asia-is-spreading-terror-in-the-region/article14624919.ece (accessed on 12 May 2017).

———. 'Pakistan Army Chief Lashes out at India'. *The Hindu*, 6 October 2016. Available at: http://www.thehindu.com/news/international/Pakistan-Army-chief-lashes-out-at-India/article15472417.ece (accessed on 15 May 2017)

———. 'We Stayed Closely Connected with India after Uri attack'. *The Hindu*, 9 October 2016. Available at: http://www.thehindu.com/todays-paper/tp-national/We-stayed-closely-connected-with-India-after-Uri-attack/article15621510.ece (accessed on 15 May 2017).

The Indian Express. 'India Warns Pakistan as Tension Escalates at LoC: Our Forces Will Make Cost of Your Adventurism Unaffordable'. *The Indian Express*, 9 October 2014. Available at: http://indianexpress.com/article/india/india-others/indias-stern-warning-to-pak-over-border-firing-our-forces-will-make-cost-of-your-adventurism-at-LoC-unaffordable/#sthash.vIQu1RPC.dpuf (accessed on 15 May 2017).

———. 'We Have Responded with Courage to Ceasefire Violation by Pakistan: PM Narendra Modi'. *The Indian Express*, 9 October 2014. Available at: http://indianexpress.com/article/india/india-others/we-have-responded-with-courage-to-ceasefire-violation-by-pakistan-pm-modi/#sthash.kFp9EiJt.dpuf (accessed on 15 May 2017).

The Indian Express. 'As Writers Continue to Return Award, BJP Says Check Their Ideological Inclinations'. *The Indian Express*, 13 October 2015. Available at: http://indianexpress.com/article/india/india-others/as-writers-continues-to-return-award-bjp-asks-to-check-their-ideological-inclinations/ (accessed on 15 May 2017).

The New Indian Express. 'Talks with Pakistan Is to Try and Turn Course of History'. *The New Indian Express*, 15 December 2015. Available at: http://www.newindianexpress.com/nation/Talks-with-Pakistan-is-to-Try-and-Turn-Course-of-History-Modi/2015/12/15/article3179202.ece (accessed on 15 May 2017).

The Times of India. 'Text of Modi Speech at SAARC Summit'. *The Times of India*, 26 November 2014. Available at: http://timesofindia.indiatimes.com/india/Text-of-Modis-speech-at-Saarc-summit/articleshow/45283865.cms (accessed on 12 May 2017).

———. 'We Didn't Build Nukes to Fire on Shab-e-Baraat', Musharraf Says'. *The Times of India*, 11 June 2015. Available at: http://timesofindia.indiatimes.com/world/pakistan/We-didnt-build-nukes-to-fire-on-Shab-e-Baraat-Musharraf-says/articleshow/47628510.cms (accessed on 15 May 2017).

———. 'Modi Running External Affairs Ministry on Whims: Khurshid', 21 July 2015. Available at: http://timesofindia.indiatimes.com/india/Modi-running-external-affairs-ministry-on-whims-Khurshid/articleshow/48156660.cms (accessed on 15 May 2017).

———. 'Pakistan Army Chief Raheel Sharif Warns India of "Unbearable Cost" in Case of War'. *The Times of India*, 7 September 2015. Available at: http://timesofindia.indiatimes.com/world/pakistan/Pakistan-army-chief-Raheel-Sharif-warns-India-of-unbearable-cost-in-case-of-war/articleshow/48854094.cms (accessed on 15 May 2017).

———. 'India Cautions Russia and Iran against Engaging with Taliban'. *The Times of India*, 16 December 2016. Available at: http://timesofindia.indiatimes.com/india/india-cautions-russia-iran-against-engaging-with-taliban/articleshow/56010317.cms (accessed on 15 May 2017).

The Tribune. 'India, Pak Say Yes to Dialogue, No to Cricket'. *The Tribune*, 9 December 2015. Available at: http://www.tribuneindia.com/news/nation/india-pak-say-yes-to-dialogue-no-to-cricket/168758.html (accessed on 29 May 2017).

Tremblay, Reeta Chowdhari, and Julian Scofield. 'Institutional Causes of the India–Pakistan Rivalry'. In *The India–Pakistan Conflict: An Enduring Rivalry*, edited by T.V. Paul, 225–50. New York, NY: Cambridge University Press, 2005.

Tse-tung, Mao. *Selected Military Writings of Mao Tse-tung*. Peking: Foreign Languages Press, 1966.

United Nations. 'United Nations Official Documents: Resolutions and Decisions of the Security Council 1948, Security Council Official Records, Third Year'. United Nations, New York (1964), 3. Available at: http://www.un.org/en/ga/search/view_doc.asp?symbol=S/RES/51(1948) (accessed on 29 May 2017).

Varshney, Ashutosh. 'India's Watershed Vote: Hindu Nationalism in Power'. *Journal of Democracy* 25, no. 4 (2014, October): 44.

Zakaria, Fareed. 'Vladimir Putin Wants a New World Order. Why Would Donald Trump Help Him?' *The Washington Post*, 15 December 2016. Available at: https://www.washingtonpost.com/opinions/vladimir-putin-wants-a-new-world-order-why-would-donald-trump-help-him/2016/12/15/ad12a046-c30d-11e6-8422-eac61c0ef74d_story.html?utm_term=.c16a11629db1 (accessed on 15 May 2017).

Index

About the Authors

Reeta Chowdhari Tremblay is Professor of Comparative Politics and Global South in the Department of Political Science at the University of Victoria, Canada. She holds an MA and a PhD degree in Political Science from the University of Chicago, IL, USA. She also has an MPhil degree from Jawaharlal Nehru University, India, and an MA and a BA degree from the University of Kashmir, India. Her major areas of research are identity-based politics and secessionist movements (Kashmir) in South Asia, the politics of subaltern resistance and accommodation in post-colonial societies, democracy and governance, and comparative federalism. During her career, she has held several administrative positions, including Vice-President Academic and Provost at the University of Victoria, Canada; Vice-President (Academic) and Pro Vice-Chancellor (Pro Tem) at Memorial University of Newfoundland, Canada; Dean of the Faculty of Arts at Memorial University; and, Chair, Department of Political Science at Concordia University, Montreal. She is the Past President of the Canadian Political Science Association (CPSA), Canadian Asian Studies Association (CASA) and the Canadian Council of Area Studies of Learned Societies (including CASA, Latin American Studies, African Studies and the Middle Eastern Studies). She has also served or is serving on editorial boards of several disciplinary journals, including *PS: Political Science & Politics* (APSA), *Pacific Affairs*, *Canadian Journal of Law and Society*, and *Politics and Governance*. She has authored or co-authored six books, including *State Autonomy and Public Policy in India; Human Rights: Global and Canadian Perspectives* and *Mapping the Political Landscape*. Some of her recent essays include 'Contested Governance, Competing Nationalisms, and Disenchanted Publics: Kashmir Beyond Intractability?', 'Kashmir's Contentious Politics: The More Things Change, the More They Stay the Same' and 'Labor Migration, Citizenship, and Social Welfare in China and India'. Her work is widely reviewed and cited—in particular her writings on Kashmir and India–Pakistan relations, a subject on which she is widely considered to be the leading North American expert. She has been recognized for her exceptional teaching at both the graduate and undergraduate levels and has received the Concordia University Alumni Association Award for Excellence in Teaching in 2002. She also regularly contributes commentaries on South Asia, in particular on Kashmir and on South Asian regional politics to South Asia Monitor (projects of the New Delhi-based think tank, Society for Policy Studies). In 2015, she was recognized as one of the top 40 prominent Indo-Canadians and was profiled in The Indian Diaspora' A-List.

Born in Lahore, **Ashok Kapur** had his early schooling in Shimla and then he went on to earn a BA Honours degree in Political Science from Panjab University, India, and MA in International Relations from The George Washington University, Washington, DC, and a PhD degree in Political Science from Carleton University, Canada. He is the author of several notable books such as *Pokhran and Beyond*, 2nd edition, *Pakistan's Nuclear Development, India and the South Asian Strategic Triangle* and *India's Strategic Problems*. His research and conference travels include visits to countries such as China, India, United Kingdom, United States, USSR, Iran, South Africa, Sweden, Norway, Israel and Pakistan. He taught foreign policy at the University of Waterloo, Canada, for 35 years and retired from the University as a Distinguished Professor Emeritus, a position he still holds. Ashok Kapur has held visiting appointments at several universities, including a Visiting Fellow, Department of International Relations, Australian National University, Canberra; Visiting Professor in Disarmament Studies, Jawaharlal Nehru University, New Delhi; Senior Associate Member, St. Antony's College, Oxford; Visiting Fellow, Centre for Security, University of Pittsburgh, PA, USA; Visiting Fellow, Institute of Commonwealth Studies, University of London, UK. He was also a member of the United Nations Committee to study Israel's nuclear capability.